AUDACIOUS SCOUNDRELS
Stories of the Wicked West

STEVEN L. PIOTT

TWODOT®

GUILFORD, CONNECTICUT
HELENA, MONTANA

A · TWODOT® · BOOK

An imprint of The Rowman & Littlefield Publishing Group, Inc.
4501 Forbes Blvd., Ste. 200
Lanham, MD 20706
www.rowman.com

Distributed by NATIONAL BOOK NETWORK

British Library Cataloguing in Publication Information available

Library of Congress Cataloging-in-Publication Data available

Names: Piott, Steven L., 1948– author.
Title: Audacious scoundrels : stories of the wicked West / Steven L. Piott.
Other titles: Stories of the wicked West
Description: Guilford, Connecticut : TwoDot, [2021] | Includes
  bibliographical references and index. | Summary: "Relying on secondary
  sources, magazine and newspaper articles, and personal accounts from
  those involved, this volume captures some of the sensational true
  stories that took place in the western United States during the late
  nineteenth and early twentieth centuries. The theme that runs through
  each of the stories is the general contempt for the law that seemed to
  pervade the culture at the time and the consuming desire to acquire
  wealth at any cost"— Provided by publisher.
Identifiers: LCCN 2020045463 (print) | LCCN 2020045464 (ebook) | ISBN
  9781493058648 (paperback) | ISBN 9781493058655 (epub)
Subjects: LCSH: Swindlers and swindling—West (U.S.)—History. |
  Businesspeople—West (U.S.)—History. | West (U.S.)—Economic
  conditions—19th century. | West (U.S.)—Economic conditions—20th
  century. | Mineral industries—West (U.S.)—History. | Political
  corruption—California—San Francisco—History.
Classification: LCC HV6698.W47 P46 2021 (print) | LCC HV6698.W47 (ebook)
  | DDC 364.16/3097909034—dc23
LC record available at https://lccn.loc.gov/2020045463
LC ebook record available at https://lccn.loc.gov/2020045464

∞™ The paper used in this publication meets the minimum requirements of American National Standard for Information Sciences—Permanence of Paper for Printed Library Materials, ANSI/ NISO Z39.48-1992.

CONTENTS

INTRODUCTION

THE FOUR STORIES THAT APPEAR IN THIS VOLUME CAN TRACE THEIR origins to the early twentieth century, when the rise of the earliest mass-circulation magazines first began to reach a middle-class readership. What was new about the major articles that appeared was their message of social concern. In perhaps a dozen or so new magazines like *McClure's*, *Everybody's*, *Cosmopolitan*, and *American*, readers found their attention being drawn to the widespread influence being wielded by big business either through political corruption, legal chicanery, or ruthless and immoral commercial practices. The magazines did this through a type of investigative reporting that critics, fearful that the negative style of reporting might contribute to political, social, and industrial unrest, would try to denigrate as "muckraking."

Often through an ongoing series of articles, the writers/reporters exposed some form of wrongdoing and did so in most cases with firsthand knowledge of their subject. Some had visited factories, others explored the sparsely populated regions of the West and the Territories, while still others interviewed the managers of great industries and vividly described the methods by which they operated. Most provided an overview or history of the country to try to find out how we had arrived at the age of monopolies and corruptionists. These so-called "muckrakers" wanted to heighten the social consciousness of their readers and sought to do so with evidence—facts, figures, names—all in a style that sought to maintain a neutral perspective. Without an ax to grind or any prescription to offer, they merely told stories. They reported on conditions and then left it to the reader to make value judgments and decide what should be done. And when they wrote honestly and fully about the sordid conditions they uncovered, the average reader found the writing to be as gripping as it was educational.

During the late nineteenth and early twentieth centuries, a growing number of ordinary citizens had the feeling that all was not as it should be. Men who were making money made prodigious amounts, but this new wealth somehow passed over the heads of the common people. As this new breed of journalists began to examine their subjects with scrutiny, they soon discovered that those individuals were essentially "simple men of extraordinary boldness." And it was easy to understand how they were able to accomplish their sinister purposes: "at first abruptly and bluntly, by asking and giving no quarter, and later with the same old determination and ruthlessness but with educated satellites who were glad to explain and idealize their behavior."[1] "Nothing is lost save honor," said one infamous buccaneer, and that was an attitude that governed the amoral principles and extralegal actions of many audacious scoundrels.

The first story in this volume, "The Nome Conspiracy," was originally told by writer Rex Beach in his melodramatic novel *The Spoilers*. Serialized in *Everybody's* in 1905, and then published in book form in 1906, the novel was Beach's firsthand account of the Nome gold conspiracy by one who actually watched it unfold. As a young college student in the early 1890s, Beach had focused his attention on science, athletics, and editing the Rollins College literary magazine. Leaving school shortly before earning his degree, Beach moved to Chicago where he worked in the law office of his two brothers while attending the Chicago College of Law and preparing himself to take the bar exam. But before he could finish, Beach, like thousands of others, was struck with gold rush fever in 1897 and dropped everything to try his luck in the Klondike.

Beach spent five years in Alaska and, although he never struck it rich, he did find a wealth of excitement and adventure on America's remote, far-western frontier. Beach lived for two years in the town of Rampart before moving on to Nome. In describing Rampart, Beach stated: "We were some fifteen hundred souls and twelve saloon keepers, all dumped out on the bank of the Yukon to shift for ourselves in a region unmapped and unexplored." It was at Nome, however, that he witnessed what one reporter called "one of the most amazing conspiracies . . . known in the history of jurisprudence" and "the brazen effrontery displayed by [Alexander] McKenzie, his tools, hirelings, and henchmen."[2] The greed and corruption, and the actions of good and evil men, inspired Beach to become, like Jack London, a literary chronicler of the Alaska Gold Rush era.

The tremendous popularity of *The Spoilers* encouraged Beach to follow it up with the nonfiction details of the Nome conspiracy in a five-part series that appeared in *Appleton's Booklovers Magazine* during 1906 entitled "The Looting of Alaska." The novel and articles, presented as a scandal and related as an adventure story, caused a sensation. What readers got was a morality tale set in a democracy where so much depends on the rectitude of judges, politicians, and businessmen.

If personal experience informed the writing of Rex Beach, so too did it influence the career of C. P. Connolly. Connolly, who had grown up in Newark, New Jersey, with very little formal education, worked for a time in New York City as a court reporter and then as a stenographer and general secretary for a banking firm. When the firm failed, Connolly moved to Montana Territory and again found work as a stenographer while he studied law. He gained admission to the bar in 1890, the year after Montana became a state, and began a career as a practicing attorney. His big break came in 1897, when he won election as district attorney of politically corrupted Silver Bow County (Butte), Montana. Eventually forced out of office as a result of the turbulent nature of Montana politics at the turn of the twentieth century, Connolly turned to writing and quickly made a name for himself among the rising group of investigative journalists. His first literary effort involved a five-part series that ran in *McClure's* magazine in 1906 called "The Story of Montana." He then extended the series with "The Fight of the Copper Kings" and "The Fight for the Minnie Healy" the following year. Taken together the articles offer a critical look at what the editors described as "the legal and business wars which have kept the State of Montana in turmoil from the beginning of the rivalry between Marcus Daly and William A. Clark, in the early '90s, up to the compromise of the legal and commercial differences between the Amalgamated Copper Company and F. A. Heinze, in the early part of the present year [1906]."[3] The story originally told by Connolly and then amplified by others is presented in chapters 2 and 3.

The lust for gold in Alaska and copper ore in Montana seemed to draw the attention of yet another investigative journalist, Lincoln Steffens, to a new source of corruption, timber. Aware of the frauds involved in the distribution of public timber lands being exposed by prosecutor Francis J. Heney and Detective William J. Burns in California and Oregon, Steffens journeyed to Portland to write the story for an unsuspecting public. What he found was that a department of the federal government (the Department of the Interior), which had been created to carry out land, timber, and mineral laws in the public interest, was being corrupted by federal appointees "bought by systematic bribery to take the part of the land grafters, timber thieves, and big mine-jumpers." Steffens's notable exposé appeared in *American* magazine in 1907 as "The Taming of the West." His general story is presented in greater detail as chapter 4.

Lincoln Steffens had made his initial claim to fame as an investigative reporter by publishing a series on municipal corruption for *McClure's* beginning in October 1902. Published in book form in 1904 as *The Shame of the Cities*, the collected articles established Steffens as an expert on the topic. With that expertise in hand, and with his interest piqued by the successful land fraud prosecutions by Heney and Burns in Oregon, Steffens followed them to San Francisco, where they were about to undertake the sensational San Francisco graft investigation. Although the San Francisco newspapers covered the investigation and prosecutions in great detail, Steffens sketched the outlines in more general terms for a national readership with two articles that appeared in *American* magazine in 1907 as "The Mote and the Beam: A Fact Novel." That classic story of bribe giving and bribe taking in a major American city is retold here as chapters 5 and 6.

In January 1903, in an editorial appended to that month's issue of *McClure's*, publisher S. S. McClure drew the readers' attention to three particular essays and noted that the inclusion of them was merely "a coincidence that may set us thinking." What he meant was that the three articles had, by sheer chance, underscored the same theme—"the glaring American contempt for law." In his editorial indictment, McClure charged that capitalists, workers, politicians, and citizens were guilty of conspiring to break the laws, and that the courts were for sale to the highest bidder. As historian Louis Filler has noted, "With this issue of *McClure's* muckraking was thus created, defined, and set on its historical way." What followed was "a moral, concerned writing up—or rather writing down—of American ways and institutions and leaders." "The people," said Filler, "particularly in the big cities and in the West, liked it immediately."[4] The four stories of the West included here are typical of that era and representative of that dominant muckraking theme, but they are also just great stories that seem eerily relevant today.

CHAPTER ONE

The Nome Conspiracy

WHEN NEWS BROKE THAT GOLD HAD BEEN DISCOVERED IN CANADA
close to the Alaska border in 1897, it set off a stampede to the Klondike. The richness of that strike also encouraged gold digging in parts of
Alaska, including the Seward Peninsula on the barren, rock-girded western coast of Alaska only fifty miles across the Bering Strait from Siberia.
In that remote location, accessible by boat only part of the year (June to
October), a group of eight prospectors discovered gold in March 1898
along Melsing and Ophir Creeks, both tributaries of the Niukluk River.
Staking their claims, they worked at placer mining, a process by which
dirt is washed away from surface gravel to reveal valuable gold particles.
Others, primarily whalers who deserted ship and a number of Laplanders
who had been imported as deer herders, soon flocked to this spot near
what became known as Council City. By the summer of 1898 there were
roughly several hundred men in the district. It was at Council City that
three individuals—miner John Brynteson, tailor Erick O. Lindblom,
and reindeer herder Jafet Lindeberg—happened by chance to meet and
agreed to enter into a prospecting partnership.

John Brynteson was a native of Artemark, Sweden, a historic mining
district. Coming to the United States at age 16, he journeyed to the upper
peninsula of Michigan where he worked in copper and iron mines. He
became naturalized as an American citizen in 1896 and two years later
ventured to Alaska. It was there that he heard a rumor of a gold discovery on the Sinuk River by a government reindeer herder.[1] Intrigued by
the report, Brynteson, along with three others, headed north in a small

boat in July 1898. Becoming stormbound near the present site of Nome, they decided to prospect the Snake River area and, in late July, unearthed trace amounts of gold. But most of the party considered the find to be insufficiently encouraging and decided to continue on to their original destination on the Sinuk. When nothing was found there, they returned to Golovnin Bay. Brynteson, however, believed that the gold particles found along the Snake River warranted a second look and, in mid-September, decided to return to the same area with two new partners— Erik Lindblom and Jafet Lindeberg.

Erik Lindblom was a native of Dalarne, Sweden. The son of a Stockholm schoolteacher, Lindblom learned the tailoring trade. After saving enough money, he journeyed to California, settled in the San Francisco–Oakland area, and became a naturalized citizen in 1894. Although he had been working as a tailor, in the spring of 1897 Lindblom decided to ship north to Alaska as a sailor. One story has it that while drunk in San Francisco, he had actually been shanghaied and transported north as an impressed deckhand. Either way, he jumped ship at Port Clarence and made his way down the coast to Golovnin Bay, then up the Fish and Niukluk Rivers to Council City where he eventually met up with Brynteson and Lindeberg.

Jafet Lindeberg was a native of Baddeven, Norway. His family had a background in reindeer herding and his uncle worked as a copper miner. Lindeberg was educated in English, French, German, and Russian as well as his native language. In January 1898, he signed a contract with Dr. Sheldon Jackson, superintendent of the US government's reindeer enterprise in Alaska, who was on a recruiting mission to Norway in search of reindeer herders. Jackson initially intended to send Lindeberg to Plover Bay in eastern Siberia to trade for more reindeer. However, when Lindeberg arrived at St. Michael, a central trading post on Norton Sound, he learned that hostile natives had disrupted the Siberian trading operation. Now left without a suitable position, Dr. Jackson gave him permission to leave government employment. Convinced that prospecting for gold promised greater rewards than reindeer herding, Lindeberg set out for the diggings in the Council City area. It was there that he met his future mining partners. Not then a citizen of the United States, Lindeberg had declared his intention to become a citizen before the US commissioner at St. Michael.

The three men prospected for a time in the Council City district, but, as the area was overrun with stampeders and already completely staked out, concluded that they needed to broaden the range of their search if they hoped to find richer diggings. Returning to Golovnin Bay, they acquired a large, flat-bottomed boat and an outfit of provisions and, on September 11, 1898, started up the coast. Stopping at various rivers to prospect along the way, they found traces of gold but not in paying amounts. They finally found an encouraging sign of gold at the mouth of the Snake River. Establishing a camp, they proceeded to prospect along a tributary of that river that later became known as Anvil Creek (named after an anvil-shaped rock that stood at the summit of a nearby mountain). It was there, on September 22, that these three inexperienced prospectors made their famous discovery. They staked out a placer mining claim of about twenty acres and designated their find as "Discovery Claim," a collective holding that would later be incorporated as the Pioneer Mining Company. Each of the three "lucky Swedes," as they would soon erroneously be known, also staked out a separate claim in his own name on the creek (which was allowed by law) and, following local custom, marked the boundaries with stakes and stone monuments. After locating on Anvil Creek, they proceeded to stake additional claims on Snow Gulch, Dry Creek, and Rock Creek. After panning for several days, they managed to glean a quantity of gold dust valued at about $50. With the evidence of their discovery concealed in a shotgun shell, they returned to Golovnin Bay. They kept news of the find to themselves, but understanding that they would need to organize a mining district, it became necessary to let others in on their secret. Using some discretion, they selected Dr. Albert N. Kittilsen, a physician, G. W. "Gabe" Price, an experienced miner from California, P. H. Anderson, a Swedish missionary, and Johan S. Tornanses, a Lapp reindeer herder, to join their venture.

After chartering a small schooner and purchasing as many supplies as they could take with them, the party returned to Anvil Creek in mid-October. Upon their arrival, the group held a miners' meeting and organized the Cape Nome Mining District. They also re-staked the original

In placer mining, sand and gravel are placed in a trough where rapidly moving water washes away lighter material allowing gold of a higher density to sink to the bottom. The operation shown here was typical at Nome.
COURTESY OF THE LIBRARY OF CONGRESS, PRINTS & PHOTOGRAPHS DIVISION

ground as required by law, marked additional claims, drew up a set of rules to govern the new district, and elected Dr. Kittilsen as the first recorder. Kittilsen, who had been educated at the University of Wisconsin and the Rush Medical College in Chicago, had originally come to Alaska in 1896 after being appointed by the US government as physician for the Lapp reindeer herders stationed at Port Clarence. Although ice was forming in the streams and the ground was beginning to freeze, they were able to construct a crude rocker from materials they brought with them and collect gold dust valued at roughly $1,800. Elated with their early success and the bright prospects that lay ahead, the party returned overland to Golovnin Bay for winter quarters. At that point, the mining claims that had been previously "located" were officially recorded and filed. The group then began making preparations for next season's operations, which meant ordering and transporting supplies from St. Michael. Although the Seward Peninsula was practically cut off from communication with the outside world (the closest post office was at St. Michael one hundred miles away) rumors of the strike gradually reached other parts of Alaska and prospectors from Dawson, Eagle, Circle, Forty Mile, and Rampart began to travel down the Yukon that winter with dog teams to the Nome area. By the time of the spring thaw, Anvil City had a population of several hundred hopefuls living in rough cabins and tents scattered along the beachfront. The wild stampede to the treeless tundra of the Seward Peninsula was poised to begin.

On the fifth day of June 1899, Robert Chipps, a US citizen, challenged the original Discovery claim as invalid and asserted his own claim to the same bonanza site. In the terminology of the time, he "jumped" the claim of the lucky Swedes. This was nine months after the initial filing. Chipps's action was seemingly motivated by his understanding that Brynteson, Lindblom, and Lindeberg were aliens (non-US citizens) and that their claims were nullified by that fact. Chipps's interpretation of the law was in error. Section 2319 of the Revised Statutes provided that all valuable mineral deposits in land belonging to the United States were free and open to exploration and purchase, and the lands in which they were found to occupation and purchase, by citizens of the United States and those who had declared their intentions to become such. But that did not seem to deter Chipps in the least.

After the discovery of gold on Anvil Creek, the first prospectors to arrive by sled, dog team, snowshoe, skiff, skin boat, and kayak were the Swedes, Norwegians, and Laplanders who lived in the vicinity, and they quickly proceeded to cover the creek with their claims. Anvil Creek was about six miles in length but only about three and one-half miles of the creek bed appeared to have "pay gravel." Claims were usually about six hundred feet in width and about 1,320 feet in length (about twenty acres), which was the limit allowed by law. Four claims would extend a mile along the length of the creek and twelve claims would cover all of the area of suspected value.

As news of the gold strike spread during the 1899 spring thaw, hordes of hopefuls converged in the new gold area of Anvil City, now known as the seaside town of Nome. If an outsider had heard anything at all about this region, it was probably similar to the description of one early twentieth-century chronicler who described Nome as a desolate and barren region where "the north winds blew blizzards out of leaden skies and rioted all winter long; and south winds blew tempests that lashed the shallow Bering Sea into fury creating an omnipresent peril to the navigators of these waters."[2] To writer Rex Beach, Nome appeared as a "bleak, open shore, pounded by surf and backed by sodden miles of tundra, rising to low rolling hills barren of all but the ever-present moss, with here and there gnarled willows groveling in the creek bottoms."[3]

When the first vessel, the *Garonne*, arrived at this desolate and forbidding spot carrying passengers from the States, they saw a few cabins constructed from the drift logs on the beach and a number of tents. The most prominent cabin was the deputy recorder's office. The adjoining tent was a restaurant and barbershop. The next tent was a store owned by the Alaska Commercial Company. One tent, festooned in blue stripes, housed a crudely constructed bar and dispensed liquors. Although it was late June, the snow had not entirely disappeared and could be seen piled in deep drifts along the beach. From the beach to the edge of the tundra one could see a mass of driftwood and logs and timber carried down to the sea by the flooded rivers and then deposited on the shore.

But the newcomers were eager to begin and optimistically believed that gold might be found in every stream. As a result, they staked claims from beach to mountaintop in their own names, for relatives and friends, or as agents or having powers of attorney for others. Seasoned veterans called these newcomers "pencil and hatchet" miners because they spent most of their time with a pencil and location notices and a hatchet with which to cut willows to serve as stakes to mark their claims. Vessels loaded to the hilt brought more prospectors down the Yukon, while a rickety fleet of gasoline- and steam-powered stern-wheelers and side-wheelers, used to transport hordes to the Canadian Klondike gold rush two years before, now brought the adventurous to Nome.

Still others came by ocean steamers from Seattle and San Francisco. Author Rex Beach colorfully remembered the migration: "Gamblers and women were close upon the heels of the first comers, as is ever the

Writer and actual gold seeker Rex Beach (shown here in a Stetson) first told the story of the Nome conspiracy in a 1906 magazine series entitled "The Looting of Alaska."

case. Saloons and dance halls appeared. Music and the rattle of dice sounded through the canvas walls. The workers swarmed over the hills, and although the signs of gold were everywhere, there was no vacant ground left. The Swedes had taken it all."[4] To these latecomers it seemed "wickedly unfair that the rich claims, so few in number, should fall to a few 'lucky Swedes' and Lapland rein-deer-herders [*sic*], and loud protests began to rise above the warm stoves in the straggling town. Then some 'sea lawyer' raised the question whether these aliens could legally locate and hold mining claims in Alaska."[5] That was all it took. These late arrivals were, like claim-jumper Chipps, ignorant of the law and easily convinced by the argument that foreigners or aliens had no right to the land and that no one had a right to locate more than one claim on the same creek. Anger at perceived injustice and greed encouraged a wild scramble for property; claim-jumping and relocating became common practices.

With passions inflamed by their own cupidity, a group of discontented miners decided to take direct action to dispossess the original preemptive claimants. Calling themselves the "Law and Order League," they convened a miners' meeting at a saloon in Nome, now the official name for Anvil City. As Rex Beach remembered the gathering, "It comprised as desperate and disappointed a crew of adventurers as may well be pictured: strong, rough men who felt that they were the law of this land and that there was no other, that in their might lay the right to do as they chose. They had grown to rely on themselves and to despise restraint, true products of the frontier, many of them, and dangerous to balk."[6] Their intention was to advance a set of resolutions stating that the district had not been properly organized, that a great deal of illegal staking had been done, and that mining claims located by aliens and more than one mining claim located by the same person on one creek were invalid and therefore open for relocation. Awaiting a signal that the meeting had been a success (a bonfire would be set ablaze in the town), accomplices stationed in the distant hills above Anvil Creek near the initial claims stood ready to proceed directly to the claims and take possession of them. But rumor of the intended action reached Dr. Kittilsen. He quickly alerted Lieutenant Oliver Spaulding, who had been sent with a squad of soldiers from the military post at St. Michaels to maintain order and prevent claim-jumping until an official court could be established. When the resolution was offered, Lieutenant Spaulding and his men, armed with pistols and fixed bayonets, disrupted the meeting and cleared the hall. No bonfires burned that night.

Although the threat of mob activity remained, the volatility of the moment was soon defused a few days later by a most extraordinary occurrence. As the story goes, a pioneer miner of the north country by the name of John Hummel, too weakened with scurvy to travel into the hills with his partners to search for gold, remained behind in his tent on the beach at Nome. Weakened as he was, he still managed to test the sand with his gold pan and discovered, quite by accident, that the beach bordering the town of Nome was rich with gold. It was soon apparent that an individual could make good money employing a primitive rocker apparatus set up on the beach. Mining had suddenly become easy. Using a pick, a shovel, and an ample amount of water, a prospector could place the rich sand into the rocker, where it could then be shaken down to reveal gold particles trapped in the bottom. Upon hearing this news, most of the two thousand dispirited latecomers immediately turned their attention to Hummel's new discovery, and mining operators on the creeks around Nome had difficulty in keeping their workers. Because claims were not allowed on the beach, prospectors could be seen working the sands between the low- and high-water marks shoulder to shoulder for several miles. Following the "pay," eager prospectors were soon tunneling under the local graveyard, ripping up the streets in town, and tearing down the houses that were still under construction. The collective yield of the beach placers was estimated to be more than $1 million, but that much gold was practically all taken out with hand rockers in less than two months. Although temporarily diverted from the diggings at Anvil Creek, the claims there were too rich to be forgotten or to be abandoned to foreigners without a struggle.

As news of the strike at Anvil Creek reached the outside world, it drew others who sought to develop its riches. One of those was Californian Charles D. Lane. No neophyte, Lane had not only been in Alaska before but also possessed a deep knowledge of the country. Wealthy, a man of some standing in the business community, and known for his fair dealings in the commercial world, Lane was also a savvy businessman and practical miner with fifty years of experience in gold and quartz mining in Nevada, Idaho, California, and Arizona. While some of the original locators were undoubtedly frightened by the pending litigation, Lane, who had learned how to protect his mining interests from schemers, was confident that he could fight off the claim-jumpers in court. Then, by utilizing the proper equipment for conducting placer mining on a large scale, he could tap the full potential of the Anvil Creek site. After negotiating with some of the original locators, three of whom were Laplanders, for their possessory rights and procuring four claims for which he was rumored to have paid $300,000, Lane began to work the claims with modern equipment. He proceeded to establish a steamship line from San Francisco to Nome, erected warehouses at Nome, built a pumping plant to bring water from the Snake River to the summit of Anvil Mountain, and constructed a narrow-gauge railroad from Nome to Anvil Creek. All of these enterprises he soon incorporated as the Wild Goose Mining Company. In a short time over $3 million in gold had been taken from the Nome area and the town had expanded to a population of twenty thousand. But the fabulous profits being realized by the Wild Goose and Pioneer Mining Companies only served to enhance the desire of others to undo their efforts.

Anticipating a protracted legal struggle against the lucky Swedes and entrepreneur Lane for the Anvil Creek gold, the claim-jumpers hired the Nome law firm of Hubbard, Beeman, and Hume to represent them. With firsthand knowledge of the potential richness of the claims and armed with the proxies of the claim-jumpers, Oliver P. Hubbard soon concocted a scheme whereby he and his partners could also garner a portion of the Anvil Creek riches. Hubbard had been private secretary to Attorney General William Miller during President Benjamin Harrison's administration and was familiar with the procedures of the Justice Department and governmental operations in Washington in general. To him, the conditions seemed perfect for an attempt at the Great Steal—fabulous mineral wealth held by men who were largely ignorant of the laws, claims about to be smothered in a confusion of lawsuits, a US Congress about to draft a legal code for Alaska that knew nothing of the land, the conditions, or the wealth that was at stake, and a well-connected law-yer (Hubbard) who knew how to navigate the Washington bureaucracy. He just needed a little outside help to set the plan in motion. Toward that end, Hubbard, along with claim-jumper Robert Chipps, traveled during the winter of 1899 to 1900 to New York City and Washington, DC, where they were introduced to Alexander McKenzie.

Known as "senator-maker" of the Dakotas and political "czar" of the Northwest, McKenzie had a reputation for savvy business instincts and bold business dealings. He was also known to have invaluable political connections. McKenzie was an influential member of the national com-mittee of the Republican Party and, as political boss of North Dakota, was closely allied with railroad companies, grain elevator firms centered in Minneapolis and St. Paul, and lumber and insurance companies doing business in the upper Midwest.

Much of McKenzie's early life is a bit of a mystery. He was born on April 3, 1850, in Ontario, Canada, to Scottish parents. Poverty limited young McKenzie's educational opportunities, and he quit his formal education at the age of eleven. Various stories have him sailing the Great Lakes to Duluth to work on the Northern Pacific Railroad, journeying by wagon train from St. Paul to Fort Rice on the Missouri River about fifty miles southeast of the future city of Bismarck, North Dakota, carry-ing dispatches through 250 miles of Sioux territory to Fort Buford, and serving as a scout for Custer's cavalry. He eventually arrived at Fargo in Dakota Territory as a spikeman on the Northern Pacific Railroad. By the summer of 1872 he was in charge of laying track on that line as it moved westward toward the Missouri River. When the Panic of 1873 temporarily halted construction on the railroad, McKenzie found himself in the small, remote outpost of Edwinton, which would later become Bismarck. He began to acquire real estate, multiplied his capital through smartly managed Wall Street investments, and became the Northern Pacific's go-between with local politicians. He soon opened a business in the rough frontier town, and when a local druggist supplied him with a formula for a carbonated beverage (soda pop), he had it delivered by wheelbarrow to stores, restaurants, and hotels. To enhance his success as a businessman, McKenzie learned to sign his name, to write, and to spell, although never expertly. Although poorly educated, he was a man blessed with a good bit of natural genius and remarkable business acumen.

McKenzie began his political career in 1874, when the sheriff of Burleigh County and his deputy drowned when ice in the Missouri River collapsed under them. Tall, broad-shouldered, handsome, and imposing in demeanor, McKenzie parlayed the look of a lawman into an appointment to finish out the unfortunate sheriff's term. When the discovery of gold in the Black Hills attracted bandits, desperados, and an assortment of nefarious criminals, McKenzie proved he was tough enough to handle any problem that came his way. Popular, he eventually served five terms in office as sheriff and also won election as councilman when Bismarck was incorporated in 1875. In the early 1880s McKenzie became an active Republican and soon demonstrated a keen mind for politics. He quickly rose to prominence in the party, displaying unique abilities as an organizer, coalition builder, and tactician. And opportunities for a well-connected individual with a mastery of the political process were plentiful. North Dakota depended on outside interests to supply its needed services. St. Paul railroads and Minneapolis milling companies provided the transportation and storage facilities for the movement of grain. Eastern banks and capitalists controlled the money needed for investment and access to credit.

Selected to the nine-man commission empowered to choose the site for a new capital of the Dakota Territory (Yankton, the current capital, located on the southern border, was being elbowed aside for a more central location), McKenzie successfully maneuvered his election as chairman of the commission's executive committee overseeing the relocation question. An interesting incident involving this debate offers some insight into the character of the man, the boldness of his methods, and the seemingly cavalier disregard he had for the law. The statute empowering the commission called for it to hold its organizational meeting in Yankton, but hostility to the removal idea was so strong in the town that McKenzie decided to work a trick. When the commissioners boarded the special train from Sioux City, Iowa, to carry them to Yankton for the meeting, McKenzie had the train stop at the outer limits of Yankton (his agents had marked the city limits with white flags). A meeting was quickly called to order, a date and site for the next meeting agreed to, and, after complying with the law's stipulation that a meeting be held in Yankton, the meeting adjourned. Deputy sheriffs and officers of the court with writs to prevent the commission from holding any formal meeting in the town could only stand by helplessly on the depot platform as the train carrying the commissioners passed through without even stopping at the Yankton station.

As chairman of the relocation commission, McKenzie called for bids for the new capital from towns in the territory and eleven applied—including Bismarck. Working closely with the Northern Pacific Railroad (which had donated a 160-acre tract of land on which to locate a new capitol in Bismarck, the northern terminus of its line), McKenzie handed out $10,000 checks to each of ten members of the legislature to gain their votes. Although the final vote required thirteen ballots, the legislature ultimately selected Bismarck. McKenzie was charged with complicity in the capital removal plan, but a federal grand jury investigation failed to indict him for bribery. The coup, which critics have called his "theft" of the territorial capital, brought McKenzie much notoriety and served to magnify his reputation as a power broker and enhance his ever-growing political influence. Although statehood reduced the physical size of McKenzie's territorial Dakota domain, he continued to control politics in the state—who got elected to office in North Dakota and most of the federal appointments in the state, in the region, and beyond—for well over a decade, from 1889 until progressives staged a successful revolt against his control in 1906. It was said that seven of the first eight Republican governors had ties to his political machine, and that he selected nearly every US senator from North Dakota during the first twenty-four years of statehood. This last category included Senator Henry C. Hansbrough, who would become a key player in McKenzie's Alaska scheme.

On January 8, 1900, at the Everett House in New York City, McKenzie and North Dakota Senator Henry C. Hansbrough met with attorney Hubbard and claim-jumper Chipps, who said they had valuable mining claims to sell. As a result of that discussion, McKenzie "purchased" a hundred properties held by Hubbard and organized the Alaska Gold Mining Company. McKenzie capitalized the new venture at $15 million and had it incorporated under the laws of Arizona. As president and general manager of the new enterprise, McKenzie kept 51 percent of the shares for himself, to be distributed among his moneyed political connections, and used the remaining 49 percent to buy out the "jumper" titles to the contested claims, which included the Chipps claim to Discovery. Chipps was paid $750 and given $300,000 in stock for his contested title, while Hubbard exchanged his half-interest in the jumper claims for shares of the Alaska Gold Mining Company and became the company secretary. Part of McKenzie's controlling interest was also shared with Senator Hansbrough, Senator Thomas H. Carter of Montana (a former chairman of the Republican National Committee and an expert on mining law), a St. Paul banker, and a Minneapolis-St. Paul attorney by the name of Arthur H. Noyes. By distributing potential rewards to his political and financial friends, McKenzie expected to have his scheme actively supported in Congress and on Wall Street.

Judge Arthur H. Noyes, who would soon prove to be a key member of the conspiracy, was born on April 15, 1853, at Baraboo, Wisconsin. He received an LLB degree in 1878 from the University of Wisconsin. After his younger brother, Rolla Noyes, graduated from law school in 1879, the two brothers established a law practice in Grand Forks, North Dakota, and quickly became active in Republican politics. The brothers eventually moved their practice to Minneapolis-St. Paul. In the meantime, McKenzie had built up a powerful political machine in North Dakota. With political leaders there willing to do his bidding, McKenzie had time to develop other ambitious plans and moved his headquarters from Bismarck to the Merchants Hotel in St. Paul.

McKenzie's plan was to obtain title to the rich Anvil Creek claims that had been jumped, either by legislative action in Congress or by decisions of the local judicial system yet to be established for the area of Alaska that included Nome. If the rightful owners of the mines resisted his takeover, the mines could be placed in the hands of a receiver who, conveniently, would be appointed by a judge controlled by McKenzie. While the litigation was being deliberated in the courts, gold taken from the mines could be sent to New York for display with the view of generating the sale of $15 million worth of stock in the Alaska Gold Mining

Company to an unwary public. Plan A was to get Congress to enable the law in his favor. If that failed, plan B would be to gain the appointment of a compliant judge like Arthur H. Noyes.

During the early part of 1900 Congress began to consider a bill to provide a civil government and a code of laws for the Territory of Alaska. The bill, as reported out of the Senate Committee on Territories on March 5, 1900, by its chairman, Senator Thomas Carter of Montana, followed the laws of the State of Oregon as they had been found to apply to Alaska under an act of Congress dating back to May 17, 1884. Among its provisions relating to mining claims and mineral locations, the bill reiterated that aliens should have the right to acquire and hold lands in Alaska on the same basis as citizens of the United States and that the title to the lands conveyed should not be questioned. When consideration of the bill commenced in the Senate, Senator Hansbrough moved to strike out that provision and insert an amendment that would deny aliens the right to locate, hold or convey mining claims in Alaska, and also disallow any title to a mining claim previously acquired by location or purchase through an alien. The amendment also expanded the law relating to the appointment of receivers for placer mining claims and the granting of injunctions to restrain the working and operation of those claims. The amendment was also made retroactive, declaring null and void all claims located by an agent or attorney in fact. This last provision was undoubtedly directed at the successful Californian Charles Lane, who had acquired many of the original claims and was a leader of the opposition. In fact, Lane had many friends in Washington as well. As chairman of the National Free Silver Committee, he had the attention of politicians in mining states who favored the remonetization of silver.

What followed were nearly two months of acrimonious debate over the proposed amendment. Senator William M. Stewart of Nevada and Senator Henry M. Teller of Colorado, both Lane allies, led those who opposed the amendment on the grounds that the provision would have violated the Fifth Amendment by taking one's property without just compensation. They were joined by Senator Knute Nelson of Minnesota, a native of Norway, who opposed the retroactive nature of the amendment on the grounds that it robbed honest Scandinavian miners of their legally acquired property and that it denigrated Scandinavians and Laplanders. In general, opponents charged that claim-jumpers, as an ilk, were contemptible scoundrels ("blackmailers or thieves" and the "curse of every mining camp") and implied that the amendment was being paid for by get-rich-quick lawyers for the jumpers.[7] Senators Carter and Hansbrough, both known to be McKenzie loyalists, led those who favored the amendment. Their position was that it would protect American citizens and that opposition to the amendment was being directed by wealthy speculators. Angry charges were hurled back and forth across the Senate floor as each side accused the other of being controlled by special interests. One day's *Congressional Record* was filled with such violent personal accusations and recriminations from one senator to another that the comments were later expunged from the record to protect the dignity of that body. In the end, with not enough votes for approval, and with the fear that if the debate continued it would result in the defeat of the Alaska government bill, supporters of the offensive amendment agreed to have it withdrawn. Congress approved the final bill providing a civil government for the Territory of Alaska on June 6, 1900. The measure established a federal district court for Alaska and the appointment, to be made by the president, of three federal judges to reside in various divisions of the territory. The judge assigned to District No. 2, which included Nome, was to reside at St. Michael and hold at least one term each year there, beginning with the third Monday in June. Judges were allowed to hold special terms of court at other times and places in their district, provided that public notice was given at least thirty days before such a special term was held.

Having been thwarted in his attempt to get Congress to enable the law in his favor, McKenzie decided that he would try to steal the rich placer claims at Anvil Creek by using the federal courts. To accomplish this, he depended on his political connections within the highest level of the Republican Party. A North Dakota politician close to McKenzie reportedly made the comment that railroad baron James J. Hill, Wall Street financier J. Pierpont Morgan, Senator Simon Guggenheim of Colorado, and Senator Thomas C. Platt of New York were all aware of McKenzie's scheme, and that President McKinley, who would formally make the judicial appointments, was privy as well. One will never know the exact strings that McKenzie pulled to realize his goal, but the extent of his political connections seemed extraordinary. He convinced President McKinley to appoint Arthur H. Noyes of Minnesota as one of the three Alaska district judges. As mentioned earlier, McKenzie and Noyes were old friends, and the "boss" knew him as someone who would take orders. They had been seen together in Washington during the Senate debates on the Alaska bill. Noyes's jurisdiction would be Alaska's Second Judicial District, the division that included Nome and the gold claims that McKenzie coveted. Relying on his political connections, McKenzie was also able to get President McKinley to appoint Cornelius Vawter of Montana as US marshal for Nome, Joseph K. Wood of Montana as US district attorney for Nome, and R. N. Stevens as US commissioner (a post that combined the functions of justice of the peace, probate judge, and lower court judge) at Nome. Vawter and Wood were nominated for their positions by Senator Carter of Montana while Stevens was the senator's brother-in-law. With this group of co-conspirators in place, McKenzie would be able to completely control the courts at Nome. In the words of one judicial official who later became familiar with the details of the unfolding scheme: It was clear that McKenzie was "intent on capturing a fortune by piratic force from a few simple-minded Lapp reindeer-herders and hard-digging Scandinavian miners. It looked to the boss like an easy job!"[8]

McKenzie and Noyes traveled together from Seattle, ironically aboard the steamer SS *Senator*, and reached Nome on July 19, 1900, long after the time for holding a term of the court at St. Michael had lapsed. Arriving at Nome just a month before the conspirators, author Rex Beach remembered that tremendous changes had taken place in the "camp" during the winter. Instead of a "naked little town clinging forlornly to the edge of the Northland" characterized by fifty or sixty frame and galvanized-iron buildings scattered along both sides of a muddy thoroughfare roughly a mile in length, and several hundred tents and low driftwood cabins following the coastline, there was now a veritable city "peopled by the landing thousands." The shallow harbor was crowded with ships unloading freight and men under the midnight sun. One observer counted seventy ships in the harbor at one time—large steamers and ships lying at anchor, and tugs and gasoline schooners busily towing barges loaded with freight from the ships. An army of longshoremen carried heavy boxes or bales of goods, walking the gangplanks from the barges to the beach. Freight was stacked along the beach and streets were clogged with traffic. Hotel accommodations were inadequate and there was a lack of places for people to sleep. "We slept, when we got too tired to work" said Beach, "on floors—if we had friends—if not, on the ground or a borrowed board." Every hour seemed to see new machinery being brought ashore. In place of the primitive rocker devices that had littered the beach the year before, there was now a line of dredges and gasoline-powered pumping plants, and huge cranes that reached out into the sea. New buildings—hotels, French restaurants, steam laundries, and Turkish baths—could be seen everywhere. Pack trains carried goods to the mines where the previous year food would have been carried on the backs of gum-booted men and dogs. A railroad had been constructed from the coast to the placers in the hills, and the "cross-ties were laid on planks which now and then disappeared in the mud." Prices were high, in fact, said to be from two to five times higher than in Seattle or San Francisco. Men were busy, and "the country was developing like magic."[9] It seemed as if the town had grown from three to thirty thousand overnight.

Others were less boosterish. One historian described Nome in 1900 by saying: "Honest men and women jostled with gamblers, con men, whores, pimps, thieves, and trigger-happy gunmen on the crooked streets. . . . Shootings, muggings, and saloon brawls were endemic in what was . . . as turbulent a community as ever existed in the Old West."[10] The report of one governmental employee in Nome rendered a similar verdict.

To this place has flocked thousands of people attracted by the riches of the gold diggings, and thousands more have followed them to engage in every sort of business and scheme that would be liable to run into their pockets some of the proceeds of the miners' labor. With them have come some of the sharpest criminals, the most dangerous cutthroats and bad men that civilization has produced, and it is a conservative thing to say that Nome has within its limits the worst aggregation of criminals and unprincipled men and women that were ever drawn together in this country.

Compared with Nome, today Butte, Montana, which is famous as the wickedest city in the United States, is a righteous and law-abiding community.[11]

Reaching Nome was far easier than the trek to the Klondike because the would-be prospector could simply wade ashore from a steamer and be at his destination. As one observer put it, "there was no winnowing of the persevering and enterprising from the shiftless and indolent as at the Chilkoot Pass [the gateway to the Klondike]."[12] As a result, many who crowded to Nome were less fitted for frontier life than those who had ventured to Dawson two years before. Many in the town, in fact, were neither boosters nor reprobates but actually novices chasing a dream. As one historian writing about Nome in 1905 remembered it:

A great many of the new arrivals pitched their tents, sat around, cooked and ate up their food, and, later in the season, like the Arabs, 'quietly folded their tents and stole away,' without accomplishing anything or trying to accomplish anything. The crude sidewalks of Nome were securely held down by a great army of men who discussed mining, the resources of the country and the prospects of the town, but never went to the creeks nor hit the ground hard enough to kill a snake. Sanguine but inexperienced men, whose only resemblance to miners was their garb, hastily put together pieces of new-fangled devices for mining. Their story was told later in the season when the beach was partially covered with abandoned nondescript mining machinery. There were other men with pack trains. These pack trains, loaded, could be seen nearly every day for a fortnight or more starting from Nome on prospecting trips to the great interior. Men had arrived in Nome to follow the directions of fortune-tellers and sooth-sayers; others had quiet tips purporting to come from early Government surveying expeditions; the truth is not stretched in the assertion that nine out of ten of the people that arrived in Nome during the summer of 1900 were visionary and impracticable, lacking knowledge of mining and mining methods.[13]

While Judge Noyes rested in his stateroom aboard the steamship anchored in the harbor a mile off the beach, McKenzie immediately went ashore and proceeded to the law offices of Hubbard, Beeman, and Hume. There, in conference with William T. Hume and Edwin Beeman, McKenzie informed them that their partner, Hubbard, had transferred to him his 50 percent contingent interest in the claims of the jumpers should they prevail in court and that Hubbard had assured him they would do likewise. McKenzie told them that he controlled the newly appointed judge and district attorney for the district, and that if they wished to see those cases heard in court they would have to transfer their interest in the suits to his Alaska Gold Mining Corporation and receive in lieu thereof shares of stock in his company. Left with little choice, they accepted the "offer." McKenzie then insisted that the attorneys transfer an additional one-fourth interest in their law firm to Joseph K. Wood, the district attorney, and that Wood would become a silent partner in their business. In return, Hume would be named deputy district attorney. This, too, was agreed to. Immediately after making these arrangements, McKenzie then demanded another one-fourth interest in the firm to be held in trust for Judge Noyes. Hume and Beeman protested this last holdup, but when McKenzie threatened to ruin their legal practice and sabotage the interests of their clients, they acquiesced. Partnership articles were then quickly drawn up and signed.

The claim-jumping lawsuits would provide McKenzie with the legal protection he needed to gain control of the rich Anvil Creek mining claims. Having manipulated his control of the firm of Hume, Beeman, and Hubbard, the only thing that remained in McKenzie's carefully calculated scheme was to have the attorneys prepare papers for the appointment of a receiver. Normally, the duty of a receiver in a property dispute is to act as a disinterested party holding a contested property in trust so that its value will not be compromised until the court can adjudicate the contested claims to title in a fair manner. In this particular case, obviously, the best way to preserve the gold was just to leave it in the ground. But McKenzie's conception of the duties of a receiver was quite different.

It was at this juncture that Alexander McKenzie revealed the full extent of his audacity as he summoned Judge Noyes ashore to officially begin his duties. On July 23 Hume met with Noyes in his hotel room and presented him with petitions asking that the disputed claims be placed in the hands of a receiver appointed by the court. When Hume began reading the affidavit setting out the facts that might justify the appointment of a receiver, however, Judge Noyes stopped him short saying that such a reading was unnecessary. Without notifying the defendants or waiting to hear arguments from their side in the dispute, Noyes declared that as he was a stranger to the territory, he preferred to appoint someone he knew. With that, he named Alexander McKenzie as receiver. Continuing this travesty, instead of charging McKenzie to hold the disputed properties in trust, Noyes directed him to take immediate possession of the mines. He then granted McKenzie permission to operate those properties and to hold the gold dust and proceeds from the claims! Any defendants were enjoined from interfering with the management of the mines in any way. As a further indignity, the court required that McKenzie post bond of $5,000 for each property, a woefully inadequate amount for the rich placer claims where the output of each mine was known to be from $5,000 to $15,000 of gold each day. With the likelihood of a long, drawn-out legal battle that could last for years, the "court's" order opened the door to McKenzie's full exploitation of the land, the legitimate claim-holders, and the law. By the time the so-called claim-jumpers had run out of legal options, Alexander McKenzie would have exhausted the gold in Anvil Creek.

Having orchestrated the judge's decision, McKenzie was poised to pounce. When informed that Judge Noyes had signed the petitions, McKenzie and his men, accompanied by a deputy marshal, boarded waiting wagons and raced to Anvil Creek. McKenzie found Jafet Lindeberg asleep in his tent on the mining claim and quickly ran him off. Some of Lindeberg's men, however, were quick enough to distract McKenzie while others sneaked in the back window of the mine office and recovered most of the gold nuggets in the safe before McKenzie's men were able to respond. By midnight McKenzie had all the properties in his possession. All this had come as a total surprise to the rightful owners, who, having not been notified, were denied even the opportunity to appear in their own defense and argue why such orders should not be issued. Without a telegraph line to carry reports of McKenzie's actions to the United States or to the circuit court of appeals in San Francisco, Lindeberg, Lane, and others were helpless in the face of McKenzie's appropriation of their properties.

With as close to lightning speed as possible, McKenzie began mining gold. He hired every available man he could find to work the claims around the clock. Within weeks of taking possession of the claims, McKenzie's men extracted more than $130,000 in gold dust. McKenzie also allegedly confiscated more than $200,000 in gold dust that belonged to the original locators. They later sued McKenzie for $430,000 in damages that included the value of their claim, their mining rights, and their wrecked equipment. But in fact, the rightful owners of the mines had no idea how much gold McKenzie was taking from the gravel along the creek. It was a sum later rumored to be $600,000. This brazen seizure of the properties had a ripple effect. Serious work halted on other claims in the area because many owners feared that if they found gold, Noyes and McKenzie would just steal it through some specious legal argument. At the other extreme, others reasoned that Noyes must know the law, so they began jumping every potentially valuable claim they could in hopes that they would later be able to prove that the original claim had not been staked according to the letter of the law. Claim-jumpers jumped claim-jumpers until some mining sites had as many as twelve people asserting ownership. McKenzie had not only committed fraud, he had also triggered mayhem.

On the day following the appointment of McKenzie as receiver of the Anvil Creek claims, Samuel Knight and William Metson, two leading San Francisco attorneys representing the original locators, called on Judge Noyes to request that he revoke the order appointing a receiver. He cavalierly put them off until August 10, and then denied them a hearing. A few days later they applied to Judge Noyes for orders allowing them to appeal to the Court of Appeals for the Ninth Circuit in San Francisco. Noyes denied this request as well, claiming that the orders of his court were not appealable, and, in effect, that he had exclusive jurisdiction in the case. Offended by the legal challenge to his authority, Noyes told the attorneys, "I am going to tie your people up all around."[14] He then proceeded to punish their clients by expanding the powers of the receiver to seize all their personal property on the claims—business records, money, tents, beds, and clothing. This sweeping order was in direct violation of the law, which limited the power and authority of a receiver to take possession of other than specific personal property. In fact, the entire proceedings from the very first order to the last were either in violation of the law or of well-established rules of procedure. Concerning this last order of Judge Noyes, the circuit court of appeals at San Francisco would later state that it was "so arbitrary and unwarranted in law as to baffle the mind in its effort to comprehend how it could have been issued from a court of justice."[15] Writer Rex Beach assessed the scheme at this point as "a perfect piece of political jobbery, backed by the weight of the United States courts and enforced by the troops in blue. Mines wrested from their owners, laws construed to suit the gang, personal property purloined to cripple the victims, the right of appeal denied—!"[16]

Stymied by the unwarranted actions of Judge Noyes in Nome, lawyers Knight and Metson then decided to send certified copies of the recent court proceedings to US Attorney General John W. Griggs in Washington in the hope that he would remove Noyes for incompetence. Griggs ignored their petition. The two attorneys finally realized that they only had one avenue left and that was to make an emotional appeal to a higher court outside of Alaska for allowance of their appeals and writs of supersedeas to stop the execution of Judge Noyes's orders. To carry out this plan, they decided to dispatch a special messenger armed with papers and affidavits disclosing the record of gross judicial unfairness by the court at Nome to the circuit court of appeals in San Francisco. The plan had to be carried out with utmost secrecy so as to elude federal agents under McKenzie's control. Although the circuit court was not officially in session, Judge William Morrow agreed to read the legal documents and remarked that the actions of Judge Noyes appeared to be "high-handed and grossly illegal."[17] He then issued writs of supersedeas for the purpose of overriding Noyes's rulings and commanding him to stay all further proceedings. Morrow also ordered McKenzie to restore the mining claims to the original locators together with the confiscated gold and all their other personal property. Armed with certified copies of Judge Morrow's orders, the messenger hurried back to Alaska.

A terrible storm prevented the messenger from immediately disembarking when the ship arrived at Nome on September 14 and delayed the delivery of the papers. When McKenzie learned that the writs were about to be served, and while the ship was still storm-bound in the harbor, he hurried to the Alaska Banking and Safety Deposit Company to retrieve his hoard of gold dust. But the original claim owners were watching his movements and surrounded McKenzie inside the bank. There, by sheer force of numbers, they compelled McKenzie to abandon his mission and leave the bank empty-handed. Rex Beach has provided a vivid description of the dramatic scene.

> *Violence threatened and it looked bad for the Czar of the Dakotas, for he was hemmed into a room by the men he had betrayed.... Virtually they had the Dakotan's back to the wall at last. He faced them—one wily and determined man against fifty wronged and angry ones. He made oily excuses. . . . He did not dream of removing the Anvil Creek dust. How ridiculous! Perish the thought! The mob was loathe to believe this and would not let him leave the bank—at which righteous indignation flamed up within him. Who were they to stop a peaceful, honest person? He turned on them like a great bear, crying dramatically: 'I am an American citizen. I have committed no crime and I am going out of here. Stand aside!' He raised his empty hands above his head and walked out through the press, glaring at them, eye to eye. One man dropped a gun in his excitement, but no one stopped him. The man's physical daring excites admiration. What a superb villain he is!*[18]

All this happened while the storm was most intense. As the rain continued with unabated fury, the streets became muddy quagmires. Sections of the town were under water, and houses and wreckage could be seen drifting everywhere. Tugs, floating piers, and small boats lay tossed on the beach, while all the machinery which had been located on the beach was buried in the sand. The storm provided an excellent backdrop for a dramatic event.

When finally served with the writs from the higher court, McKenzie refused to comply with them and Judge Noyes declined to enforce them. Two of McKenzie's strategically placed co-conspirators, Joseph Wood, the US district attorney for Nome and partner of McKenzie, and C. A. S. Frost, who had been sent to Alaska as a special examiner by the Justice Department and then gained appointment as assistant US district attorney before being co-opted by McKenzie, encouraged him to adopt a defiant position. Instead of enforcing the order of the appeals court, Wood and Frost ordered another McKenzie man, US Marshal Cornelius Vawter to swear in a *posse comitatus* to prevent anyone from trying to enforce the writs. Tensions were high and individuals on both sides carried guns. It was reported that Frost also hired three private detectives at government expense to shadow the movements of Charles Lane, the lucky Swedes, and their lawyers, and to report their findings to McKenzie. Pressed on the matter, McKenzie allegedly boasted: "I am not stealing pennies."[19] Attorney Metson alleged that McKenzie offered him a $1 million bribe to desert his clients. Equally uncooperative, Judge Noyes held that the court of appeals had no right to allow the appeals or issue the writs of supersedeas. In private, Noyes allegedly declared: "Our company made a great mistake not to have had someone to look after the San Francisco end of this litigation; if it had these writs would have never been issued."[20] At first Noyes argued that the writs might not be genuine, and then advanced the argument that they only required him to maintain the status quo of the receivership. Maintaining the status quo, of course, meant that McKenzie would continue to exploit the Anvil Creek claims. Instead, in what one writer called "the very burlesque of law," Noyes called on troops to guard the gold kept in the vault of a local bank to prevent the plaintiffs from taking it.[21] Equally concerned, the original locators stationed guards with shotguns and Winchester rifles in an upstairs room in a building directly across the street from the bank. The guards had instructions not to allow anyone suspected of being connected to the McKenzie ring to take pokes of gold dust out of the bank.

When Judge Morrow in San Francisco learned that the receiver, the US district attorney, the assistant US district attorney, the US marshal, and a federal judge had disdainfully dismissed his court orders, he immediately sent two federal marshals to Nome to enforce the writs and arrest Alexander McKenzie for contempt of court. They had to hurry as it was already October 1, and Nome would soon be locked in ice and unreachable until the following summer.

The federal marshals arrived at Nome aboard the SS *Oregon* on October 15 and confronted McKenzie while he ate breakfast. In typical bravado McKenzie insisted that no "son of a bitch" could arrest him.[22] The comment was typical of others he had arrogantly made in public, claiming at one time or another that: "Nobody can hurt me. I am too strong at *headquarters*," and "the strongest in public life" were backing him.[23] But the marshals refused to be intimidated and, despite warnings from McKenzie's allies that violence would develop if they tried to arrest him, placed McKenzie in custody. That same afternoon McKenzie sent for Judge Noyes and asked him to issue a writ to set him free, but Noyes refused knowing that such an action would now place him in jeopardy. It was the first indication that the judge had decided to distance himself from the boss.

McKenzie had given the keys to the vault boxes of the Alaska Banking and Safe Deposit Company, along with some confidential papers, to US District Attorney Wood. When the marshals requested that Wood relinquish the keys, he refused even to admit that they were in his possession. Undeterred, the marshals called upon the army at Fort Davis who sent a contingent of soldiers to assist them. They then used sledgehammers to break into the safe-deposit boxes. The marshals then handed the gold dust, valued at over $200,000, to the original locators as directed by Judge Morrow. With McKenzie safely in their custody, the marshals hurried to catch the *St. Paul*, the last ship leaving Nome before the grip of winter ice in the Bering Sea closed off the harbor. Also being transported on the vessel were the certified copies of the court records (the evidence of conspiracy) that had been secured by attorney Samuel Knight. Judge Noyes had ordered that Knight be arrested and placed in jail for suborning perjury, but Knight managed to evade arrest by smuggling himself out of Nome on a small launch. He then waited at sea to catch the *St. Paul* as it left the harbor. At the end of the three-thousand-mile sea voyage back to San Francisco, McKenzie would have to face the trial that he boasted would never take place.

Upon arriving in San Francisco on November 7, 1900, McKenzie vowed that he would never go to prison. Representing McKenzie was a team of impressive legal talent that included Frank B. Kellogg, a future secretary of state. His attorneys immediately petitioned the Supreme Court of the United States to put aside the prosecution, but after a hearing on December 7, the higher court ordered a trial. The gathering of evidence for the contempt trial took several weeks and then preparations for oral arguments and consideration of the evidence several more. Finally, on February 11, 1901, the court found Alexander McKenzie guilty of contempt of court. In arriving at their decision, the three judges of the Ninth Circuit Court of Appeals—William W. Morrow, Erskine Ross, and William B. Gilbert—rejected the claim of McKenzie's lawyers that he had refused to obey the writs of supersedeas because his legal counsel had advised him that they were void. Instead, they found McKenzie's actions to be "intentional and deliberate" and commented that the "grossly illegal proceedings initiated almost as soon as Judge Noyes and McKenzie had set foot on Alaskan territory at Nome . . . may be . . . said to have no parallel in the jurisprudence of this country."[24] The court then sentenced McKenzie to a term of one year in the Alameda County jail. The three judges agreed that there was obvious evidence of a criminal conspiracy to use the federal judicial system for the theft of gold mines and that McKenzie's actions merited far more severe punishment, but since he was only on trial for contempt of court, additional punishment must await another trial for conspiracy. But that was unlikely to happen. McKenzie was one of the most powerful political bosses in the country and had an array of supporters on Capitol Hill and influence with President McKinley. And the McKinley administration was not about to press a case for conspiracy that might reach back to fellow Republicans in Washington.

As soon as their client entered jail in Oakland, California, McKenzie's attorneys began to work overtime to gain his release. They immediately applied to the US Supreme Court for a writ of habeas corpus, which would allow argument of the case before the higher court. They intended to argue that McKenzie's actions as receiver were based on the order of a federal judge, his old friend Noyes. But the US Supreme Court rejected the application for a writ and upheld the lower court's ruling on all points. McKenzie's supporters then launched a campaign to free him by bringing pressure to bear on President McKinley. Senator Hansbrough, who had attempted to amend the federal mining law to the conspirators' advantage, and Senator Richard F. Pettigrew of South Dakota defended him on the Senate floor. Senator Mark Hanna of Ohio, a close confidant of McKinley, reportedly called McKenzie's conviction a "high-handed outrage." Meanwhile, the North Dakota legislature petitioned the president for clemency, supported by scores of telegrams from loyalists in North Dakota and Minnesota in support of its action. Another petition by senators, congressmen, and US judges stated that they believed McKenzie would not intentionally break the law. Mark Hanna, along with railroad magnates James J. Hill of the Great Northern and Daniel S. Lamont, vice president of the Northern Pacific and a former secretary of war, consulted with the president about the case. Leaving no stone unturned, Senator Matthew Quay of Pennsylvania put pressure on Attorney General Philander C. Knox to exert his influence in the matter. Feeling the political heat, President McKinley reportedly remarked that in his entire political career "he had never before been subjected to such tremendous pressure from influential men as he had been to pardon McKenzie."[25]

Yielding to pressure, McKinley, who happened to be in California to commission the battleship *Ohio*, asked the judges at San Francisco what they thought about the propriety of a presidential pardon. The judges had rejected Attorney General Knox's suggestion that McKenzie's sentence be commuted to time served. To put additional pressure on the judges, Senators Hansbrough and Porter J. McCumber of North Dakota convinced a Minneapolis doctor to certify that the prisoner's health was so frail that he would in all likelihood not survive his remaining months in jail. Although McKenzie's stay in jail had been an easy and relatively comfortable one—he had been allowed the free use of the corridors and the jail yard and was able to receive many visitors—his doctor argued that he was suffering from dilation of the heart and nervous prostration. Questions concerning McKenzie's health were also supported by three other Oakland doctors who declared that the "climate" of the Alameda jail was harmful to the prisoner's well-being. Finally, on May 23, after conferring with President McKinley and a representative of the Justice Department, the judges gave in to McKinley's initial request and agreed to clemency. As part of the "arrangement," McKenzie was induced to issue a statement of contrition and compelled to return another $9,000 in gold that he had stolen and shipped to Seattle, supposedly on the orders of Judge Noyes. After serving a mere three and one-half months of his twelve-month sentence, McKenzie was released from jail the next day, and within a few hours was reportedly seen "sprinting" down the railway platform of the Southern Pacific station in Oakland to catch the first train out of town.[26]

In summing up the McKenzie portion of the contempt of court proceedings, James Wickersham, US district judge for Alaska from 1900 to 1908, stated: "McKenzie now ceased to be an active defendant in the Nome contempt cases. Having made such restitution as the court demanded and complied with its orders, his notorious criminal activities as the head of the most flagrant prostitution of American courts known in our history, and his other offenses were all forgiven by the President's pardon."[27] McKenzie returned to North Dakota, where he quickly "recovered his health" and resumed his activities as a leading citizen. When the counterclaims filed by McKenzie on behalf of the claim-jumpers finally reached the court of appeals, the judges ruled in favor of the original locators in every case. The Pioneer and Wild Goose Mining Companies were able to recover all the claims in question.

Proceedings against Judge Noyes and the other members of the ring in Nome were deferred while the McKenzie case tracked through the courts. In the meantime, Noyes and US District Attorney Wood continued to hold office through the winter months. But the judge, apparently hampered by heavy drinking, made little progress in dealing with the backlog of cases that had built up over the previous year. When the Ninth Circuit Court finally got around to citing Noyes for contempt, the Justice Department suspended him from making further decisions pending the outcome of his case and assigned his docket to the more capable district judge for Division No. 3, James Wickersham. During the winter

Wickersham tried fifty-six jury cases and 140 equity cases. He also dismissed 226 cases for want of evidence, most of which had been filed on a whim by claim-jumpers who intended to use the threat of litigation as a means of extortion. Noyes received his contempt citation from the court on July 5, 1901, when the shipping lane to Nome reopened. His initial reaction was to posture as the outraged innocent. In a letter to Senator Hansbrough, he claimed: "I never did a dishonorable thing in my life, and never spent a dishonorable dollar in my life and I never expect to. The golden opinions of my fellow men are treasures far too rich to be swapped for gold dust."[28] He placed the blame for all the false accusations against him on the owners of the Pioneer and Wild Goose Mining Companies, whom, he said, had slandered him after he had refused their bribes.

When Judge Noyes was finally ready to leave Nome on August 13, he reportedly stumbled drunk onto the deck of the SS *Queen*, dropping a heavy package onto the deck, where it remained while he secluded himself in his cabin. Late the next day someone on board examined the package and found two sacks of gold nuggets, more than one hundred pounds of gold. How a federal judge could possess such a treasure was patently obvious to those familiar with the judge and his methods. A few days after Noyes sailed from Nome, two petitions—one from the general public and the other from fifty-four attorneys of the Nome bar—were sent to President McKinley asking that Noyes be removed from his position and a fair, honest, and capable judge be appointed in his place. The petition from the lawyers argued that removal was necessary to "prevent riot and bloodshed" and charged that Noyes was "vacillating," "dilatory," "weak," "petty," "negligent," "careless," and "absolutely incompetent."[29] In plotting strategy, the judge still harbored hope that influential political allies in Washington would find a way to transfer the investigation to the nation's capital where, among friendly senators, he might have a better chance of eluding punishment. But after traveling to Washington to lobby on his own behalf, he failed to secure a change of venue. His trial finally began in San Francisco in October and followed the same format as the McKenzie prosecution. After taking several thousand pages of testimony, the court delivered its decision on January 6, 1902.

Noyes had been charged with contempt for refusing to enforce the supersedeas writs ordering McKenzie to relinquish the gold dust that he had confiscated from the claims along Anvil Creek. His attorneys argued in his defense that he believed all matters relating to the receivership had moved beyond his control. The court thought otherwise. Although the three judges trying the case expressed no official opinion on the existence of a conspiracy, they left little doubt that they believed one existed. In the words of the court: "Much of [the evidence] tends strongly to show the existence of a criminal conspiracy between some of these respondents and McKenzie and others to use the court and its process for their private gain, and to unlawfully deprive the owners of mines who were in possession thereof of their property under the forms of law."[30] In fact, the court's summary of Judge Noyes's offense focused more on the unseemly deeds of the Nome ring in stealing gold than on the specific actions that justified a contempt conviction. Surrounding the contempt charge in this manner may have been unnecessary in reaching a decision on the narrow legal issue presented by the case, but in such a politically charged litigation it probably served as a pragmatic approach for the court to take. By including the full scope of Noyes's misdeeds in its opinion, the court guarded itself against any accusations of bias by Judge Noyes's defenders. At the same time, their detailed presentation of wrongdoing could add strength to the argument for a new trial should Justice Department officials decide to take stronger action.

Although the judges unanimously found Judge Noyes guilty of contempt, they disagreed on the appropriate punishment. Judges Morrow and Gilbert recommended the imposition of a $1,000 fine in lieu of imprisonment. Judge Ross disagreed and recommended that Noyes be sentenced to eighteen months in the county jail. Morrow and Gilbert, however, acting as the majority, concluded that imprisonment would have been tantamount to removal from office—a punishment that they believed they were not authorized to impose. As a result, Noyes was fined and the question of further punishment (removal from office) left up to President Theodore Roosevelt, who had assumed office after the assassination of President McKinley.[31]

When the convictions of Noyes and the other corrupt officials were finally reported, Alaskans rendered their opinions on the verdict. Editor J. F. A. Strong of the *Nome Nugget* described the machinations as one of "the most amazing conspiracies to obtain gold by legalized robbery that has ever been known in the history of the jurisprudence of this or any other country," and marveled at "the brazen effrontery displayed by McKenzie, his tools, hirelings, and henchmen." He also offered no sympathy for the "freebooters who foolishly imagined themselves the people."[32] In the mind of the editor, they had all made a mockery of the law. To writer Rex Beach, the story was the "Looting of Alaska" where a territory had been "ruined, rifled, and degraded by such practices as have seldom blackened the pages of American corruption." To accomplish Alaska's "debauch," said Beach, "our judiciary has been capitalized, and American courts of law exploited as a commercial investment." Taking the long view of the events that unfolded, Beach saw a tale of "intrigue and pillage originating in the fertile brains of statesmen beneath the shadow of the Washington Monument, stretching out to the westward and ending among the gold-bottomed placers of Nome"[33]

The Ninth Circuit Court came under heavy criticism for its decision in the Nome scandal. Miners in general were upset that the spoilers got off so easily. After his conviction for contempt, a grand jury in Nome wanted to indict Judge Noyes on criminal charges. But neither the Justice Department nor President Roosevelt in Washington nor Judge Wickersham in Nome were eager for a new prosecution. It seemed as if all parties believed that any vindication would not be worth the embarrassment to the government, the courts, or to certain leading politicians. As a result, Judge Wickersham resisted efforts in Nome to seek a grand jury indictment. Although it might be argued that the action smacked of an administration cover-up, Judge Wickersham adamantly defended the position that it was better to let the matter drop and accept the disgrace of a contempt conviction as sufficient punishment. "The quicker the people of Nome and the court forgot those black days," said Wickersham, "the better it would be for the administration of justice in that district."[34]

Others in Washington were not as easily convinced. The *Washington Post*, which had taken a leading role in exposing the shameful affair in its entirety, led the call for a special investigation and for the current administration to explain why Judge Noyes had not been removed from office. In response, Attorney General Knox agreed to undertake a new evaluation of Justice Department documents. During that review process, David H. Jarvis, the collector of customs at Nome and something of a confidant of the president on matters pertaining to Alaska, wrote to President Theodore Roosevelt from his post in Alaska. In the opinion of Jarvis, only "the immediate removal of everybody connected with this conspiracy will give the people confidence in the good intentions of the administration and restore confidence and stability to the business of that part of Alaska." Roosevelt then scribbled a note to the bottom of the memorandum which read: "Atty Gen'l, This is from Jarvis, who certainly knows Alaska. TR."[35] Understanding the meaning of the note, Attorney General Knox removed Noyes from office on February 24, 1902.

Strange as it might seem, the Nome scandal did not receive widespread national exposure until 1905 to 1906, when writer Rex Beach published a novel and then a series of articles on the subject. Beach, who had lived in Nome during the gold rush and was well acquainted with the McKenzie-Noyes saga, published a fictionalized version of the story in 1905 as *The Spoilers*. The popularity of that best-selling novel (it sold eight hundred thousand copies in the first ten years of publication) led Beach to follow it up with the nonfiction details of the remarkable events in a five-part series he wrote for *Appleton's Booklovers Magazine* that appeared between January and May 1906, entitled "The Looting of Alaska." Beach charged that the scandal had been "smothered and the public kept in ignorance." "Criminals," said Beach, "were pardoned, records expunged, thieves exalted to new honors. Your Alaskan remembers it, though—remembers when he was bound, gagged, and gone through by the basest officials that ever disgraced an appointment. He remembers how at headquarters the wheels of justice were mysteriously clogged, and how, when judgment of a feeble kind overtook the gang, they squirmed out of punishment." Beach also wondered how such actions could have occurred, and then asked rhetorically if they had been made possible "by our territorial policy, by our system of official appointments, by the moral degradation of our professional politicians, or by an indifferent, calloused public sentiment?"[36]

The novel and articles caused a sensation, especially in Washington where some politicians cringed at the public revelations of their complicity. The publicized scandal had a startling effect on readers as great as the best of the current muckraking exposés that were then in vogue. *The Spoilers* was eventually transformed into a stage play and then five times made into a movie. The most successful of the latter was a version that starred John Wayne, Randolph Scott, and Marlene Dietrich in 1942. Although the roles played by Wayne and Dietrich were the inventions of screenwriters, Scott played Alexander MacNamara, a character based on the real-life villain Alexander McKenzie.

Although Judge Arthur H. Noyes seems to have disappeared from the historical record after his conviction and removal from office in 1902, the same cannot be said of Alexander McKenzie. After a progressive revolt in North Dakota politics ousted the McKenzie-controlled political machine in 1906, their leader merely turned his attention to other lucrative pursuits. He speculated in real estate, became a contact man for a St. Paul construction company where he acted as sort of a "rainmaker" securing contracts for the firm, and formed a partnership with Richard B. Mellon to deal in securities. He also owned a ranch with two thousand head of cattle as well as various mining properties. When he died in 1922, arrangements were immediately made for a state funeral for private citizen McKenzie in North Dakota. A Northern Pacific train carrying his body back to Bismarck was met by an honor guard of the North Dakota National Guard and by Masonic and Catholic delegations. A funeral service befitting a "state-builder" was held in the chamber of the House of Representatives. McKenzie's role in the Nome scandal seemed to be excused and/or completely forgotten.

Chapter Two

The Montana Copper Wars (Part I)

The Clark-Daly Feud

SITUATED ON A HILLSIDE BENEATH THE CONTINENTAL DIVIDE IN THE northern Rocky Mountains of southwestern Montana is the town of Butte. Overlooking the Silver Bow Valley at an elevation of 5,800 feet, this remote location offers little to suggest that it would become a major commercial center. But, as one historian has noted, it was "geology, not geography, that made this isolated valley such a remarkable place."[1] At the northern end of this mountain basin lies a russet-colored hill that became the site for a town which took its name from a nearby promontory called "Big Butte." The hill, roughly six hundred acres in size, sits atop one of the greatest mineral formations to be found anywhere in the world. Its riches would lure thousands of fortune-seekers and attract millions of dollars in investments, and one day one of the world's greatest mining centers would surround it. The millions of dollars in profits taken from what has been called the richest hill on earth would build some of America's great fortunes, besmirch the political life of the state and the nation, lead to an epic battle against the "Copper Trust," and, ultimately, shake the financial world on Wall Street.

Intricately interwoven into the history of this part of Montana are the personalities and careers of three individuals—William Andrews Clark, Marcus Daly, and F. Augustus Heinze—known to Montanans as the "Copper Kings." How these three individuals vied for fame and fortune became, according to one chronicler, part of "one of the most corrupt political and commercial conflicts known to history." As muck-raking journalist C. P. Connolly rather dramatically put it in his serialized account "The Story of Montana" for *McClure's* magazine in 1906, the struggle between these three mining kings "made hundreds of men, and ruined thousands; . . . perverted the moral sense of entire communities; . . . placed scores of prominent men within the shadow of prison walls; [and] . . . destroyed promising political careers. . . . It . . . corrupted the machinery of justice to the core, and placed the law-making power of the State upon the auction block."[2]

The first of the three individuals to make his mark on the state was William Andrews Clark. Small in stature and slight of build, Clark stood only five feet, seven inches tall and weighed a scant 140 pounds. Serious, grim, somewhat supercilious and aloof, Clark seemed not to want friends and made few. One observer remarked that he appeared cold and calculating: "his heart is frozen and his instincts are those of the fox: there is craft in his stereotyped smile and icicles in his handshake. He is about as magnetic as last year's bird's nest." Vain in his mannerisms and neat and precise in his attire, he hardly looked or acted like someone who could establish a loyal following among the "common people." But Clark was exceptionally intelligent, self-taxing in his work habits, and a genius in business. And there was a tenacity beneath that rather modest veneer which suggested a relentless, all-consuming ambition. The off-color remark: "There is no force in nature more terrible than a young Scotsman on the make" is perhaps applicable in Clark's case. His drive, determination, and his desire to be successful and to have that success acknowledged would make him one of the richest men in the world, but it would also lead to his disgrace.[3]

Clark was born in 1839, the son of John and Mary Clark, two struggling dirt farmers in Fayette County, Pennsylvania. Looking to improve their circumstances, in 1856 the family moved west to Van Buren County, Iowa, where young Clark was able to acquire enough frontier schooling to attend Iowa Wesleyan College for two years. He taught school for a few years in Missouri, but the outbreak of the Civil War and the news that gold had been discovered in Colorado convinced him it was time to pull up stakes and move west once again. Clark had little success prospecting in Colorado but joined three companions who decided to try their luck at the booming gold camp of Bannack in present-day Montana. To make the seven-hundred-mile journey, Clark drove an ox team. Upon arrival, two of Clark's associates decided to move on to the rich diggings at Alder Gulch, while Clark and a friend acquired a claim in Jeff Davis Gulch, near Horse Prairie Creek. The two greenhorns took up placer mining, built sluices and a cabin, and managed to do quite well. At the end of the year, the partners sold their claim and realized a profit of roughly $2,000.

Using that money as his bankroll, Clark decided to put down his pick and shovel and become a freight merchant buying up large supplies of goods, transporting those goods by wagon, and then reselling them at inflated prices in the mining camps. Clark hauled goods from Salt Lake City to Bannack and Virginia City in Montana, purchased a bulk shipment of tobacco in Boise, Idaho, for $3,000 and then transported it to Helena, where he sold it for $10,000, and even brought large shipments of goods from the Pacific coast. He made trips to the east and consigned more goods for Montana, procured a valuable mail contract between Walla Walla, Washington, and Missoula, Montana, and eventually established a store in Helena. He began to act as purchasing agent for other merchants and eventually formed commercial partnerships in Helena and in Deer Lodge, where he made his home, specializing in wholesale and retail merchandising. His wholesale supply house soon controlled the trade of central Montana. He also entered into the profitable business of buying gold dust for resale to eastern banks and began to operate as a moneylender. Loans and gold purchasing eventually led Clark into banking.

Having established himself as a very successful merchant capitalist and banker, and with a keen eye for new investments, Clark began to focus his attention on the all-but-dormant mining camp of Butte, located forty miles east of Deer Lodge. He visited the camp in the summer of 1872 and listened to the optimistic assessments of the few miners still working claims. He examined carefully the ore that had already been exposed in the few shallow shafts and concluded that it might be worked for a profit. Excited by the potential of Butte as an investment opportunity, he purchased four major claims—the Original, Colusa, Mountain

Chief, and Gambetta Mines—all of which would one day become great ore producers. Without perhaps realizing it, Clark had shifted his career track to vein mining. Taking samples of ore from his new properties, Clark ventured to New York where he enrolled for an intensive course in assaying and metallurgy at the prestigious Columbia University School of Mines. Clark would soon have a more scientific understanding of local mining problems than most of the so-called practical miners at Butte.

As Clark's interest in mining intensified, he came to play a major role in improving mining technology in Montana. In 1877, he sent 150 tons of high-grade ore from his Original Mine at Butte to the Boston and Colorado's Blackhawk smelting operation near Central City, Colorado. The Boston and Colorado had imported German and British metallurgy to master the reduction of that state's complex silver ores which were somewhat similar to Montana's. Intrigued by the ore samples that Clark had sent them, the Boston and Colorado dispatched one of its experts to Butte to examine the situation there. The result was the creation in 1878 to 1879 of the Colorado and Montana Smelting Company with Clark as vice president and co-owner. Utilizing the modern techniques that worked in Colorado, the new company built a state-of-the-art smelter on the south side of Silver Bow Creek, below the town of Butte. Smelting operations began in the late summer of 1879. Clark made handsome profits both as co-owner of the smelter and owner of the major mines that fed their ores to it. His future looked bright indeed.

The second of the three personalities to leave his mark on the state was Marcus Daly. A practical miner and mine developer, Daly looked the part. Stocky in his build, stooped in his shoulders, and brusque in his manner, he appeared as a man of simple tastes that underscored his Irish peasant roots. Unlike his nemesis William Clark, Daly was hearty, likeable, and unpretentious. It has been said that he never pretended to be more than a working miner who happened to make it big. The essential simplicity and openness of the man made him immensely popular among his hard rock miners. But Daly's easygoing manner, ready wit, and relaxed charm covered up a sharp intelligence, a tactical ruthlessness, and an explosive temper. He was loyal to his friends but hateful toward his enemies and, like Clark, never forgot a slight or let go of a grudge.

Marcus Daly was born in a small village near Ballyjamesduff in County Cavan, Ireland, in 1841. His parents were poor, and young Daly received very little education, a deficiency about which he was extremely self-conscious for the rest of his life. With few opportunities in an impoverished land, Daly joined thousands of his Irish countrymen who emigrated to America, arriving alone in New York City at the age of fifteen in 1856. He worked at odd jobs for two years and then took his savings and purchased a ticket on a steamer to California. Once in the Golden State, he found work on farms and ranches until he and a friend decided to set out for Calaveras County to prospect. Unable to strike it rich as a prospector, Daly found work in already established mines and quickly learned the skills of a hard rock miner. The year 1862 found him in Virginia City, Nevada, where the bonanza Comstock Lode was booming. There he met John Mackay, a mining capitalist, who gave him a job as a mine foreman. He worked at this position for the next six years and gained recognition as a master at assessing vein structures and at tunneling, timbering, and blasting. It was later said about Daly that he could see farther into the ground than anyone else.

In 1870, the Walker brothers of Salt Lake City, who had developed something of a banking-mining empire in the region, hired the highly regarded Daly as foreman of their Emma Mine at Alta, Utah, and later to manage their Lion Hill Mine at Ophir, Utah. The Walkers continued to expand their mining operations and, after examining Butte ores shipped to them for processing, sent Daly to look over the camp in 1876. Forming a partnership with Daly, the Walkers negotiated for several purchases in Butte, including a part interest in the Alice Mine, later to be one of the great silver mines in the state. With these new acquisitions, Daly moved to Butte to manage the promising properties near the top of Butte hill.

As full-time resident manager, Daly found time not only to deepen and extend the working of the Alice Mine and to improve its milling operations, but also to examine neighboring shafts and other quartz outcroppings on the hill. Located east of the town of Butte was the Anaconda Mine, nothing more than an unexceptional silver prospect in 1880. The mine was owned by Michael Hickey and Charles X. Larabie, two small-time miners who really lacked the financial means to develop the property. Daly, who was in the process of selling out his interest in the Alice Mine for a rumored $100,000, thought there was a mine in the Anaconda and bought the silver property for $30,000. Realizing that he would either need to have his ore sent to an expensive stamp mill for crushing and to a smelter for reduction, or to build or lease plants of his own, Daly turned to the San Francisco–based partnership of George Hearst (the father of newspaper mogul William Randolph Hearst), James Ben Ali Haggin, and Lloyd Tevis for financial backing. Daly had come to know Hearst and Haggin during his Comstock days. In return for a 75 percent ownership of the mine, Daly's backers extended him a generous operating budget. Workers began sinking an eight-by-twenty-foot, three-compartment shaft into the Anaconda in June 1881 and, true to Daly's prediction, soon found rich deposits of oxidized silver ore, compounded with copper.

The significant turning point in the development of the Anaconda and for Butte as a mining mecca came less than a year after serious digging, drilling, and blasting began. At somewhere around three hundred feet below the surface the millable silver ore started to play out, but as it did, the copper ores began to become more pronounced. This was due to the eroding process, which served to concentrate heavy deposits of enriched copper sulfide at that depth. When the nature of the ore changed, Daly personally went down into the mine to examine the vein. What he saw was the largest deposit of copper sulfide that anyone had ever seen. It was an exhilarating moment for Daly and one that served to spur his efforts toward further expansion and development.

Daly immediately began buying up properties—the St. Lawrence Mine (which adjoined the Anaconda and contained the extension of its vein system), the Neversweat Mine, and portions of the Rob Roy, Nipper, and other claims—that were adjacent to the Anaconda. He also continued to deepen his existing shafts and reached the six-hundred-foot level in 1883. In addition to the expanding vein of copper, the mine continued to yield appreciable amounts of silver and gold, which enhanced overall profits. Journalist C. P. Connolly has offered a colorful description of the growth of the Butte hill from that time on.

An army of men descended into the mines daily to strip them of their treasure; huge forests were despoiled of their timber to stull and shore up the excavations and protect the earth above—for these copper veins are often one hundred feet wide. Immense smokestacks began to vomit their clouds of smudge from the scores of furnaces scattered over the hill; the moan and clank of huge pumps could be heard in the depths, forcing the water to the surface; the pound of hammers and the steady impact of drills sounded everywhere, while the earth trembled and bellowed with distant underground explosions. Great hollows, like cathedral naves, were scooped out, where the treasure had lain in the rock-ribbed earth. Horses and mules were blindfolded and lowered into the mines—where their hides, like the gray beards of the old miners, soon took on the greenish color of the copper which saturates everything below the surface.[4]

In the summer of 1883 the syndicate began construction on an extensive reduction and smelting complex. Because the creeks around Butte had already largely been claimed by others, the owners decided to locate their new works at a spot where Warm Springs Creek flows out of the mountains into upper Deer Lodge Valley about twenty-six miles west of Butte. Daly personally laid out the new town site and, after flirting with the idea of calling it Copperopolis, decided to name the site after his richest prize—Anaconda. The final step in the grand plan came in the fall of 1884 when the Union Pacific–Utah and Northern Railroad completed a thirty-one-mile spur line that linked the Anaconda Mine to its mammoth Washoe Smelter. Although few would have realized it in 1884, Montana's mining future rested not with gold and silver but with copper. And from 1884 to 1900 Butte copper and its copper barons would come to dominate the economic and political life of Montana.

Since its earliest days, Butte carried a tough, no-holds-barred reputation—rough, squalid, frenetic, wild. The town has been called "the black heart of Montana" and "a sinister Baghdad in the midst of rural innocence." Author Gertrude Atherton referred to it as the "perch of the devil." As the quintessential mining town, late nineteenth-century Butte had an "air of transience, fatalism, and ribaldry, so typical of western mining camps."[5] And Butte had a wild side. Drinking, carousing, whoring, and gambling seemed to be the favorite diversions for the working class. In 1893, the city directory listed 212 "drinking establishments." These ranged in size and quality from the immense Atlantic Bar which had a block-long counter and fifteen bartenders to the more notorious haunts like the Alley Cat, the Clipper Shades, or the Bucket of Blood. Most of the saloons never closed and it was common for a miner at the end of his shift to stop in for a "one-bit" shot of whiskey, a "growler" (a bucket of beer to go), a nickel beer that came with free food, or a ten-cent "Shawn O'Farrell" (an ounce of whiskey with a beer chaser). Even after impressive business blocks grew up to signify Butte's financial success and urbanity, locals still referred to the emerging city as a "camp." Butte was a place where people had a difficult time accepting their new riches and remained rather self-conscious of the town's ugliness and squalor, its cultural backwardness and isolation, and its open-all-night atmosphere. Following a visit in 1888, a reporter for *Harper's* found that the "very activity of Butte is sometimes wearisome. It never ceases."[6]

At the end of the 1880s Butte still seemed rough and untamed. Shabby wooden plank sidewalks wound down the hill, and mud presented a constant problem. A central business district had begun to take shape around Park and Main Streets and an affluent residential area had sprouted on the west side of town. Directly to the east of the downtown area was the Anaconda Hill, marked by the seven smokestacks of the Neversweat Mine. Novelist Gertrude Atherton described the hill as a "tangled mass of smokestacks, gallow[*sic*]-frames, shabby grey buildings, trestles . . . [looking] like a gigantic shipwreck." Sprawling down from the hill into town was Dublin Gulch with its Irish and Slavic populations. To the south and southwest could be found the brick and frame houses of the working class. At the bottom of the hill, in an area called "the flats," was an array of mills, breweries, and dumps that fronted on Silver Bow Creek and the tracks of the railroad. The notorious "Cabbage Patch" area covered six blocks of the town's southeast quadrant. The patch was one of America's worst slums, a "congestion of cabins, lean-to's, hovels, saloons, and whorehouses squatting amongst waste dumps and rubbish."[7]

Taken as a whole, Butte offered a unique sense of place. When journalist Ray Stannard Baker visited in 1903, he found that the town gave "one an impression of tremendous disorder, of colossal [human] energies in play."[8]

Most outsiders who visited Butte in the late nineteenth century were struck by the stark desolation and general ugliness of the place. The air was polluted with the sulfur and arsenic-laden smoke caused by the open roasting and smelting of ore from the mines. Labor leader "Big Bill" Haywood had a vivid memory of the first time he approached Butte: "I marvelled at the desolation of the country. There was no verdure of any kind; it had all been killed by the fumes and smoke of the piles of burning ore." It was common practice for mining companies to dump their sulfide ores into huge pits, toss in logs for fuel, and then let it burn for days to eliminate as much of the sulfur as possible. According to one mining engineer, the ores being smelted at Butte gave off from 260 to 300 tons of arsenic-laden sulfur every day. If westerly breezes were prevalent, the smoke blew away with minimal side effects. But a temperature inversion or a shift in the wind direction from the east created a more ominous set of problems. On such days one could see clouds hanging low over the hill, creating a darkness that required streetlamps to be lit. Uptown, one could barely see across the street, while down in the flats movement was nearly impossible. In the darkly humorous words of the *Engineering and Mining Journal*: "the unfortunate traveler from South Butte traces his way not by landmarks, for these are utterly invisible, but by the hacking cough of his forerunner, who though a few feet away is completely veiled in smoke."[9] The smoke caused respiratory problems that compounded the common mining camp concerns for diseases such as tuberculosis or miners' consumption. It also killed off most of the city's vegetation. According to the *Anaconda Standard*, only four of the city's trees remained alive in 1890. One local humorist joked that cats actually died licking arsenic from their whiskers. An anti-smoke crusade in the early 1890s led to the passage of an anti-roasting ordinance and the installation of primitive pollution abatement devices on most smelters. But the smoke problem did not really subside until the early twentieth century, when most of the smelting operations were transferred to Anaconda and Great Falls.

Butte possessed one other noteworthy characteristic, a rather unique social order. An essential component of western mining camps with their get-rich-quick attitude was a basic, unassuming democracy in which residents seemed to have an unquestioning tolerance of each other. "Millionaires, bums, working stiffs, well-groomed ladies, and whores all bumped elbows on common terms, and Butte seldom bothered to any pretenses." Describing a typical gaming house in Butte, one reporter commented: "Enter such a place and you see everybody: Mr. Jones, lawyer; Mr. Smith, banker; Mr. Brown, miner; a street fakir 'dropping' on black and white the proceeds of his night's wrestle . . . two or three women, likely to be French or African; a heathen or two, silent, patient, but usually lucky, huddled in a lump watching the mechanical movements of the long-bearded elderly chap as he slides this card that way and that card this way." Mining camp democracy meant "social commonality," a wide-open tolerance of social vices and a uniquely unrestrained kind of individualism. As one journalist noted: "Butte was a town of personalities. Don't tell me democracy doesn't make for the development of the individual! That camp was the most democratic place I've ever lived in."[10]

As Butte's residents watched their colorful boomtown come to dominate the economy of Montana, they were also drawn to the titanic struggle between William A. Clark and Marcus Daly on the political front. Bitterly personal and crassly and ruthlessly fought, the feud, which lasted a dozen years between 1888 and 1900, seemed like a clash of uncontrollable egos. In the end, their backroom dealings and willingness to resort to unheard-of levels of bribery and chicanery would debase the new state of Montana and, ultimately, reach the United States Senate, where it would attract national attention. In the words of one historian: "Montana gained in all of this an unenviable reputation as a political and economic pawn—bought, sold, and sullied by mining wealth."[11]

Of the two protagonists, success had changed Marcus Daly very little from his early days in Montana. Amiable, unassuming, an uncultured man of simple tastes, he lavished his attention on the town of Anaconda and viewed the town and its works with pride as his fiefdom. As others handled the operations of his businesses, he increasingly spent his time raising and racing horses. He eventually established a twenty-thousand-acre stock farm in the Bitter Root Valley about 150 miles west of Butte and constructed an impressive mansion to go with it. He called the showplace the Bitter Root Ranch. Cold and distant, William A. Clark was Daly's opposite and sought to leave his common roots behind him. Even with all his money and financial successes, he still craved status and schemed constantly to gain high political office. He seemed to be almost obsessed with the need to show the world that he was something—a wealthy, cultured, respected statesman. One of America's wealthiest individuals, Clark owned mines, mills, and smelters at Butte, banks, retail stores, newspapers, coal mines, water, electrical, and street railway franchises, and large timber holdings in the Big Blackfoot and Missoula Valleys. One of his truly great acquisitions was the United Verde Mine in Jerome, Arizona, which at its peak yielded $10 million a year in profits. Over time, as his cultural interests grew, he became an art enthusiast and spent lavishly on fine art. But he also craved public adulation and hoped that a successful political career would bestow that kind of civic distinction.

Most observers suggest that the origins of the Clark-Daly feud can be found in earlier business dealings that strained relations, but, regardless of how that hatred began, it burst forth in open, public battle during the election of 1888. In that campaign, the territorial Democratic convention nominated William A. Clark for the territory's highest elective office—delegate to Congress. It looked like an easy victory for Clark who had little to fear from his little-known Republican opponent Thomas H. Carter, a Helena attorney. In the campaign, Clark followed the lead of the National Democratic Party led by Grover Cleveland and supported the party's call for a lower tariff. A Democratic victory seemed certain. But behind the scenes, Marcus Daly secretly plotted to defeat Clark. Even though Daly was an ardent Democrat and had dutifully supported the party, his connection with the Montana Improvement Association created a problem. Like other freewheeling timber companies in the West, the company followed an aggressive policy of logging on unsurveyed public timberlands. The Cleveland administration had taken exception to such practices and had filed federal suits against a number of timber companies. Because it seemed like the Republican Party, led by Benjamin

Harrison, would adopt a more permissive public lands policy and actually looked to have a better chance of winning the election, Daly and his timber allies decided to dump Clark and support Carter. On election day, even as one thousand of his mine and smelter workers traveled to Butte to take part in a pro-Clark rally, Daly's shift bosses and political operatives worked their coup. Employees of the Anaconda and the Montana Improvement Company turned in their thousands of ballots to election officials with Carter's name pasted over Clark's. Because there was as yet no secret ballot, shift bosses could inspect ballots to see how their workers voted. Even in Clark's home precinct, gangs of Daly's hirelings went to the polls as repeaters. In the final tally, Carter beat Clark by a vote of 22,486 to 17,360 and carried fourteen of the territory's sixteen counties.

After the election, the Republican *Butte Daily Inter Mountain* simply claimed that "The Issues Settled It." In other words, the general unpopularity of Cleveland's low tariff policy dragged the party and Clark down to defeat. This was partially true as many stockmen in the territory tended to favor the high-tariff, protectionist stance of the Republicans. But Daly's subterfuge was crucial. Although he denied any culpability, others concluded differently. According to the Clark-owned *Butte Miner*, Clark's defeat was the result of "the deepest kind of treachery among the supposed friends of Mr. Clark." The Democratic *Great Falls Tribune* agreed, stating: "The perfidy of these men will not soon be forgotten." Hardly a naïf, Clark understood that he had been "played." "The conspiracy," he said, "was a gigantic one, well-planned, and well carried out . . . the day of retribution may come when treason may be considered odious." Clark would never forgive the affront and always remember it as an attempt on the part of Daly to destroy his political influence in Montana.[12]

Now that the political battle lines had been drawn, Daly took one other ancillary action that had broader implications for Montana. Since Clark already owned a major newspaper, the *Butte Miner*, Daly realized he needed his own mouthpiece and decided to create a better one. With a verbal promise to invest $100,000 in the new enterprise, Daly convinced John H. Durston, former owner-editor of the *Syracuse Standard*, one of New York's oldest newspapers, to be his managing editor. Durston then purchased an elaborate printing plant, hired some of the best journalists available, and proudly announced the arrival of the first issue of the *Anaconda Standard* on September 4, 1889. As the voice of Daly and Anaconda, the newspaper developed into one of the better-known papers in the region. There was a negative side to this new endeavor, however. As one historian aptly noted, "the appearance of the *Standard* signaled an ominous fact that few recognized at the time: mining money was seeping into and beginning to contaminate the workings of the free press."[13]

When Montana finally gained statehood in 1889, the question uppermost to those interested in the politics of their new state was who would represent them in the United States Senate. Still bristling from his defeat in 1888, Clark was determined to secure one of the two new seats. Because state legislatures rather than voters chose US senators at that time (direct election of US senators would come with the passage of the Seventeenth Amendment in 1913), Clark realized that his fate was tied up with that body. Both the Democratic and Republican National Committees poured money into Montana's legislative campaigns because they knew what was at stake. But at a time of Republican resurgence in a normally Democratic-dominated state, the new legislature found itself deadlocked—eight legislators from each party in the state senate (with the Republican lieutenant governor holding the tie-breaking vote) and twenty-five legislators from each party in the state house of representatives with five seats in dispute. The result was a farce. Each party refused to surrender its position in the house, while in the senate Democrats at first refused to attend or vote, hoping to keep the Republicans from forming a quorum and then meeting with the house to elect the US senators. From November 23, 1889, to February 20, 1890, the Montana legislature remained deadlocked and passed no legislation. In the end, members of the legislature from each party met separately and selected their own two US senators. Clark was one of the Democratic choices. This action, however, merely transferred the problem from the Montana legislature to the United States Senate where the Republicans with a small majority voted to seat their political brethren and send the Democrats packing. Although Daly played no role in the theatrics, Clark had to watch from the gallery as the US Senate rejected him.

With the election of the 1893 state legislature, the process of selecting a US senator proved once again to be problematic. This time, however, mining money and intrigue were featured more prominently. Because incumbent Republican Senator Wilbur Fisk Sanders had been elected to the short three-year term in 1890, his seat was now up for reelection. As expected, the various factions jockeyed for position. When the Democratic caucus endorsed William A. Clark, eight Daly Democrats bolted and supported William Wirt Dixon, Daly's chief attorney, instead. Balloting for a US senator remained stalemated from January 11 to February 10, 1893. The Daly people said they would agree to a compromise if Clark would drop out, but Clark's backers refused the offer. Clark's only hope was to reach out to Republicans.

At this point, Clark's agents began to offer bribe money to win the support of Republican legislators, while Daly's men spent just as wildly to buy them back. It was alleged that Daly even hired Pinkerton detectives to uncover compromising personal information that might be used to coerce a legislator's vote. One lawmaker commented: "It is said some of the legislators will go home ten thousand dollars richer than when they came to Helena this winter." No one ever proved that bribes were given, but no one really doubted that they were. In the end, Clark's money won the crossover votes of six Republicans and two previously anti-Clark Democrats, but he still remained three votes short of the thirty-five he needed to secure victory. It was yet another bitter defeat for Clark who had sullied his reputation in the process. When legislators, described by one veteran of territorial politics as a "band of bribe takers and bribe givers . . . a stench in the nostrils of all honest men, and a by-word and jeer throughout the Union," finally adjourned, they failed to choose anyone. As a result, it remained to Republican Governor John Rickards to either call the legislature back in session or to exercise his power to appoint someone to fill the vacant seat. He chose the latter and appointed politician-businessman-newspaperman Lee Mantle to the US Senate. But the national body was reluctant to allow gubernatorial appointments in cases where state legislatures had simply failed to act, and on August 28, 1893, the US Senate voted 31–28 to deny Mantle a seat. Left with the option of calling the legislature back in special session where a Democrat would most certainly be selected, Governor Rickards decided to do nothing. This time the Clark-Daly feud had not only debauched and stymied the state legislature, it had cost the new state full representation in Congress.[14]

The election of 1894 proved to be yet another donnybrook for Montana voters and another round in the battle between Clark and Daly. This time voters were asked to choose a permanent site for the state capital and to select two US senators. The "capital fight," as it was called between the cities of Anaconda and Helena (the current territorial capital), offered Clark a chance to get back at Daly. For his own selfish interests and to gratify his personal vanity, Daly wanted to enthrone Anaconda as the state's capital. Clark, on the other hand, itching to spite Daly, saw a chance to do so and also become the champion of Helena, regarded by most Montanans as the commercial, monetary, transportation, and social center of the state, and win the support of that city's powerful political order. Clark, supported by Helena's financial leaders, had the advantage from the start in both money and in Helena's more centralized geographic location. But both sides took nothing for granted and sought to reach out to all parts of the state for support. This time the contaminating influence of money, which had previously been showered on the legislature, flowed throughout Montana. No one will ever know the exact amount of money spent by the two copper kings in the contest. Daly later testified that his side spent $450,000, while Clark set the total amount of money spent at approximately $1 million. Regardless of the rough estimates, money flowed freely in the battle.

The contest quickly turned into a grudge match. Each side sought support from wherever they could get it. The Northern Pacific Railroad backed Helena, which lay astride its main line, while James J. Hill and the Great Northern Railroad backed their commercial partner Anaconda. Mudslinging reared its ugly head as well. Clark's *Butte Miner* charged that Daly was the head of an "alien, soulless corporation" and asked its readers if the state capital should be located in a town that was owned and operated by one corporation. In turn, the *Anaconda Standard* charged the Helena crowd with being completely under the thumb of the Northern Pacific—that "land-thieving octopus."[15] Anaconda supporters also took issue with what they charged to be Helena's cosmopolitan airs and its pretentiousness as the home of ostentatious millionaires and imposing Victorian mansions. Each side reached out to every community in the state—waving money, making promises, and, on occasion, leveling threats in a frantic quest for votes. The Clark people produced thousands of little copper collars with the obvious message: A vote for Anaconda was a vote for being forever yoked to a despotic corporation. Daly supporters, in turn, handed out thousands of specially made cigars labeled "Anaconda for the Capital." Clark's supporters, hoping to prejudice the staunchly unionized miners of Butte and Anaconda against Daly, countered with the charge that the cheroots had been made by "scab" labor. Both sides plastered broadsides and doled out trinkets and favors on the streets of key towns like Butte. They also staged parades, band concerts, and fireworks displays. Agents for the two camps bought drinks for patrons of the town's saloons to win supporters and sometimes even handed out greenbacks to voters passing by on the street.

On election day, November 6, 1894, the Republicans won a sweeping victory in Montana, due largely to the sinking popularity of Democratic President Grover Cleveland and the effects of the current economic depression. As a result, William A. Clark had no chance of realizing his election to the US Senate in the 1895 legislature. In the final balloting for the capital, Helena won a narrow victory by a vote of 27,024 to 25,118. The victory allowed John M. Quinn, the editor of Clark's *Butte Miner* to gloat, "Tyranny has reached its Waterloo." But, in fact, it was Helena's free-spending campaign directed by William A. Clark that carried the day and, perhaps, marked the larger significance of the campaign. As one historian has noted: "In the final analysis, the real importance of the capital fight lay less in geopolitics than in the fact that mining money and manipulation was now spreading like a cancer through the body politic."[16] In victory, Helena gave Clark and Quinn a hero's celebration. When Clark's train arrived in the city, grateful townspeople unhitched the horses from his carriage and pulled his conveyance through the streets of the city amid the blare of band music and a carnival of fireworks. Daly was not as fortunate. Helena's celebrants dressed a mock-up of his body in funeral garments, placed it in an improvised hearse, and jeered it through the streets of town. It was an insult Daly never forgot.

The climax of the Clark-Daly feud came with the legislative session of 1899. Having lost three contests for high office (once to the US Congress and twice to the US Senate), time seemed to be running out for the sixty-year-old multimillionaire. The Clark Democrats were able to win control of the party at the Democratic state convention in Anaconda, but, as before, nomination would ultimately hinge on the outcome of legislative contests in the general election that fall. The Clark and Daly machines once again competed for voter support, but it seemed that the stakes had gotten higher. John Neill, the owner-manager of the Clark-subsidized *Helena Independent*, was reported to have made the comment that "he [Clark] is disposed this time to be absolutely unlimited in the amount of money that he will put up for the election of democratic [*sic*] members of the Legislature in this State." Democrats triumphed in the election on November 8, 1898, and would hold a sizeable majority in the balloting for a US senator. But Daly's Butte-Anaconda-backed Democratic candidates had won as well, and that meant that Clark could only count on forty-three firm Democratic votes—well short of the required majority. Confident that Clark had been stopped again, Daly headed off to New York on business. But the Clark machine was not ready to admit defeat, and secretly started "buying up some newspapers and offering favors to others, offering lucrative business deals to legislators, throwing money wherever it promised to return political gain."[17]

The sordid political spectacle that followed got under way in January 1899 when the legislature convened. Clark had already set up his headquarters in the Helena Hotel and had turned his operation over to his two chief agents—John B. Wellcome, his principal attorney, and Charles W. Clark, his twenty-six-year-old son. Wellcome was well known, well liked, good natured, and completely devoted to Clark's success. Although he had never held political office, he was the advisor Clark trusted most. According to one contemporary, "He was the sort of man who, if he were so disposed, would be likely to do successful business in the underground passages that lead to the private offices of high officials." Normally "shrewd" and "judicious," he became "in his dealings with members of the legislature, thoroughly reckless." Although still quite young, Charlie Clark "had inherited a certain political sagacity, [and] had wide experience in the uses to which money might be put." He was ultimately responsible for the success of the plan to corrupt the legislature.[18]

There were rumors of bribery even before the session opened. Two of the most persistent of those rumors were that William Clark would pay out $1 million, if necessary, to get elected and that lawmakers could count on making an easy $10,000 if they chose to hawk their vote. And all this talk seemed to take place in a surreal atmosphere. The city's residents, ever loyal to the man who had won the capital fight for them, seemed to condone and even defend what was certainly happening. C. P. Connolly described the incomprehensible mood quite well: "The business men of Helena were almost a unit in declaring that bribery was a necessity, and in defending it. . . . The man who stood out against bribes found that his old friends held aloof from him. . . . He became conscious of a lack of sympathy, of a curious isolation on the streets and at his club; found himself marooned upon a cold eminence of virtue."[19]

With rumors of bribery in the air, and with anti-Clark newspapers fueling the rumor mills, the two houses of the legislature were forced to create a joint committee to investigate the allegations. On the night of January 9, the night before legislative balloting for a US senator was to commence, the committee heard the testimony of three state senators—Henry L. Meyers of Ravalli County, William A. Clark of Madison County (no relation to William A. Clark of Butte), and Fred Whiteside of Flathead County. Whiteside, who became the key witness in the investigation, had a solid reputation. He had come to Montana in the late 1870s as a buffalo hunter and stayed to become a successful architect and building contractor. He had also served as a member of the legislature several years earlier, and had been a member of the committee appointed to investigate corruption in the State Capitol Commission. In testifying before the committee, Whiteside produced $30,000 in crisp $1,000 bills which he alleged had been given to him by John B. Wellcome, the alleged manager of Clark's boodle fund, to purchase his vote and those of Myers and Clark. In addition, Whiteside charged that he had been cornered by

Wellcome, Charlie Clark, and a group of Clark men just hours before coming to the committee with his story. He stated that the group, suspicious of his intentions, had first threatened him and then offered him $300,000 to change his mind. It was only by protesting his innocence and affirming his loyalty to Clark that he was able to get away without physical harm.

The Whiteside charges and the submission of the investigating committee's report to the joint session of the legislature the next day, created a sensation. But a large majority of the state's newspapers, many of which had been either purchased or subsidized by the Clark machine during the prior election campaign, defended Clark and assailed his accusers. Feeling pressure to bring a speedy resolution of the accusations, the joint session called upon the district attorney of Lewis and Clark County to impanel a grand jury to investigate the charges. During a two-week period beginning on January 11, the grand jury called forty-four witnesses as the public eagerly awaited a verdict.

Clark knew that Marcus Daly held the loyalty of enough Democrats to deny him the nomination in a straight party vote. In order to win, he would have to garner the votes of Republicans. This would be difficult to do in the midst of publicity connected to an ongoing bribery investigation. Still, Republican stalwarts urged their members to stand by their party. Publicly, Clark tried to woo members of the opposition by suggesting that he had common ground with them on key issues—especially that he was sympathetic to their views on the tariff and protectionism. But the real cajoling went on behind the scenes. As would later be revealed in another investigation, Clark's agents were offering bribes of as high as $20,000 and, on one occasion, even $50,000 per vote. It was said, however, that as Clark's agents worked one side of the street, Daly's men worked the other. Daly himself remained on the East Coast during the legislative session dealing with serious medical problems and negotiating the future sale of his business operations, but he kept in touch with the situation in the capital. But Daly could not stop the flow of Clark money. Then, on January 26, Clark got a break. The Helena grand jury, rumored to be treated with the same bribe offers as the legislators ($10,000 for each member and $15,000 for the foreman) but probably reflecting the pro-Clark bias of the community, exonerated Clark. The jurors concluded that, despite the existence of $30,000 in allegedly tainted money, there was not sufficient evidence of bribery on which to base an indictment of William A. Clark. The decision was deserving of derision which was quick in coming. C. B. Nolan, the state's attorney general, violently denounced it. But because he was known to be a Daly man, his opinion lacked resonance.

The reprieve from the grand jury only seemed to increase Clark's boldness. When the minority Republican Party met in secret caucus on the crisp, clear morning of January 28, 1899, Clark was still well short of the forty-seven votes he needed for nomination. But a strange thing happened. When asked how they would vote, eleven Republicans stood up and walked out of the room, signaling that they would not support their party. Amazingly, only four regular Republicans—J. R. Mckay, Tyler Worden, W. A. Hedges, and William Lindsay—held out against the lure of Clark money. As lawmakers formally announced their votes during the roll call later that morning in the hall of the Merchants Hotel, which served as the temporary capitol, the galleries resounded with cat calls, hisses, and applause. Hecklers shouted out charges of bribery and even yelled out the amounts of the individual bribes. Daly's lieutenants were furious. Others were openly disgusted. Representative E. D. Matts scolded his colleagues: "I am sorry to see this man [Clark] go to the Senate of the United States, like Richard III, over the bodies of disgraced men." Newspapers throughout the country gave the scandal front-page coverage and seemed genuinely shocked by the revelations. Trying to add some humor to the appalling spectacle, the *St. Paul Dispatch* ran a front-page cartoon that showed a stack of $1,000 bills with the caption: "The kind of bill most often introduced in the legislature of Montana." But Montanans, in general, did not seem to be as shocked by the events as the rest of the nation, and one writer thought he knew why. "Montana had already been demoralized by easy money, open gambling, quick and unearned fortunes, low moral standards in the proletariat, subsidized newspapers, complacent representatives of the law. It might howl about bribery and conspiracy but it was not shocked."[20]

For their part, the Clark partisans took to the streets. Much like the victory party that followed the capital fight in 1894, Helena celebrated on Clark's tab. Saloons handed out free champagne and fireworks and bonfires lit the sky. Clark's champagne bill for the night was said to have totaled $30,000. But his other expenses were more grotesque. According to the Daly crowd, Clark had purchased forty-seven votes of the state legislature for $431,000, not including the $30,000 that Whiteside had turned over to the investigating committee. Clark had allegedly offered another $200,000 to thirteen other lawmakers who refused to take the bribe. Clark gloated over his victory and denied all the charges that had been leveled against him. He repeatedly referred to the Whiteside money as a Daly "trick," a frame-up, and stated that his victory meant "vindication" against his enemies. The eleven Republicans who crossed over to support him at the end, he said, did so as a matter of principle: "The people have risen in their majesty and power and have forever set the seal of their condemnation on a merciless combination which sought to subjugate the people of this state."[21]

The fight, however, was not over. Daly, galled that Clark had won and outraged that he had attempted to shift blame back on him, decided to fight against the seating of Clark in the US Senate. Promising to bankroll that effort, Daly voiced his anger: "The crime of bribery . . . was bad enough, but to try to fix that on some innocent people was still worse, and I think we should satisfy Mr. Clark with an investigation."[22] Daly's plan was twofold. He would start disbarment proceedings against John B. Wellcome, Clark's lawyer and alleged bagman with the legislature, whose conviction would serve as a precedent in the national hearings, and then have charges filed against Clark from the floor of the US Senate.

Fred Whiteside, accused by the Clark forces as being the agent of the Daly interests in the plot to defeat Clark, filed the motion to disbar Wellcome before the Montana Supreme Court in May 1899, charging him with conduct unbecoming an attorney in the bribery of eight legislators. According to their later testimony before the US Senate Committee on Privileges and Elections, the justices of the state supreme court were then approached by individuals acting on behalf of Clark and Wellcome.

Dr. William Treacy, a Helena physician twice offered Judge William H. Hunt $100,000 if he would vote to dismiss the case. Rebuffed by Hunt, Treacy then approached state Attorney General C. B. Nolan, in charge of the trial against Wellcome, and offered him $100,000 to drop the proceedings. Clark attorney Frank Corbett discussed the case with Judge William Pigott in a suspicious manner, while Reverend A. B. Martin, another Clark ally, strongly lobbied Chief Justice Theodore Brantly in an unethical manner although he offered no money. Unfortunately for Clark, he had finally encountered honest men who could not be swayed. In the end, the court voted to disbar Wellcome. It was an ominous precedent.

William A. Clark formally took his US Senate seat on December 4, 1899. On that same day, Senator Thomas Carter of Montana presented two petitions from his state calling upon that body to investigate the election of William Clark and declare it void. One petition was from Governor R. B. Smith and other prominent Montana citizens and included the names of individual legislators who had allegedly accepted bribes as well as evidence that had been gathered in the grand jury investigation and in the Wellcome disbarment hearings. Three days later the US Senate referred the matter to the Committee on Privileges and Elections chaired by Republican Senator William Eaton Chandler of New Hampshire.

The Chandler Committee began its investigation on January 5, 1900, and finally concluded its hearings three months later on April 6. The committee eventually called ninety-six witnesses to testify where they were given a tough grilling by its members. The testimony, argument, and documentary evidence presented to the committee comprised 2,702 pages and filled three volumes of government reports. Testimony revealed that a sordid political culture existed in Montana and many of the witnesses actually defended the use of large sums of money to attain their political ends. Clark and Daly both testified. Daly offered to open the books of his mining companies and to provide records of his private accounts and vouchers for inspection by the committee. Clark did not, stating that he had destroyed his checks as was his customary business practice, and that he could not produce vouchers for the money spent by his agents. But their public statements were disingenuous. Clark stated that his expenditures had gone only for proper methods of political organization and never knowingly for bribery. Daly denied that he had used coercion in any way and that he did not have any significant political power in the state or any major involvement in the fight against Clark. The committee did, however, find a great deal of evidence of wrongdoing on both sides. It was evident that Clark's agents had spent his money wildly and to argue that he had not known about it rang false. Even though he had destroyed his checks, the committee was able to subpoena and examine his bank statements which showed heavy expenditures. The committee also found that both sides spent significant sums of money in the purchase of Montana newspapers in their battle to influence public opinion. Ultimately, it was the disgraceful testimony of those legislators who appeared before the committee to explain how they had acquired such sudden riches that hurt Clark's cause the most. With downcast eyes and unbelievable stories, they generally forfeited any credibility and, in the process, embarrassed themselves and their state. In responding to the overall testimony, the *Yellowstone Journal* of Miles City offered a common sentiment: "THEY ARE ALL LIARS."[23]

The Committee on Privileges and Elections held its final deliberations on April 10, 1900, and announced that it found the election of William A. Clark null and void on account of "briberies, attempted briberies, and corrupt practices." Although the committee's decision was unanimous, it did find evidence of wrongdoing on both sides. The committee made special note of one incident in which an agent of the Daly camp had secretly broken into the hotel room of a key Clark supporter and illegally opened his mail. The report also made mention of the amount of money that both sides poured into the purchase of Montana newspapers in their competitive battle to sway public opinion. One perhaps typical example of this tactic involved the *Bozeman Chronicle*. The newspaper had backed Daly until Clark gave $2,500 to its owners, who promptly changed their editorial position. Daly responded to this bit of knavery by simply buying the paper for $11,000.

The committee presented its findings to the full US Senate on April 23, asking that it concur with its recommendation. Clark had to make a decision—to resign his seat or wait for the upper chamber to vote him out. He chose the former and announced his resignation in a tearful speech before his colleagues on May 15, 1900. In the speech, he again reviewed the persecution he felt he had suffered at Daly's hands and defended his use of money against his archrival. He declared that a situation had been created in which the city of Anaconda had become totally dependent for its commercial livelihood on the great smelter works there. As a result, Daly ruled Anaconda like a despot and his power placed the entire state at his mercy. He noted as well that after his own critical examination of the evidence taken by the committee, he was still convinced that his friends had not resorted to dishonorable or corrupt means to influence the actions of members of the Montana legislature in their choice of a United States senator.

But there were still games to be played. If Clark had not resigned, and if his senate colleagues had proceeded to expel him, the law stipulated that there would not have been an election and, as a result, there could be no vacancy. In other words, there would be no US senator from Montana until voters chose one at the next senatorial election. But if Clark resigned before any action by that body, it would create a vacancy which the governor of Montana could fill by temporary appointment. Clark might then compel the governor to appoint him to succeed himself! Having studied the situation for some time, the Butte millionaire and his agents began to hatch an audacious ploy by which pro-Daly Governor Robert B. Smith would be inveigled out of the state and Lieutenant Governor A. E. Spriggs, a friend of Clark, would then exercise his authority as acting governor to reappoint Clark to his own vacated senate seat.

For their plan, in effect a political conspiracy, to work, they had to find a way to get Governor Smith to leave the state. Through the agency of one Thomas Hinds, they convinced Smith to travel to California to assess a mineral property there for mine owner Miles Finlen. A lawyer by profession, Smith owed Finlen $2,000, a debt that would be discharged through this favor. The California property was located about sixty-five miles from the nearest railroad, which meant that Smith would be cut off from communications. Spriggs, for his part, happened to be attending the Populist National Convention in Sioux Falls, South Dakota, to which he was a delegate. Once Smith had departed for California, the Clark people sent Spriggs a cryptic telegram: "Weather fine, cattle doing well." It was the signal that he should hurry back to Montana. Charlie Clark, who had been holding his father's formal letter of resignation, inserted the correct date and, at almost the exact moment his father was standing before the US Senate in tearful departure, handed it to acting Governor Spriggs. A few hours later he appointed Clark to the position from which he had just resigned.

Embarrassed at being duped, Governor Smith hurried back to Montana. Protesting his own innocence in the ploy, Smith told the press: "This is only another one of the many dirty tricks, perjuries and crimes resorted to by Clark and his minions to fasten him on the state as a senator, and no just or fair minded man can look upon this whole proceeding with anything but contempt and a sense of shame."[24] Back in Montana, Smith immediately revoked Spriggs's appointment of Clark, stating that it was tainted with collusion and fraud, and appointed former congressman Martin Maginnis in his place. But since Spriggs had actually held the legal authority to make such an appointment, the credentials of both Clark and Maginnis were placed before the US Senate for determination. Since it looked like another major fight looming at a time when Congress was anxious to adjourn, both the friends and enemies of Clark decided to let the issue lie. Clark was again denied a seat in that body and, as had happened in 1893 to 1894, Montana was again left with an unfilled seat in the United States Senate.

The sordid affair brought responses from every front. Clark's nurturing of a friendly press in Montana softened some of the criticism there. The *Billings Gazette*, however, seemed to speak for the agrarian, eastern part of the state when it denounced both sides and concluded that Daly and "his crowd are just as corrupt as Clark and we will never have any decent politics in Montana until both are shorn of power." The response from the national press was harsher. The *Boston Transcript* captured the outraged tone of many when it stated that the episode "shows what a war between two not overly scrupulous multi-millionaires can accomplish for the political degradation of a commonwealth."[25]

For most observers, the feud between Clark and Daly seemed to have finally come to an end. Marcus Daly's health was rapidly failing and he would not live out the year, while the political career of William A. Clark seemed ruined and disgraced beyond redemption. But just as the political battle in Montana faded from view, another contest for economic supremacy in the state took its place. It would be a titanic struggle between two new adversaries—F. Augustus Heinze and the Amalgamated Copper Company. This time the legislature would no longer be the primary battleground of the two combatants. The fight, although it would still have an impact on Montana politics, would largely be transferred to the courts. And, yes, William A. Clark would have a nefarious role to play in this drama as well.

CHAPTER THREE

The Montana Copper Wars (Part II)

F. Augustus Heinze's Battle with the "Copper Trust"

As Butte's importance as a copper center grew, it naturally attracted other outside investors. Two companies that would later play a role in the war of the copper kings were the Boston and Montana Consolidated Copper and Silver Mining Company and the Butte and Boston Consolidated Mining Company, founded in 1887 to 1888 by very successful and powerful Boston and New York copper men. Under the control of Albert S. Bigelow, head of a wealthy Boston copper family, and the five Lewisohn brothers of New York, the companies were well managed and amply financed. The "B. & M." owned a number of highly valuable mining properties in Butte and eventually constructed a large smelting and refining complex in Great Falls. The Butte and Boston likewise owned a valuable cluster of mines in Butte, but lacking a reduction works for its ore had to ship the unrefined product to the Boston and Montana's smelter. Over time the "B. & B." evolved into something of a subsidiary of the larger Boston and Montana. Taken together, the two companies represented one of the strongest and most profitable mining operations in the United States.

At about the time the two Boston companies were getting established in Butte, the third of Montana's larger-than-life personalities arrived in Butte to begin his sensational career. At first glance, F. Augustus Heinze was young, athletic, and handsome. Standing five feet, ten

Butte, Montana (c. 1905) taken from the mining operations at the top of the "richest hill on earth."
COURTESY OF THE LIBRARY OF CONGRESS, PRINTS & PHOTOGRAPHS DIVISION

inches tall and weighing two hundred pounds, he had the look of a powerful Yale fullback. Locals initially found him to be an amiable but rather lazy fellow who seemed mainly interested in having a good time. He frequented Butte's saloons and gambling haunts and his hard-drinking and fun-loving attitude quickly made him a favorite. Women also liked his shy demeanor and his polished manners. As one writer put it: "He possessed brains in abundance, a fine address, a strong physique, tireless energy, boundless egotism, was a 'good mixer,' a prudent spendthrift, and had no moral restrictions."[1] But there was more to Heinze than that. Coupled with his keen intelligence was an audacity—a brashness, shamelessness, boldness, and daring—that would catapult him to the top ranks of Butte's entrepreneurs.

Unlike Clark and Daly, Heinze came from a wealthy and cultured background. His father, Otto Sr., a German immigrant, had made a small fortune as a New York importer. His mother, Eliza Marsh Lacey, was from a distinguished Irish-Episcopal family. Born in 1869, young Fritz (a name he disliked so much that he dropped it) received an excellent education in Brooklyn, New York, and then in Germany, where he studied at gymnasia in Leipzig and Hildesheim. Along the way, he acquired a deep interest in geology that would eventually shape his future. In the cultured world in which he was raised, it was easy for Heinze to exude the confident air of an urbane aristocrat. After returning from his study in Germany, Heinze completed his education at the Brooklyn Polytechnic Institute and then at the Columbia University School of Mines, from which he graduated with a degree of engineer of mines in 1889. Itching to start his career, Heinze decided to head west—first to visit the booming quartz towns of Colorado and then on to Salt Lake City. In September 1889, still not yet twenty years old, Heinze stepped off the train in Butte.

With his excellent academic credentials Heinze quickly found a job as a mining surveyor with the Boston and Montana Company at a salary of $250 a month. His position afforded him valuable practical experience in the most productive and extensive copper mining field in the country, and he quickly acquired a thorough understanding of the underground conditions at Butte. He diagrammed underground vein structures, talked to informed people, and thoroughly familiarized himself with "the hill's" intricate geology. He also became especially well acquainted with the various holdings of the Boston and Montana Company. He eventually concluded that a small smelting operation that utilized the latest technology and offered low rates to small-scale mining operators could return a good profit. A year after his arrival, Heinze quit his job and ventured east to raise capital to implement his plan. When investors, including his own father, proved to be reluctant to support his project, Heinze took a position working as a reporter for the prestigious *Engineering and Mining Journal*. Although he remained for only a year, the job afforded him the opportunity to study stock market practices and finance and to make contacts with men interested in mines and mining that would help him going forward. Finally, after convincing his brothers Otto Jr. and Arthur to join his venture, and after traveling to Europe to line up additional creditors and take a quick course in engineering and metallurgy at the University of Freiburg, Heinze was ready to launch the Montana Ore Purchasing Company and to market Butte copper on the Atlantic coast. With the 1894 opening of his first smelter, which eventually cut the refining costs of the independent mines almost in half, Heinze immediately became their champion.

To keep his smelter running at efficient capacity, Heinze leased mines and accepted ores from independent miners. It was not long, however, before he demonstrated an amazing knack for locating rich ore bodies in mines that had previously underperformed. Rumors soon began to circulate that Heinze had Daly's gift for finding ore. But Heinze could also be shrewd and deceitful. When he leased the Estella Mine from millionaire mine owner James Murray, he made an arrangement with Murray whereby he would give Murray 50 percent of all ores running 15 percent copper, and nothing on so-called second-class ores running at less than that amount. Because the mine was then running only first-class ores, the offer seemed attractive to Murray. But as soon as the contract was signed, every ton of ore taken from the mine ran at under 15 percent. Heinze's miners simply mixed in waste rock with the vein ore to be sent to the smelter. Murray soon investigated, found he was being duped, and promptly sued. Heinze responded by hiring the best attorneys available and won in court. It was Heinze's first legal victory, but only the first of scores of lawsuits that he would become involved in in the years to come. Profits came to Heinze and his investors so quickly that he was able to purchase the Rarus Mine for $300,000 in 1895, a deal that later confirmed his suspicion that the mine held the eastward extension of the Anaconda lode. In just two years, Heinze had developed mines that cost him $1.5 million and turned them into properties that were worth from $20 to $30 million.

When Heinze's business ventures took him away from Butte, he left his chief engineer, C. H. Batterman, in charge of his Butte operations.

After returning from a trip to the Kootenay mining district of British Columbia, Heinze learned that his chief engineer had signed on as a consulting engineer with the Boston companies. Batterman had apparently become convinced that Heinze's Rarus Mine actually "apexed" on the Butte and Boston Company's neighboring Michael Davitt property. As he left for his new position, Batterman took with him many of Heinze's maps and mining notes concerning the geological formation of the Boston properties. The information had been collected by Heinze during his employment as a surveyor for the Boston and Montana Company and by his own independent explorations in a number of Butte mines. The issue of concern in all of this was whether the Rarus Mine or the adjacent Michael Davitt Mine held the apex of the valuable ore suspected to lie underground.

The Apex Law, originally championed by Senator William Stewart of Nevada, was written into the federal law code in 1866 and then revised and updated in 1872. Prior to that time, the ownership of mineral deposits was established simply by extending the surface boundary lines of a property downward. The apex theory changed that. As before, a miner was blocked from exploring or mining beyond the boundary of his claim on the surface of that claim. But under the new interpretation, whoever owns the ground where the vein of ore comes to the surface or apexes owns the entirety of the vein. If this vein should meander beneath the surface beyond the sidelines of the surface claim and into that of a neighbor, the owner may follow it and take out the ore. It belongs to him, not to his neighbor. The property is, in a literal sense, in the vein. The surface ground becomes merely the entry point of operations. Lawmakers and the public tenaciously clung to the law at the time because of the incentive that it afforded the prospector in the search for mineral wealth.

The Apex Law would cause endless litigation in the mining West and nowhere more so than in Montana. The question for the courts was whether the surface outcroppings or apexes belonged to the veins being worked hundreds if not thousands of feet below the surface. In Montana, this crucial question was usually submitted to the judges of the district court rather than to a jury. It was up to the judge in these so-called equity cases to decide the fact of ownership based upon the testimony of mining experts employed by each side in a suit. The judge's decision, barring some error of law, was final. The only recourse for the loser in a suit was either to make an appeal to a higher court in hopes of having the decision reversed or waiting for the results of the next election in the hope that there might be a change of judges. The marathon of legal wrangling that occurred between 1896 and 1906 in Butte would eventually shut down mining properties worth tens of millions of dollars, throw thousands of employees out of work, push animosities to the verge of outright warfare, and place investors on the brink of financial ruin.

When Batterman absconded with his maps, charts, and papers, Heinze sued him in court and won. Meanwhile, he proceeded to deepen his Rarus shaft and found rich ore near the vertical side wall of his claim. He then continued his excavation through that side wall into the adjoining property of the Boston and Montana Company where the ore became even richer. Working his men around the clock, Heinze rushed the ore to the smelter as fast as possible. The bustle of new activity soon caught the attention of the Boston and Montana. Thinking that Heinze was up to no good, they sent spies into the Rarus and concluded that Heinze was stealing their ore. When asked for an explanation, Heinze informed them that he was merely following the vein that apexed on his own Rarus property. The Boston and Montana disagreed with Heinze's logic and brought suit to enjoin him from further mining through his new shaft.

Heinze, perhaps knowing that he held the more tenuous legal position in this dispute, offered to settle the controversy by paying the Boston and Montana $250,000 for the contested property (the Michael Davitt), which he claimed had cost the company only $25,000 and had been allowed to lie idle until he located valuable ore beneath the surface. But ore had now been found in such quantities and of such high grade that mining experts estimated its value at perhaps $20 million. To A. S. Bigelow, president of the Boston companies, Heinze's offer was nothing more than brazen effrontery, especially coming from someone who only five years earlier had been working for him as a surveyor at $5 a day. According to a later account, Heinze then took his maps and charts to the Boston Company and spread them out on Bigelow's big mahogany desk to support his contention that the Boston ore apexed in his Rarus property. But Bigelow was having none of this. He implied that Heinze's proposal was a form of blackmail, and that he would stand for no more of such treatment. He would see Heinze in court. Heinze's boastful retort has been often quoted: "Very well, Mr. Bigelow, you have a great deal of property in Montana which is subject to the same kind of litigation as that which you say you will thrust on me. If your program is fight, you will find I am prepared. Before you and I have finished, I will give you a fight that will be heard from one end of this continent to the other."[2] Heinze's boast was no idle one. At the height of the war on Butte hill, Heinze would have thirty-seven attorneys in his employ. Many of them were assigned the single task of finding new lawsuits to pursue.

The case was finally heard by Ninth Circuit Federal District Court Judge Hiram Knowles at Butte early in 1898. At that time the attorneys for the Boston companies argued that the major ore vein of Heinze's Rarus Mine actually apexed in their Michael Davitt Mine. Judge Knowles, who had allegedly once worked as a lawyer for the Boston companies, directed the jury to find for the Boston concern. But the jury refused to act against the popular Heinze and failed to reach a verdict. In ordering a retrial, Judge Knowles issued an injunction and closed down all operations in the area bordering the two mines. The case, which became stalled in federal court, would not be retried again in Butte until 1900 and then in different circumstances.

As the Rarus–Michael Davitt case languished in the courts, Heinze learned that he had a bigger problem to contend with. He would have to deal with an attempt from Wall Street to consolidate all the other copper mining properties on Butte hill into one giant Copper Trust. Marcus Daly is given credit for first dreaming of a great copper corporation that would monopolize the copper holdings on Butte hill, but it was Thomas Lawson who gave that vision real form in 1896. Lawson, a shrewd promoter, wily speculator, and impetuous stock plunger by trade, had first gotten interested in copper by successfully speculating in the stock of the Butte and Boston Company. Through his newly acquired position as a major stockholder in that company, he soon gained entry into the halls of its management. From that vantage point he came to envision a corner in copper, a corner at first centered on the two Boston companies at Butte, but quickly expanding to the other properties there and then on to the control of the other copper mining centers as well. But Lawson needed capital to launch his scheme and eventually found two potential backers—Henry H. Rogers and William Rockefeller—key figures in the Standard Oil Trust. H. H. Rogers and William Rockefeller, along with James Stillman, president of New York's First National Bank, were known to insiders as the "Standard Oil gang." Already engaged in the process of reinvesting their fantastic petroleum profits in railroads, gas utilities, and steel, they listened with interest to Lawson's copper scheme, did their own exhaustive research, and decided to take the plunge. They began buying heavily into copper operations in Michigan, Utah, and Montana. At Butte, they set their sights, as Lawson had suggested, on acquiring the two Boston companies. But when the Boston and Montana–Butte and Boston became mired in litigation with Heinze, they altered their plan of action. They would focus on acquiring the Daly's Anaconda operations first and come back and grab the Boston companies later. They began buying heavily into Anaconda stock, and quickly gained a growing voice in its management.

It was at this point that the logic of copper consolidation came full circle. Instead of being the consolidator, Marcus Daly decided he would sell the Anaconda and its sister corporations to the Rogers-Rockefeller crowd for $39 million and agree to accept the position of president of the new corporation. Daly's presence was merely window dressing, reassurance for the copper world that the new creation would remain under expert management. The result was the formation of the Amalgamated Copper Company, incorporated at Trenton, New Jersey, on April 27, 1899, and capitalized at $75 million, with 750,000 shares at $100 each. Investors rushed to buy shares in the new "trust," in reality a holding company that would get around antitrust law by owning and controlling the actual operating companies that it acquired. The first subscription of Amalgamated stock ran to $130 million as eager shareholders obviously concluded that anything created by Standard Oil money must surely yield riches.

The Rogers-Rockefeller group had acquired their Butte holdings for $39 million, which they covered with credit from Stillman's

National City Bank. The so-called "crime of Amalgamated" came when they grossly overcapitalized their new holding company at $75 million (approximately twice its proven assets). In what could only be termed the callous swindling of the public, the directors of the Amalgamated then issued their subscribers one share for each five shares solicited in the over-subscription. This brought them an additional $26 million. Taken against the original purchase price, this meant that the investing public paid for two-thirds of the real cost of the acquired properties. But these same investors had acquired with their $26 million only slightly more than one-third of the heavily watered shares of Amalgamated stock. Put another way, the Standard Oil gang had invested only $13 million of their own money and now held nearly five hundred thousand shares of Amalgamated worth roughly $50 million!

Rogers and his associates continued to prey on Amalgamated shareholders in the months that followed. After their initial offering, they began cashing in by unloading their inflated stocks. Amalgamated stock quickly fell to $75 a share on a wave of selling as many small holders sold out at a loss. The insiders then resumed buying and added to their profits. In 1901, in the midst of much ballyhoo similar to that of 1899, the directors brought out a second subscription of stock, triggered this time by their long anticipated takeover of the Boston and Montana–Butte and Boston Companies. Again, with little regard for the true value of the newly acquired firms, they increased the capitalization of the "trust" from $75 million to $155 million and increased the value of each share from $100 to $130. Once again, gullible investors paid for watered properties while the insiders took the real profits. The directors then cut the dividend and unloaded vast amounts of stock, this time driving down the market value to $33! Thousands of small investors were once again taken to the cleaners while insiders bought back the stock at bargain prices and took another round of profits. It was symbolic of the Wall Street morality at the time. As one angry investor complained to the US Bureau of Corporations, "Rogers has taken more millions from the Amalgamated minority stockholders than all the thieves in the 46 state prisons."[3]

By the time the Rarus–Michael Davitt case came to trial again in 1900, the public had become aware of the recent efforts toward the consolidation of copper operations at Butte. They also knew that the Boston companies had been targeted for inclusion in the new Copper Trust. Demonstrating his savvy political grasp of the changing corporate climate in Montana, Heinze instructed the editors of friendly newspapers like the *Helena Independent* to attack the Standard Oil–Amalgamated as an "alien" trust trying to take over the state. On one occasion, the editors of the *Independent* characterized Rogers and his Standard Oil associates as "a crew of political cut-throats . . . employing all the tactics of sea pirates to throttle and destroy the liberties and the property of all who do not bow the knee in abject servility to them and give tribute to their rapacity."[4] The tactic worked, and, after a forty-five-day trial, the Helena jury found in favor of Heinze. Claiming unfavorable publicity as sufficient grounds for appeal, the Amalgamated then won another retrial. At this point there was a truce in the case, which lasted for years. While the case lay in limbo, both sides were under an injunction forbidding them to work the disputed veins.

Another legal tangle occurred between Heinze and the Boston Companies in the so-called Pennsylvania cases. These suits were tried before two judges of the Second Montana District Court (a third judge would be added in 1900). Most of the cases that were of vital importance to Heinze, however, seemed to find their way into the court of one of Montana's most colorful justices, William Clancy. Something of a political accident, Clancy had slipped into office when the Populists fused with the Democrats to gain control of state politics in 1896. Illiterate and coarse (he would often spit streams of tobacco juice into a brass cuspidor during hearings), the portly, curbstone lawyer and occasional saloon lounger seldom demonstrated much expertise in the law. One critic noted that the judge had not the slightest understanding of the meaning of the geological terminology being used by geologists and mining engineers on the witness stand. But along with his Missouri backwoods humor, deep, bear-like voice, and flowing white beard, he possessed a good deal of cunning and shrewdness. Most importantly, he had an unfailing loyalty to F. Augustus Heinze, who understood his importance and became his political patron.

The litigation began when Heinze asserted that the Boston and Montana's Pennsylvania veins apexed on his Johnstown and Rarus properties. In late 1899, Judge Clancy found in favor of Heinze on every point, but the Boston and Montana immediately filed another suit asking for $600,000 in damages. Suits and countersuits keep the issue tied up in the courts for years. At one point, the Montana Supreme Court almost jailed the officers of Heinze's Montana Ore Purchasing Company for ignoring its injunctions and continuing to mine the disputed veins. The court eventually allowed Heinze to mine along the "contested peripheries" of the Pennsylvania under a bond to cover possible losses to the Boston and Montana in future decisions. Alarmed that Heinze was stripping out the veins as fast as possible, the Boston and Montana–Amalgamated successfully petitioned the court to significantly raise the amount of Heinze's bond, surmising that they could defeat Heinze by exceeding the limit of his credit. If Heinze could not furnish bonds, he would be forced to close down his operations and probably face bankruptcy. But Heinze outmaneuvered them by having his brother Otto set up a dummy corporation called the Delaware Surety Company, in actuality a shell corporation with few assets. When the court accepted the bond of this bogus company, Heinze resumed mining. The Pennsylvania litigation would continue to drag on until the final stages of the copper wars.

Perhaps the most outrageous of Heinze's legal maneuvers was the so-called Copper Trust case. This stratagem unfolded in the spring of 1899 when one of Heinze's engineers discovered two small triangular patches of land that remained unclaimed between the meeting points of a number of Anaconda mines. The entire parcel measured about 0.009 of an acre or about the size of a small room. Heinze immediately filed patent on the plot and, with a sense of humor, named his claim the Copper Trust. Then, in a burlesque of the Apex Law, Heinze sent one of his lieutenants before Judge Clancy with the unbelievable argument that the Copper Trust held the apexes of a major portion of the great Anaconda–St. Lawrence lode! The *Anaconda Standard* referred to Heinze's action as an "astounding piece of audacity."[5] Without a moment's hesitation, Judge Clancy issued a temporary restraining order and asked to show cause why he should not grant an injunction closing down operations in portions of the Anaconda, St. Lawrence, and Neversweat mines controlled by the Amalgamated until ownership could be determined. The Amalgamated immediately closed down the affected mines and laid off five hundred of its workers. Howls of outrage and streams of verbal abuse then descended upon the judge from the unemployed miners. Facing reelection and the real fear of personal injury, Clancy quickly withdrew his restraining order. The case finally died before the Montana Supreme Court two years later. By 1900 the ever-expanding mass of Heinze-inspired litigation had reached a crisis point, and it would be in the election of 1900 that the final battle would be fought.

In that turbulent contest, F. Augustus Heinze and William A. Clark formed an alliance of mutual advantage. Clark wanted to vindicate his damaged reputation and recapture his lost US Senate seat. To do that, he would need a friendly legislature that would not have to be bribed. Heinze wanted to gain control of the state government and especially the support of the Butte judges whom he could rely on to decide in his favor in all contested legal claims against the Amalgamated. But the battle would be difficult. The Amalgamated had an unlimited political war chest and the advantage of leverage over a huge number of Montana voters—the workers employed in its mines. In 1900, the Amalgamated employed over six thousand men in Montana, while Clark employed only 428 in his Butte operations and Heinze a meager 453. But fearful of their new corporate overseers, not all of the Amalgamated's employees were loyal. Complicating matters for the Amalgamated was the reality that Marcus Daly's formidable political machine was in disarray due to his illness and absence from the state. Equally ominous from the "trust's" perspective was the obvious fact that they would be confronting two Montana copper barons who were just as tough-minded and unprincipled as they were.

Clark and Heinze also had a good deal of resources at their command. Clark had established an efficient political organization as well as business connections that stretched across the state. He also possessed enough money to bankroll any political campaign and a network of newspapers, led by the *Butte Miner*, that he either owned or controlled to influence public opinion. Heinze had his own scurrilous newspaper, the *Reveille*, or as the Butte locals called it, "The Reviler." The editor was experienced Pat O'Farrell. Heinze also proved to be a pretty savvy political boss who had a knack for politics at the grassroots level. He prudently selected a captain for each of Butte's ethnic groups and for each of its unions. He also had one of his lieutenants watching over each of Butte's voting precincts and maintained an elaborate list of deceased voters so that strangers could be employed to vote for them at election time. Heinze handed out free turkeys to his employees at Thanksgiving and Christmas, gave free candy to the kids, presented a monthly bottle of wine to housewives, and saluted his workers with a demijohn of bourbon on payday. He even sold his newspapers to newsboys at a lower rate than his competitors, and the newsboys accordingly pushed their sale on the streets.

It was essential that Clark and Heinze win the important labor vote in the election, and they accomplished the task in masterful fashion. To gain the support of the Butte Miners' Union and the Trades and Labor Assembly with their 7,000 and 2,500 members respectively, Clark and Heinze announced that they would immediately grant their workers the eight-hour workday (instead of ten) while maintaining the existing $3.50 daily wage. When the Amalgamated refused to follow suit, Heinze and Clark had scored a coup. In the Miners' Union Day parade on June 13, 1900, Clark and Heinze rode in a decorated carriage at the head of the procession and were cheered by thousands of onlookers.

The central theme of the Heinze-Clark newspapers and orators was to attack the Amalgamated as a trust and to associate it with Standard Oil domination. One special target in this campaign was the J. Hennessy Mercantile Company, the so-called company store, that Marcus Daly–loyalist Dan Hennessy had opened in downtown Butte in 1898. Critics commonly charged that Amalgamated employees were compelled to trade there or at least led to believe that their jobs would be more secure if they did so. If symbolic evidence was needed to cement the association further, the six-story department store also housed the headquarters of the old Anaconda Company on its top floor. The idea was to associate the store with similar, small-scale corporate operations that had previously exploited workers in the oil and coal regions of Pennsylvania and West Virginia by charging them exorbitant prices in a noncompetitive retail environment. Very much a part of the retail operations in Butte was the clerks' union. To get the union to support their campaign, Clark and Heinze convinced them to have a resolution passed in their body demanding that stores close their doors at 6 p.m., instead of the current hour of 8 p.m. Clark and Heinze's lieutenants worked hard to get every business in Butte to comply. All the stores eventually agreed to the new policy except Hennessy's, which immediately incurred the wrath of the clerks' union.

By the fall, Clark and Heinze had pieced together an unbeatable political coalition. After some maneuvering, Clark's allies were able to win control of the regular Democratic Party apparatus in the state and have that body declare for Clark's election to the US Senate. Clark and Heinze also picked up the support of the Populist and the Union Labor Parties, as well as a few disgruntled antitrust and pro-silver Republicans. They then worked out a "fusion" ticket that featured popular Democrat "Honest Joe" Toole for governor. Keeping their platform simple, they denounced the Amalgamated and played to the labor vote with an attack on company stores and calls for free silver and the adoption of a statewide eight-hour law. The situation appeared dire for the Amalgamated. If the Clark-Heinze fusionists should win, it would mean that the trust would have to face a hostile legislature and state government, a pro-Heinze city government in Butte, and two pro-Heinze district court judges in William Clancy and Edward Harney. With Heinze's forces seemingly unbeatable in Butte, the Amalgamated focused its energies on the out-state vote and allegedly established a war chest of $1.5 million specially targeted at acquiring newspapers. In effect, it was the old Clark-Daly newspaper war just taken to a new level of co-option.

With Clark's unlimited supply of money to draw upon, Heinze soon added another new wrinkle to the campaign—importing theatrical talent. Raiding the theatrical centers of Chicago, New York, and Boston, Heinze secured the best vaudeville songsters money could buy. Using parodies of popular songs, they told the history of Standard Oil in humorous verse to appreciative onlookers. He hired a traveling theatrical company at $500 a week to permit popular singer "Cissy" Loftus to sing one of his campaign songs between acts. Brilliant cartoonists were brought from the East Coast to lampoon the Standard-Amalgamated, in one instance depicting the trust as a rapacious gorilla scaling a mountain with the fainted form of the maiden Montana clutched in its arms. Meanwhile tallyhos roamed the streets carrying glee clubs whose most popular refrain was "We must down the Kerosene, boys," while banjo-strumming minstrels in bright red jackets and circus clowns entertained the crowds. Heinze also spent Clark's money wildly on lithographs and woodcuts that showed Amalgamated miners working ten hours a day in the hot and oppressive mines belowground, while the workers employed by Heinze and Clark put in their eight hours for the same wage.

One of the most potent weapons for the Heinze-Clark forces was Heinze himself. He had never delivered a public speech until one night in Butte early in the campaign when he took the podium and, discarding his original manuscript, told with real oratorical flair and deep pathos the story of Amalgamated's attempts to drive him from the state. His unexpected appearances on the stump and his riveting off-the-cuff addresses gave form and substance to the campaign. Portraying himself as the ally of the workers against the grasping, avaricious trust, Heinze repeatedly told his listeners: "My fight against the Standard Oil is your fight. In this glorious battle to save the State from the minions of the Rockefellers and the piracy of Standard Oil you and I are partners. . . . If you stand by me I shall stand by you. No man or woman has ever heard that Heinze ever played a friend or associate false . . . together we shall curb and crush and pulverize the machinations of the Rockefellers and the Standard Oil Trust."[6] Whereas the fancily dressed Clark had never connected with the miners clad in their shabby work clothes and about to go on their shifts, Heinze dressed in the rakish garb of the Western mining camp. From the stages of beer halls, from hotel balconies, or from the steps of the courthouse, Heinze seemed comfortable speaking to the workers and did so with ease in both English and German. They admired his boldness and sympathized with his struggle as an underdog fighting against such a powerful adversary. It was a brilliant performance. As journalist C. P. Connolly remembered it: "[S]o masterfully had he arrayed facts against Standard Oil, that his larceny of Amalgamated ores was forgiven in the belief that he was fighting a battle royal against a coterie of public enemies and judicial bribers, and was, therefore, justified in the use of any weapons. . . . The public eye was focused on this young, daring, resourceful freebooter. They cared little how selfish his motives might be—his fight was their fight."[7]

The corporation fought back but not effectively. Amalgamated officials did make convincing arguments: that they had invested $90 million in Montana; that the industry under common management was more efficient; that rationalization and centralization would eliminate waste, contention, and endless litigation; and that consolidation would benefit capital and labor alike by assuring increased and steadier profits and guaranteeing employment. But voters were not listening. When the results of the Montana election of November 6, 1900, were finally in, the Clark-Heinze fusion ticket swept to victory. The Democrat-Populist-Labor candidates won control of the governor's office, both houses of the state legislature (assuring Clark an easy election to the US Senate), the election of two pro-Heinze district court judges, and the entire slate of Silver Bow County (Butte) officials. At the victory celebration, three thousand supporters gathered at the Butte Hotel on election night to hear speeches from their heroes. Heinze set the tone by telling the crowd that they had "given the death-blow to tyranny and despotism, to coercion and blackmail, the like of which has never been accomplished in any other part of the union." It remained to be seen if that was true.[8]

After his election to the US Senate with Heinze's help in January 1901, William Clark withdrew from the alliance and joined arms with the Amalgamated crowd. There were rumors that Henry Rogers had threatened to use the influence of Standard Oil–Amalgamated to challenge his seat in the US Senate unless he abandoned his opposition to the trust, but Heinze's recklessness had undoubtedly convinced him that it was prudent to safeguard his business and financial interests now that his political goal had been attained. As one historian noted, "A conservative at heart, Clark had no real ideological quarrel with the trust and no personal quarrel with its masters now that Daly [who died six days after the election] was gone. Nor, being an unprincipled and unsentimental man, did he seem to flinch at breaking with Heinze and the others who had supported him in the recent campaign."[9] With political duties in Washington and with expanding business investments outside the state, Clark would spend less and less of his time in Montana. With his "departure," the second of the old mining barons faded from view. The desertion of Clark, however, only served to compel Heinze to fight with more energy and determination.

By 1903, the court-issued injunction forbidding Heinze to work the valuable ore bodies lying on the border of his Rarus Mine and the Amalgamated's Michael Davitt was becoming a problem. He desperately needed access to these ores, especially the rich Enargite and Windlass veins, to keep his mills and smelters running at full capacity. Caught in a financial bind, Heinze made up his mind to get those ores, court order or no court order. In August 1903, he made an audacious maneuver and transferred ownership of the Rarus from his Montana Ore Purchasing Company to another of his holdings—the Johnstown Mining Company. Heinze then made the outrageous argument that because the Johnstown Company was not part of the original injunction, he could send in his crews and work the disputed claim. Heinze's men began to drive cross-cuts into the disputed ground of the Michael Davitt and sealed off or "bulkheaded" any underground approaches from the adjoining Pennsylvania Mine owned by the Amalgamated. He then sent in hundreds of workers to blast and remove the high-grade ores as fast as possible and seal the cavities with waste rock before being ordered to stop. When Amalgamated men in the Pennsylvania Mine began to hear the rumbles of blasting coming from the adjoining Rarus, they decided to investigate. On the night of October 10, Amalgamated geologist Reno Sales and superintendent George McGee removed a bulkhead and sneaked into the contested area at the six-hundred-foot level. What they saw were armies of Heinze's men dumping Michael Davitt ore into the Rarus workings, where it was then hoisted to the surface.

Lawyers from the Amalgamated quickly petitioned Judge Hiram Knowles, who had been in charge of the litigation since 1898, for the right to enter the Rarus and inspect the illegal digging. Unfazed, Heinze increased the pace of his illicit operations and went into seclusion to avoid being served a court order. According to one account, he barely escaped the marshal by fleeing through a rear window and climbing down a fire escape. It took sixteen days before inspectors could finally gain access to the site. What they eventually found was a maze of crosscuts and stopes, filled with waste rock from the recent excavations. The court then ordered measurements to be taken of the cavities as the first step in an assessment of the amount of ore removed that would allow fines to be levied for damages. Heinze again thumbed his nose at the court by denying entry. In an ongoing attempt to further intimidate Judge Knowles, Heinze had his press spokesmen wage a personal attack on the judge as being biased against Heinze in favor of the trust.

When Heinze's appeal of the case finally reached the US court of appeals in San Francisco, that court sent Judge James H. Beatty of Idaho to Butte to assume jurisdiction. Heinze showed no more respect for Beatty than he had for Knowles despite the threat of contempt citations. When the Amalgamated's geologists finally gained access to the Rarus in December, they found Heinze's men tearing into the richest ore bodies with machine drills without making any attempt to cover up their activities. The workers did not even stop while the inspectors looked on. The inspectors found that the richest fissures of the Michael Davitt had already been robbed and that the mine, in places, had been left as a hollow shell. The most shocking revelation to come to the Amalgamated was that the Johnstown Mining Company, to which Heinze had transferred the contested ore bodies, was devoid of any assets that could be used to compensate them for the loss of their valuable ores. In most cases, before the geologists even had a chance to measure the cavities of the extracted ore bodies to calculate estimates of loss, Heinze's men had already destroyed the evidence. Setting dynamite charges, they blew up the stopes, which caved in and demolished the walls of the veins. It was obvious that Heinze intended to deplete the veins before the court could stop him, and before his credit ran out, regardless of the consequences.

When the rule of law failed to deter Heinze, the contending companies carried the battle belowground. Foremen from both sides sent their men to mine the disputed veins and to thwart any incursions from the opposition. As each side intensified its commitment, guerilla warfare broke out. Workers fouled the opposition shafts with powder smoke and poured slaked lime into the pipes which blew fresh air into the workings. They fired high-pressure steam and water hoses at each other, tossed homemade smoke grenades back and forth, dynamited tunnels, caved in drifts, stopes, and crosscuts, and even electrified the metal turn plates on which the ore cars moved around corners. In late December two miners died in an accident when Heinze men blasted a bulkhead from the opposite side. When Amalgamated crews attempted to drive crosscuts, Heinze's men drove them out with smoke and lime. Wild fistfights occurred when opposing crews unexpectedly came upon one another. At one point, Heinze's men attempted to force the opposition out of a crucial area by tapping the city's water mains and diverting the flow via a pipeline into their works. To prevent the flooding of their mine, workers employed by the Amalgamated allowed the water to accumulate behind a ten-foot-thick cement dam in one of their crosscuts. They then made plans to blast out the walls and allow the water to flood back upon the Heinze men, blowing steam whistles to warn the workers inside the mine. Hearing the whistles, a large crowd of wives and relatives rushed to the entry of the mine fearing that their loved ones were being drowned below. It was a signal that things had gone too far. Superintendents from both sides rushed to assure the crowd that the men had not been harmed, and, in doing so, defused the situation and prevented the crowd from turning into a mob. The next day representatives of the contending parties came together at the Silver Bow Club in Butte and agreed to a formal truce.

Fear of both the loss of lives and investments finally brought an end to the underground warfare in the spring of 1904. At the same time, the courts managed to reassert their authority. Judge Beatty, finally able to drag Heinze and two of his foremen into court, found them in contempt. The judge denounced Heinze's Johnstown ploy and condemned his flagrant disregard for the orders of the court. "I have been engaged in mining litigation and mining operations for the last thirty-two years," said the judge, "and in all of my experience I have never known an order of the court violated as this has been. It is simply beyond all reason."[10] Despite the stern lecture, Judge Beatty refrained from severely punishing Heinze and his men. Holding prison sentences in abeyance, he issued only a modest fine of $20,000 to Heinze and $1,000 to each of his lieutenants. The *Anaconda Standard* contemptuously dismissed the fines, saying that $20,000 was about what Heinze could have made in six months' interest on the stolen ore. In truth, Heinze had made out like a bandit. In tapping the rich deposits within the Michael Davitt, it was estimated that he had pilfered over $1 million worth of high-grade ore.

One other epic battle between Heinze and the Amalgamated, the fight over control of the Minnie Healy Mine, led the two combatants to descend into the world of political corruption. The Minnie Healy was a small mining operation that lay next to the Piccolo and Gambetta claims of the Boston and Montana Company. Miles Finlen, a regular Butte investor and ally of Marcus Daly, held a working lease on the mine. As part of the lease arrangement, Finlen was to extend the shaft two hundred feet with the option to purchase the claim for $100,000 at the end of two years. Finlen had no luck finding ore in the Minnie Healy and one day told Heinze that he had spent $54,000 on the property and he wanted to get out. Heinze had no knowledge of the mine's value but wanted it because of its location next to the Piccolo and Gambetta claims. He had the idea that the rich veins of those two claims apexed in the Minnie Healy which, if true, would give him cause to file suit against the Boston Company. Allegedly, Heinze and Finlen reached an oral agreement whereby Finlen would sell his rights and leasehold to Heinze for the amount of money ($54,000) he had already invested. A few days after he took possession, Heinze struck a huge body of immensely rich ore.

Knowledge of the Finlen-Heinze deal reached Daly in New York, where he and H. H. Rogers had just formalized their plan for bringing the Boston and Montana Company into the Amalgamated. The news that a new, rich mine had appeared outside their control and that preliminary reports suggested that the rich veins of their neighboring properties probably apexed within the boundary of the Minnie Healy caused them a great deal of concern. Daly immediately ordered Finlen to back out of the deal. No luck. Finlen then tried to take the mine back by force, but his men were met by Heinze's armed guard at the entrance to the Minnie Healy and repulsed. The only recourse was to take Heinze to court and try to have the agreement nullified. Finlen then signed his rights over to the Boston and Montana Company (which became part of the Amalgamated in 1901) and that company took over the suit.

The case of *Finlen v. Heinze* was to be tried without a jury by Judge Edward W. Harney, who, along with Judge Clancy gave Heinze control over the district court in Butte. Harney had a reputation for being a skilled lawyer, but also of being a hard drinker who frequently appeared on the bench in an intoxicated condition. On June 18, 1901, after a two-month trial, Judge Harney handed down a decision in favor of Heinze. But the Amalgamated appealed the decision to the Montana Supreme Court and won a reversal based on the personal misconduct of Judge Harney. In justifying its decision, the higher court stated that Harney had shown himself to be "completely lost to all sense of decency and propriety, and that he made of the occasion, while off the bench, a carnival of drunkenness and debauchery."[11]

Evidence that came out during the trial before the Montana Supreme Court, and which eventually found its way into the partisan press, showed that the judge had engaged in some rather risqué behavior during the 1901 trial. It seems that Judge Harney, although married, had entered into an affair with Mrs. Ada Brackett, a public stenographer in Butte who had worked for Heinze's Montana Ore Purchasing Company. She lived in a small house in town, and Judge Harney became a regular visitor. An agent of Heinze's Montana Ore Purchasing Company actually rented the house from the owner, and a detective in the employ of the same company guarded the house while Mrs. Brackett lived there. During the Minnie Healy trial, Mrs. Brackett carried on a secret correspondence with Judge Harney. The letters were apparently sent to one another via a courier by the name of George B. Dygert. Dygert was an attorney whose office adjoined Mrs. Brackett's and a close friend of D'Gay Stivers, an attorney for the Amalgamated. Before being delivered, each note was removed from its envelope and copied. The letters did not prove that Harney had taken a bribe from Heinze, but strongly suggested it. The most important piece of correspondence was the so-called "dearie letter" which became an important factor in the ultimate reversal of the Minnie Healy case by the Montana Supreme Court. In that letter Brackett assured the judge, "I love you," and then wrote, "all they [the Heinze group] want you to do is to be honest in every decision, whether it is for or against them. . . . As for your future, after you leave the bench, if you will allow me, I am empowered to promise you certain things which will assure that most generously." She then closed with a gentle reproof that became widely quoted: "Be very careful of this letter, dearie."[12]

The story of the sex scandal and the implied offer of a bribe eventually reached the public. The sordid affair was certainly an embarrassment to Judge Harney, and to Heinze as well. Harney, however, fought back with his own account of how the trust had tried to blackmail him with threats of exposure and impeachment unless he admitted to having been bought by the opposition. He also related in some detail an account of how he and Mrs. Brackett had been lured to a room in the Thornton Hotel by several agents of the Amalgamated, including Charlie Clark, and offered $150,000 if he would resign his position and sign a statement admitting that he had accepted bribes. Mrs. Brackett was promised $20,000. When Harney refused to make such an admission, Clark raised the offer to $250,000. According to the judge's account, when he still refused to admit wrongdoing, Charlie Clark became impatient and told him: "for a tenth of what I have offered you, you might be put out of the way when you start for home some night, and nobody would ever hear of you again."[13] But neither the offer of money nor the threat of bodily harm could bring the judge to admit to taking bribes. He was either innocent or supremely loyal to Heinze. In the end, the Montana Supreme Court remanded the case of *Finlen v. Heinze* to the lower court for retrial. That meant that the irascible Heinze loyalist Judge William Clancy would ultimately decide the outcome of the Minnie Healy dispute.

Judge Clancy finally rendered his decision in the Minnie Healy case on October 22, 1903, and awarded full legal title to the Minnie Healy to Heinze's Johnstown Mining Company. The decision gave Heinze clear access to $10 million in proven ore deposits as well as the opportunity to launch new apex suits against mines surrounding the Minnie Healy. It was a crushing blow for the Amalgamated. Just as significant, however, was a related decision delivered the same day. It had been an ongoing legal tactic of Heinze's to launch a series of minority stockholder suits against his competitors. Three pending suits had been brought against the Amalgamated by Montana Ore Purchasing Company Vice President John

MacGinniss and company attorneys James Forrester and Daniel Lamm. They had argued that their rights as minority stockholders, even though they owned only a few dozen shares, had been violated when companies in which they held stock had been absorbed by the Amalgamated and that the corporation itself was an illegal monopoly. Relying on a legal technicality, they argued that the transfer of ownership of those independent companies to the Amalgamated without their consent was illegal (the companies in question had been chartered before the passage of an 1899 law that required the consent of only two-thirds of the stockholders for such decisions). As a result, they had asked the court to restrain the holding company from issuing dividends—in effect, asking the court to dissolve the trust. In his decision, Judge Clancy accepted their argument and issued injunctions prohibiting the Amalgamated from possessing the stocks of or drawing dividends from the companies in question. In a sense, Clancy's ruling placed the Amalgamated in a situation where it could not operate any of its Montana subsidiaries. If the decision was allowed to stand, the Amalgamated was finished in Montana.

The reaction from the Amalgamated was quick and forceful. It shut down all its operations. Mines in Butte closed, shipments of coal and coke to Butte stopped, and nearly 6,500 men immediately laid off. Smelters and refineries in Anaconda and Great Falls extinguished their fires and locked their gates. It was the same in the lumber mills in western Montana and in the coal towns of Cascade, Gallatin, and Carbon Counties. Somber, ill-humored workers gathered in the railroad yards or milled in the streets of Butte, Anaconda, Great Falls, and Havre. All of a sudden, twenty thousand workers, the majority of Montana's labor force, found themselves anxiously facing a severe Montana winter without any income.

Each side tried to claim the high ground in the crisis. The Amalgamated disingenuously tried to defend its actions by arguing that since it could not issue dividends, it must, in fairness to its stockholders, suspend its operations. But the trust was already preparing appeals to the state supreme court and could certainly gain a stay of Clancy's decision pending their appeal. Heinze tried to shift the blame back on the Amalgamated by arguing that the trust had really closed down its operations for the purpose of manipulating stocks and to reduce its 150-million-pound surplus of copper and to maintain prices. The trust, he said, was trying to intimidate the state and turn it into a subservient colony. But to outsiders it seemed that mining interests had once again compromised the commonwealth of Montana. The *Engineering and Mining Journal* doubted the sincerity of either side and described the debacle as merely "the latest outcome of that bewildering tangle of litigation which has emphasized the defects of the United States mining law and debauched the politics and corrupted the judiciary of a state."[14]

In general, the workers directed their anger more toward Heinze and his "friendly" judges than at the trust, a situation that put Heinze on the spot. Looking to redirect their anger, Heinze promised to deliver a public address in front of the Silver Bow County courthouse. As he climbed the steps of the courthouse on the afternoon of October 26, 1903, he could sense the tension. A sullen crowd, estimated to be ten thousand in number and which verged on becoming a mob, spread far out into the street. The great majority of those assembled were hostile, some were reportedly armed, and most worked for the Amalgamated. Standing solemnly before the throng, Heinze then launched into the greatest speech of his life. He denied that he had been hounding the Amalgamated Copper Company in the courts, and charged, instead, that he had been fought by the trust in every conceivable way with the intention of driving him from the state. He charged that "there are within the sound of my voice a hundred men, now in my employ, who have been offered bribes ranging all the way from a thousand to ten thousand dollars to commit perjury for the purpose of defeating me in my lawsuits." He compared the Amalgamated to the worst of the trusts "in its influence and functions, and the control it has over the commercial and economic affairs of this state, is the greatest menace that any community could possibly have within its boundaries." He linked the actions of Amalgamated with the worst offenses of the Standard Oil Trust and reminded his listeners that Rockefeller and Rogers were ruthless in crushing every obstacle in their path. He then charged that the "same Rockefeller and the same Rogers are seeking to control the executive, the judiciary, and the legislature of Montana." Then, in a brilliant peroration, he concluded with the warning:

These people are my enemies, fierce, bitter, implacable; but they are your enemies, too. If they crush me today, they will crush you tomorrow. They will cut your wages and raise the tariff in the company stores on every bite you eat and every rag you wear. They will force you to dwell in Standard Oil houses while you live, and they will bury you in Standard Oil coffins when you die. Their tools and minions are here now, striving to build up another trust whose record is already infamous. Let them win, and they will inaugurate conditions in Montana that will blast its fairest prospect and make its name hateful to those who love liberty. They have crushed the miners of Colorado because those miners had no one to stand for their rights. In this battle . . . you and I are partners and allies. We stand or fall together.[15]

It was a masterful performance, a demonstration of his oratorical skills and his personal courage, but also of his cleverness—his ability to win votes through the appeal of a demagogue. Heinze had triumphed for the moment and, when the crowd departed, it was loyal to him once more. But that feeling only lasted until the reality of the situation sunk in again the following day.

The Amalgamated knew it held the stronger hand and soon decided to play its trump. It demanded that the governor call a special session of the legislature and that it enact what it called the "Fair Trial" law. The law would simply disqualify any district judge upon a charge of bias by a litigant and allow for his replacement by another judge. It was a simple and uncomplicated way to remove the likes of Clancy and Harney. But it was also a form of corporate blackmail. The Amalgamated would only put the unemployed thousands back to work if the legislature complied. Governor Joseph Toole initially resisted the company's demands and refused to call the legislature back in session. As he demurred, the freezing days of early November began to set in. In the interim, both sides continued to level charges at each other. Thomas Lawson, spokesperson for the Amalgamated, issued press statements in which he suggested that he and Heinze had been meeting in secret to negotiate a sellout to the Amalgamated, while Heinze denied that any meetings had taken place. But the pressure from labor unions and other groups to call a special session eventually became too great, and Governor Toole announced that he would convene the legislature in early December. As one historian noted, "Toole had done what he had to; for without his order, the wage earners of the state could not have survived the winter. But in doing so, he served to demonstrate the extent to which this remote, thinly populated, much-abused mountain commonwealth had become a pawn in the world of capitalist intrigue and manipulation."[16]

Legislators wasted little time before doing what they were told. After a minimum of debate, they passed two laws. The first clarified when a case might qualify for a change of venue, and the second allowed for the disqualification of a "biased" judge. This "Fair Trial" or "Clancy Law" effectively ended Heinze's control over the courts in Butte. It was a crippling blow for Heinze, but what rankled many was the means that had been employed to force its adoption. As the *New York Journal of Commerce* concluded: "It looks as tho [*sic*] the real governing power in Montana was the Amalgamated Copper Company, or likely to become so."[17] If not beaten, Heinze and his clique were certainly in retreat after 1904. Even so, he could still boast in May of that year that the copper war in Montana was wearing down the trust and causing it to lose $2 million annually, and that he would soon force the trust to capitulate on his terms. In truth, although Heinze and his newspapers still hammered at the old theme of Standard Oil–Amalgamated domination, the leader of the anti-monopoly forces in Montana was actually planning to sell out to the trust. Secret negotiations for a sellout picked up after the election of 1904 and continued, first in Butte and then at various New York hotels, for the next fifteen months. The bargainers had to agree on a buyout price, but also on what sort of company would take over the Heinze properties. Reports of a settlement finally reached the press in February 1906 and seemed to signal the end of the copper wars in Montana. In the deal, Heinze, for a rumored selling price of $10.5 million, would turn over the bulk of his Montana properties, not directly to the Amalgamated, but to something called the Butte Coalition Mining Company. An important component of the purchase price involved the dismissal of 110 pending lawsuits that were tying up properties valued at from $70 to $100 million. The Butte Coalition, newly incorporated in

New Jersey and capitalized at $15 million, would be a new holding company similar to the Amalgamated with the Heinze properties grouped together in a subsidiary known as the Red Metal Mining Company. The agreement offered at least the appearance that the two adversaries were dealing with a third party.

Historians today have generally concluded that, despite a well-cultivated image of a modern-day Robin Hood fighting the hated Standard Oil–Amalgamated Trust to a standstill, Heinze had really planned all along to force the trust to pay him an exorbitant price for his holdings. "This is not to say," said one observer, "that his antitrust crusades were altogether insincere, only that he was an especially virulent example of the ruthless capitalists of his time." By any evaluation, the Heinze-Amalgamated fight left a shameful legacy. Power had been abused and government agencies had been perverted. Big money, wielded by unscrupulous local entrepreneurs like Heinze and Clark or by an unprincipled group of Wall Street manipulators led by H. H. Rogers, debased a state and shocked a nation. The conservative *Mining and Scientific Press* echoed that sentiment: "The judiciary of a State has been debauched, its politics mired, its people obsessed, while two parties of mine-owners have twisted our awkward mining laws to the acquirement of territory and the destruction of property." In summing up the situation as it stood in 1906, one historian commented: "No longer facing real competition for mastery of the hill, the Amalgamated monolith now bestrode the state like a great, insensate colossus."[18]

After his sellout to the Amalgamated, Heinze shifted his base of operations to New York City and set out to become a Wall Street power broker. With an office complex on Thirty-Third Street and a double suite of rooms at the Waldorf Hotel, Heinze reestablished himself as an avid investor and social lion. It seemed as if the flamboyant Heinze was determined to create a mining and banking empire in the center of high finance. Heinze, along with brothers Otto and Arthur, had formed the United Copper Company, an Amalgamated-style holding company, in 1902. Chartered in South Dakota and capitalized at $80 million, the corporation had been created to control and manage the various Heinze operations. Devoid of most of its properties after the sellout, Heinze now sought to build the company back up by developing new mining operations in Montana, British Columbia, Idaho, and Utah. He also decided to enter the unregulated world of banking which could afford a buccaneer like himself almost free use of depositors' money for speculative purposes.

At the same time, Heinze established a friendly business relationship with Charles W. Morse, a Wall Street speculator. Morse controlled the American Ice Company, which some called the "Ice Trust" because of its monopoly of the ice business in New York City, and the Consolidated Steamship Company or so-called "Steamship Trust" because of its near monopoly of freight and passenger traffic along the East Coast. Morse also controlled the National Bank of North America and the New Amsterdam National Bank and was a major stockholder in the Mercantile National Bank as well. But Morse had earned a dubious reputation in financial circles for adhering to a method of operation that has been called "chain-banking." Following this strategy, Morse and his backers would purchase a controlling interest in one bank and then use the equity in that bank as collateral to borrow money to purchase shares in other banks. The goal was to create a pyramid of interlocking financial relationships. In partnership with Morse, the Heinzes purchased control of the Mercantile National Bank of New York from Edwin Gould and F. Augustus Heinze became its president in February 1907. They then linked the Mercantile National to a chain of banks already held by Morse. Heinze then heightened his presence on Wall Street by buying a seat on the New York Stock Exchange for his brothers and creating the brokerage house of Otto C. Heinze and Company. Using that company as their agent on Wall Street, the Heinze brothers then entered into a speculative arrangement with Morse in which they used shares of the United Copper Company stock as collateral.

At this point, things started to unravel for Heinze and his partners. The United Copper Company appeared vulnerable because of its lack of proven holdings and because of a tight money market and the falling price for copper. It also suffered from a form of contempt by association. After Heinze's sellout to the Amalgamated in 1906, the *Copper Handbook*, a sentinel for the industry, described United Copper as an "exceptionally daring piece of stockjobbery," the tool of an entrepreneur who "has shown himself utterly rapacious, unscrupulous and conscienceless in his mining and financial operations."[19] The word on the street was that the company was overcapitalized and controlled by a group of reckless speculators. Shares of United Copper, which had reached a high of $70 per share in 1906, had dropped to $40 by the fall of 1907. In an attempt to stem losses, the Heinzes purchased over $2 million worth of United Copper stock through various brokerages. Although this maneuver temporarily stopped the slide, a sudden wave of selling and panicked calls for margin from the brokers pushed the Heinzes toward bankruptcy by depleting their cash reserves. This led them to believe that the brokers were selling them short. In trouble, the brothers then decided to try to create a "corner" in United Copper by calling in their shares, figuring that the brokers did not hold a sufficient number of shares to meet their call and would have to bid up the price in a frantic search for additional shares in the open market. They were wrong. Other investors held large enough blocs of the stock to cover the short purchases of the brokers. In receiving their stocks, the Heinzes stood by helplessly as the price for their shares broke while they had to come up with huge amounts of cash to cover their purchases. On October 15, 1907, share prices for United Copper fell from $60 to $36 as the Heinzes desperately sold stock in an effort to raise enough capital to meet their obligations. The following day, the share price fell to $10. This precipitous drop in value immediately placed the firm of Otto Heinze and Company and the Mercantile National Bank in jeopardy as both were large creditors of the troubled holding company.

When word got out that Mercantile National was in trouble, depositors made a run on the bank to pull out their money. The stampede quickly spread to other Morse-connected banks like the Trust Company of America and the Knickerbocker Trust. Although magnates in the realm of big business, Heinze and Morse undoubtedly appeared as upstarts to more established financiers. Real financial power rested with the Morgan and Rockefeller banking interests, who, along with their allies, controlled the central New York Clearing House, a consortium that directed the flow of credit between the banks of the city that were members. Running out of options, Heinze and Morse called on the Clearing

House for help. The directors of the Clearing House agreed to come to their aid, but only if Heinze and Morse agreed to two conditions: They would immediately have to resign from the boards of their principal banks and the Mercantile Bank would have to enter into a process of slow liquidation. They agreed, finding themselves ousted from the financial system they had hoped to command.

Although Morse's National Bank of North America and his New Amsterdam National Bank had been compromised by the failed copper corner, they survived. The Knickerbocker Trust, however, one of the largest and most successful trust companies in the country, did not. On October 21, the public learned that Charles T. Barney, president of the Knickerbocker and one of the most respected financial figures in New York, had been asked to tender his resignation. They also learned that J. P. Morgan's National Bank of Commerce, the Clearing House agent for the Knickerbocker, would no longer clear checks for it. An investigation by the Clearing House into Barney's affairs revealed that he had been an associate of Charles Morse and Augustus Heinze and that he may have been a partner in their schemes. A follow-up audit revealed that the bank was actually insolvent. The fall of Charles Barney and the refusal of the Clearing House to rescue the Knickerbocker caused a run on the bank that triggered a severe, nationwide banking panic. The so-called Panic of 1907 hit the nation hard, pushing teetering banks over the edge, dragging down stock values, causing plants to close and workers to be laid off. Only the massive pouring of millions of dollars into the banks and the market by J. P. Morgan–led New York banks and the US Treasury Department saved the day. But the economic dislocation caused by the panic and the short recession that followed revealed the power of Wall Street bankers and underscored the need for closer federal regulation of the financial sector.

The panic ruined the Heinzes and their allies. Much of the blame could be placed on themselves as a result of their shady speculations and mismanagement. But some, including F. Augustus Heinze, believed that the big bankers, led by J. P. Morgan and by James Stillman of the National City Bank and of Amalgamated Copper, had a hand in the collapse through their efforts to crowd upstarts like Morse and himself out of their financial domain. The massive sales of United Copper stocks, which undercut the company's standing in the financial community, and the runs on the Heinze-Morse-owned banks looked suspicious. Although we shall never know for certain, it looked like the Rogers-Rockefeller-Stillman gang was still trying to settle some old scores with Heinze.

In the aftermath of the panic, tragedy served as the postscript for its major villains. On November 14, 1907, Charles T. Barney died from a self-inflicted gunshot wound at his home on Park Avenue in New York City. The disgrace of his fall was too much to bear. Heinze and Charles Morse had their own legal problems to confront as they both faced charges of criminal malfeasance. Morse was eventually convicted of grand larceny (misappropriating funds from the Bank of North America) in January 1910 and sentenced to fifteen years in prison. Maintaining his innocence and that his actions were no different than those commonly practiced in the financial community, Morse mounted a vigorous campaign to gain his freedom. Mysteriously, he grew ill, and when it looked like he might die in prison President Taft commuted his sentence and granted his release in January 1912. Morse then fled to Europe, where it was revealed that his "illness" was actually due to eating soap shortly before his medical examinations.

For his part in the affair, Heinze was indicted on sixteen counts of financial malfeasance and various violations of banking laws. Heinze went to trial in the spring of 1909 and miraculously managed to escape conviction. The following year he married actress Bernice Henderson, but the couple soon separated after the birth of a son, F. Augustus, Jr. Then, in the spring of 1914, Bernice died after being stricken with spinal meningitis. Other reversals followed. His efforts to rebuild his mining empire failed, and, in 1911, with its stock at 80 cents a share, United Copper fell into receivership. In October 1914, Heinze suffered another setback when a New York court awarded Edwin Gould a large cash settlement against him for incomplete payment of his earlier purchase of the Mercantile National Bank. Years of hard drinking and nighttime carousing had taken their toll on Heinze as well. When he traveled to Saratoga, New York, to vote on November 3, 1914, he had been suffering for months from internal bleeding and cirrhosis of the liver. He died suddenly the following day at the age of forty-four from a massive hemorrhage.

Any assessment of Heinze's short but remarkable life is difficult. Shrewd, bold, and unabashedly unscrupulous, he gave the piratical Standard Oil–Amalgamated the fight of its life in Montana. But the same recklessness that he exhibited in the Treasure State cost him dearly when pitted against the financial titans on Wall Street. It has been suggested that Heinze's tragedy might be best explained in terms of "lost opportunities" and "roads not taken." "Had he followed a more constructive and less nihilistic path," noted one historian, "F. Augustus Heinze might have been one of the truly great men of his generation."[20]

CHAPTER FOUR

The California-Oregon Land Frauds

THERE IS A STORY, OR MAYBE IT IS A TALE, FIRST TOLD BY MUCKRAKING journalist Lincoln Steffens as a preface to his exposé on the Oregon land fraud system that appeared in the *American* magazine in September 1907. It seems that a Catholic priest from Tillamook County, Oregon, by the name of Joseph Schell had learned from his parishioners that they were being forced off lands that they had claimed and lived on as homesteaders so that the federal government could create a new forest preserve. But Father Schell and his poor parishioners were confused. They were aware that Congress had passed laws to grant compensation to those who might be dispossessed by such a process. The Forest Reserve Act of 1897 had authorized the Interior Department to set aside land for forest preserves. Under the so-called lieu lands provision of this act, persons who settled on or owned lands to be included within proposed forest reserves would have the option of exchanging their land (the government would issue certificates known as lieu land scrip for this purpose) on an acre-for-acre basis for other public land of perhaps greater value. If homesteaders chose not to relocate, they could easily sell their valuable scrip to brokers for an agreeable price as the brokers would then resell the land to lumbering, mining, or stock-raising interests that would be eager to obtain them. In fact, speculators often invested in worthless land near proposed forest reserves in anticipation of making a profitable exchange. If they had political connections, they often persuaded or bribed officials charged with creating a reserve to include their lands within the boundaries. But when the Tillamook County homesteaders went to the land office to fill out the proper papers and receive their scrip, they were told that their claims were invalid.

Convinced that some error had been made, Father Schell visited the state land office himself. Although officials agreed that a great injustice had been done, they told him that the issue involved title faults and they were only following the letter of the law as they were required to do. Not satisfied with their rather technical explanation, however, Father Schell began to investigate. What he found was that total strangers had recently filed claims to the same homestead lands, and that the land office had honored those claims. He then learned that those same strangers had immediately signed the rights to those claims over to a Portland banker who speculated in lieu land scrip, assisted by a Portland attorney who had drawn up all the legal paperwork. The evidence suggested that fraud had occurred—that applications and entries had been forged and that officials in the land office were in league with the despoilers. Confident that justice would win out, Father Schell decided to present the results of his investigation to the proper Oregon authorities.

Father Schell took his findings back to the state land office. No luck. He then proceeded to the office of US District Attorney John H. Hall, but was brushed off with vague promises of an investigation that were not kept. He then talked to the press, but when the editors saw the names of the prominent men who were accused of being guilty of fraud, they pushed the dutiful priest aside as if he were a lunatic. Before long, his life was threatened. The Portland attorney who had abetted the swindle tried to bribe him and then tried to blackmail him with an affidavit from a woman who falsely swore to misconduct on his part. His church reprimanded him and then transferred him. He finally wrote a letter to Secretary of the Interior Ethan Allen Hitchcock, whose office acknowledged receipt of his post, but nothing more was done. By this time, the original homesteaders had long been forced off their land without compensation.

Determined to see his grievance gain some consideration, Father Schell decided to take a leave of absence and carry his case directly to Washington, DC, to talk to Secretary Hitchcock in person. But the secretary was "too busy" to see him. He then appealed to Senators John Mitchell and Charles Fulton of Oregon, but their secretaries told him they were "unavailable." He was then referred to the assistant secretary of the interior, who referred him to the assistant attorney general's office, who sent him back to the General Land Office in the Interior Department. He tried to schedule an appointment with Commissioner Binger Hermann, a fellow Oregonian, but his clerk passed him on to Assistant Commissioner W. A. Richards whose assistant sent him to the Lieu Lands Division under William Valk. Valk's secretary referred him to the Forestry Division, headed by H. H. Jones, but his clerk decided that the person to see was really Woodford D. Harlan, chief of the Special Service Division of the General Land Office, who sent him on to yet another department. Bounced from office to office in the labyrinth that is the Washington bureaucracy, Father Schell quickly became known around Washington as that "crazy priest." His persistence had made him a nuisance.

When word reached his church superiors, they decided to discipline him. They recalled him to Oregon, transferred him for a second time, and strongly rebuked him for bringing ridicule upon the Church and his position. He had tried and he had failed, stymied by what would later be known as the "land ring," composed of members of state legislatures, government officials, United States commissioners, special land agents, notaries, and private citizens of all classes. But Father Schell had been an "outsider" and, as such, his credibility could be questioned. The key to giving legitimacy to the charge of fraud was to gain the confession of an "insider." One lesson that journalist Lincoln Steffens had learned from his own investigative reporting was that corruption is often exposed by the "quarrels of the grafters over the graft."[1]

In the late nineteenth and early twentieth centuries, most of the looters of the public domain simply manipulated existing land laws to get rich. One method was taking advantage of the Timber and Stone Act of 1878. The Timber and Stone Act had been passed to assist settlers in obtaining timber and stone from lands contiguous to their claims. The law provided that lands not valuable for agricultural purposes might be sold in blocs of 160 acres for $2.50 per acre. A loophole in the law, however, allowed "dummy" entrymen to file bogus claims for the land and then turn right around and deed the land to mining and lumber companies. In the process, thousands of acres of valuable timber lands in the Pacific Northwest passed for a fraction of their real value into the hands of corporations.

Another angle involved school lands. As states gained admission to the Union, certain tracts of land were granted to them as "school land" to be sold to raise funds for public schools. State officials were allowed to dispose of this land as they saw fit. As mentioned, under the Forest Reserve Act certain public lands could be set aside as forest reserves. If the federal government created a reserve that included school land, a state would be compensated with an equal amount of unclaimed land in lieu of that withdrawn. If a state had already issued patents to private individuals for this land, the federal government would issue scrip to those holders who might exchange it for other land in the public domain. It was this turn of the law that opened the door for corruption. School lands were frequently of little value. In Oregon and California, where many of the frauds occurred, most of those lands were located in mountainous regions of the state and often worth no more than $1.25 to $2.50 an acre. Government land received in exchange, however, might easily be worth $5 to $25 an acre and sometimes more. The law stated that after an application for the purchase of school land had been filed, the applicant could then sign over the property to another party. School lands were of little value to land speculators unless they were subsequently withdrawn from forest reserves and exchanged for more valuable land. If land-grabbers knew where those forest reserves were going to be created, and if they could "secure" parcels of school lands within the area of the anticipated forest reserves, they could get very valuable scrip in exchange. The key to this conspiracy was in knowing someone familiar with the workings of the General Land Office (GLO) and knowledgeable in the area of state and federal land laws.

One such person was Joost H. Schneider. He was formerly an executive secretary in the firm of John A. Benson and Frederick A. Hyde, two wealthy California real estate promoters, and had worked in that office from 1879 to 1902. The San Francisco–based concern was a real estate brokerage business and engaged in buying and selling lieu land scrip. It seems that Schneider had quarreled with his employers after being denied a salary increase. Schneider then left the firm, moved to Tucson, Arizona, and opened up his own real estate business. Angry and embittered by his treatment, Schneider decided to seek revenge on his former employers. He wrote a letter to Binger Hermann, commissioner of the GLO , stating that Benson and Hyde had engaged in a conspiracy to defraud the government of immense tracts of state school lands in California and Oregon by a process of illegal filings while he was in their employ. Hermann, a major figure in the subsequent land fraud investigations, had held his position since being appointed by President William McKinley in 1897. Prior to that he had worked in a district land office in Roseburg, Oregon, won a seat in the Oregon senate, and served for twelve years in Congress. At the time of his appointment to the GLO, Hermann was a well-connected figure in Oregon politics. According to Schneider, Benson and Hyde would settle dummy entrymen on school lands in California and Oregon. They would then map out a forest reserve that would include those claims. B. F. Allen, the forest superintendent in Los Angeles, was supposed to do this work but he accepted their maps and followed their recommendations for creating new reserves. Benson and Hyde would secure the rights to the dummy holdings and then use those rights to take valuable timber properties elsewhere in the state.

Coming from an "insider" like Schneider, the letter should have caused a stir, but Commissioner Hermann filed it away without a response. Schneider tried again and again but still failed to receive a reply. Hermann had his reasons for ignoring Schneider. First, he resented any effort on the part of Secretary of the Interior Hitchcock to assert greater control over the GLO, which traditionally had been allowed to operate without much oversight. Second, he felt increasingly threatened by the growing conservation sentiment being expressed by McKinley's successor, President Theodore Roosevelt, and his like-minded chief forester Gifford Pinchot. Hermann was well aware that Pinchot hoped to transfer forest reserves from the GLO to his own forestry department. It would be very difficult for Hermann to resist such pressure if he had to admit that GLO operations were riddled with fraud. Hermann had one other reason for ignoring Schneider: he was intimately involved with the Oregon ring of land-grabbers.

One day, while Commissioner Hermann was on vacation, one of Schneider's letters fell into the hands of Assistant Commissioner W. A. Richards. Richards then asked S. J. Holsinger, a special agent in the land office in Phoenix, Arizona, to interview Schneider in Tucson and make a report of his findings. When Hermann learned of Richards's action, he tried to divert Holsinger to other assignments, but eventually Holsinger got around to Schneider. His report, completed in November 1902, was shocking in its details. The California real estate magnates Benson and Hyde, not content with conducting a legitimate business, decided to secure school lands by locating them under false names ("dummies"). In order to obtain names to attach to the applications, they ran advertisements in various San Francisco newspapers offering employment opportunities for stenographers and bookkeepers. With the promise of high salaries, they received many applications. Benson, Hyde, and Schneider then copied the names and forged the signatures assigned to these applications and used them as the dummy land buyers. Their first work was done in the Sierra Forest Reserve in California. A notary public, a party to the fraud, attested that the signatures were valid and that the individuals had appeared before him. These applications were then submitted to the state land office and titles secured. After a time, bogus powers of attorney were executed in favor of Frederick Hyde and the scrip secured and offered for sale. As business flourished, Benson and Hyde decided to expand their operations and create their own forest reserves. To successfully carry out this plan, they realized that they would need to have "inside" information. They sent Henry P. Dimond, a lawyer employed by Hyde, to Washington to see if he could "fix" a clerk in the General Land Office so that they might know what important actions were about to be taken. In return for his services, the clerk, who appeared in correspondence as "B," would receive two cents per acre as compensation.

Benson and Hyde waited to file the dummy locations on the school lands with the state land office until they received word from their informant that the recommendation for a forest reserve had been forwarded to the president. Those claims were then expedited through the land office by officials who, in turn, received a commission. Schneider repeated the accusation that Hyde had furnished government agents with previously drawn maps of proposed reserves, and that he had, at the request of Hyde, amended the map of the proposed Lassen Forest Reserve to exclude certain lands owned by wealthy men who threatened to mount a strong opposition to the proposed reserve if changes were not made. Among the shocking statements made by Schneider during his interview was that about three-fourths of the school entries in the Cascade Forest Reserve in Oregon were fraudulent, while in California all of the school section entries in the Lake Tahoe Forest Reserve, and most of the entries in the Zaca Lake and Pine Mountain reserves and the addition to the San Jacinto Forest Reserve, were dishonestly filed as well.

When agent Holsinger's report reached the General Land Office, Commissioner Hermann filed it away and did nothing. Unfortunately for Hermann, the report had first been seen by Assistant Commissioner Richards who made a copy before passing it on to his boss. Richards waited long enough to be convinced that Hermann intended to take no action and then saw that his copy of the report reached Interior Secretary Hitchcock. Hitchcock immediately sent for Hermann, requested that he produce the suppressed report, and demanded an explanation as to why he had not acted on the charges. Not satisfied with Hermann's response, Secretary Hitchcock asked for his resignation. Hermann asked for time to arrange his personal affairs before leaving, and Hitchcock granted his request. It was later revealed that Hermann used this time to destroy thirty-five or forty letterpress copybooks containing information that would have been useful in prosecuting land fraud cases going forward.

After appointing W. A. Richards as the new commissioner, Secretary Hitchcock dispatched Arthur B. Pugh, an assistant US attorney, and Harry Steece, a special agent in the General Land Office, to the Pacific coast in January 1903 to conduct a further investigation into the charges that had been made. Stopping in Tucson to see Schneider again, they found that he was no longer willing to talk. It appeared as if his initial claim of wanting to exact revenge against his former employers had actually been a form of blackmail and sufficient to extort some sort of settlement from them. Unfortunately, his prior statement to Holsinger had not been sworn to and since he now refused to sign a formal affidavit, his testimony was useless as evidence. Although additional information gathered after trips to Los Angeles and San Francisco confirmed what Secretary Hitchcock already knew, the evidence did not seem to be strong enough to warrant criminal proceedings against those suspected of crimes. Upon his return to Washington, Pugh recommended that Secretary Hitchcock employ a detective to dig deeper into the affair. At this point, Hitchcock called in John Wilkie, chief of the United States Secret Service. Although Wilkie noted that the problem was outside of his jurisdiction as an official in the Treasury Department, he offered to lend the Interior Department his best detective. The person he had in mind was Special Agent William J. Burns.

Born in Baltimore to Irish parents, Burns had grown up in Columbus, Ohio, where his father became a police commissioner and probably inspired his interest in the detection of crime. After entering the secret service division of the Treasury Department, Burns established a brilliant record and gained notoriety for solving a counterfeiting case in Pennsylvania and a theft at the San Francisco Mint. At the time of his appointment, Burns was forty-four years old. With his stocky build, red hair, bristling mustache, three-piece suit, gold watch chain, and derby hat, he would soon become one of the most recognizable figures in the American press.

Eager to begin his new assignment, Burns decided to start his investigation by spending a few weeks in the Interior Department learning the technical details of land office business. He showed up at the department on May 1, 1903, posing as a law professor doing academic research on public land policy in general and lieu lands statutes in particular. What he really wanted to do was to follow a typical claim from its beginning out in the field to the General Land Office, then through the proper divisions there and back again to the local land offices where the patents were delivered. What he discovered was that in hundreds and hundreds of applications for lieu land scrip and the deeds of relinquishment that often accompanied them, the name F. A. Hyde occurred repeatedly. Burns concluded that the appearance of one name on so many documents should have aroused suspicion in the minds of honest officials. And because everyone knew that Hyde was a California broker through whom bigger operators acquired immense tracts of land, they should have investigated.

Since they did not, Burns concluded that all of these officials—special agents, forest superintendents, and all the other division experts stationed along the line to prevent fraud—must be corrupt.

Determined to validate his theory, Burns decided to try and get one of the clerks who had a hand in approving a claim to confess. He picked J. J. Barnes, an expert in the school-land division who had been in the service for forty years. Burns assumed that with his intelligence and experience, Barnes would know a great deal. He confronted Barnes with a detailed account of the manipulations of the land claims known thus far and accused him of accepting bribes. Wilting under the knowing eye of Detective Burns, he confessed. It turned out that Barnes was clerk "B" whom Schneider had said Dimond hired to keep Hyde and Benson apprised of departmental business.

With the confession of Barnes, Burns headed west to California hoping to get another crooked official, someone who had personal knowledge of the graft, to turn on his employers and become a witness for the government. He decided to focus on B. F. Allen, the forest superintendent at Los Angeles. Looking for leverage to use against Allen, Burns discovered that his record contained a charge of falsifying expense accounts. Commissioner Binger Hermann had absolved him from blame, but that only increased Burns's suspicion. Digging into the matter further, Burns found that Allen had made work-related charges to the department during times when he was on vacation and that he had claimed reimbursement for railroad tickets when it was shown that he had actually traveled on a free pass. It did not take much pressure to convince Allen that the detective knew the game, and he confessed. Allen admitted to doctoring his expense accounts and that Schneider's story was true. He admitted that he had allowed Hyde to draw maps which he, as superintendent of forests, should have drawn, and that Hyde had actually written reports for him. To back up his story, Allen produced copies of his correspondence with Hyde. During his questioning of Allen, Burns asked if he had a "special" relationship with Binger Hermann. Allen replied that he was not "in" with the former commissioner, but that he had worked with his own boss, H. H. Jones, head of the Forestry Division of the General Land Office in Washington, and that Jones was also working for Benson and Hyde.

Encouraged by his success, Burns circled back to Tucson to talk to Schneider, who remained steadfast in his desire to recant his former testimony. This time Burns took with him as a witness Knox Corbett, the postmaster at Tucson. The detective found that Schneider was still obdurate, but, according to journalist Lincoln Steffens, managed to get him to reveal a great deal of information. "Burns would begin," said Steffens, "by asserting something which he knew to be false. Schneider would deny this, with heat and energy, and then he and Burns would enter into an argument. 'Well, anyhow,' Burns would say, 'this is true,' And he would state a fact, some fact that Schneider had told Holsinger, for example, or one that Allen had told Burns. Schneider would admit the fact and the argument would proceed. In this way Burns, with Corbett by, drew from Schneider the whole story."[2]

After talking to Schneider, Burns returned to California to follow his new leads. He first went after Grant Taggart, the forest supervisor for northern California. According to Steffens, "Burns had nothing on him, but his theory was highly perfected by this time, and it looked so much like knowledge to Taggart that he broke down and 'came through.'"[3] Taggart said that it was John Benson, not Benson's partner F. A. Hyde, with whom he had done business, and that he had drawn boundaries of forest reserves to suit the recommendations of Benson. It now seemed like the two major players each had their own organization—one that handled the northern part of the state and the other the southern. And each organization had its own group of corrupted officials. Burns also talked to the clients, clerks, stenographers, and messengers that had worked for Benson and Hyde. Their stories were helpful. Hyde's stenographer told him that Hyde customarily enclosed money in the letters he sent to the recorders in the local land offices and to other minor federal officials, and that he had forged names to official papers. Burns also tracked down some of the "real" people who had filed claims through Hyde's office. He learned from them that for a small fee they had made false affidavits swearing that they had settled on the claims in accordance with the homestead laws and then immediately relinquished their rights to Hyde.

By the time Burns returned to Washington, he was ready to begin a sharp examination of those clerks whom he suspected of being connected to the land ring. He already had evidence from Forest Superintendent Allen that H. H. Jones, the chief of the Forestry Division, was "bad." Logic dictated that William Valk, head of the Lieu Lands Division and W. D. Harlan, chief of the special agents, were likely corrupt as well. Burns managed to get both individuals to admit their connections with certain members of the land ring and their special relationship to John Benson. The confessions were gained none too soon because one of Burns's California operatives wired him that Benson was on his way to Washington, apparently eager to learn more about the threat that the ongoing investigation might pose for him. When Benson arrived in the city, he immediately scheduled separate meetings in his hotel room with Harlan and Valk and, after being assured that the investigation had produced nothing harmful to him thus far, presented each with a bribe. They, in turn, handed the money over to Burns, who marked it for identification. He then had Benson arrested. Benson was taken before the US commissioner and required to give $5,000 bond. But he jumped bail, forfeited his bond, and fled to New York, where he was rearrested and held under $20,000 bond. In the meantime, a grand jury in the District of Columbia indicted him on the charge of bribing Harlan and Valk. A few weeks later, Hyde, Benson, Dimond, and Schneider were all indicted for conspiracy to defraud the government of large tracts of public lands. In an effort to gain convictions against the major schemers, the Justice Department decided to grant immunity from prosecution to several of the corrupted officials in return for their testimony as government witnesses.

Around the time that Secretary Hitchcock dispatched agents Pugh and Steece to California to conduct a further investigation into the alleged Benson-Hyde ring, he sent Special Agent Alfred R. Greene to Oregon to see if he could substantiate Schneider's claim that Benson and Hyde had extended their operations to that state as well. Although Greene failed to find evidence relating to the Benson-Hyde ring, he uncovered a second land fraud conspiracy. This so-called Oregon ring, a newer and smaller operation than that conducted by Benson and Hyde, seemed to be directed by three individuals. At the head of the ring was Franklin Pierce Mays, a prominent Portland attorney and state senator. His two experienced operatives were Stephen A. Douglas Puter, a timber assessor or "cruiser" (someone who is expert at estimating the standing timber on a tract of land), and Horace Greeley McKinley, a minor speculator in timber lands. Interestingly, as had occurred in California, this Oregon fraud came to light as a result of a quarrel among the conspirators.

It seems that Horace McKinley had entered into a private land deal with the Lloyds, a father and son who wanted to invest in timber lands. Clyde Lloyd, the son, commissioned McKinley to obtain forested lands for him in western Oregon. For reasons that are not entirely clear, McKinley found himself in a financial bind and in need of cash. He and Puter had just completed a land swindle upon the government for lands in the anticipated Cascade Forest Reserve. They had transferred their title to that land to a third party while they awaited sale, but they had not yet recorded the deeds. But McKinley desperately needed money and, in a panic, sold one of the unrecorded claims (to which he did not hold title) to Clyde Lloyd. When McKinley, still short of funds, found that his partner, Puter, was delaying his cut of the proceeds from another transaction, he found it necessary to sell two additional parcels to Lloyd, for which he collected a grand total of $1,800. When Puter learned what McKinley had done, he rushed to the recorder's office to file his own deeds before Lloyd. When Lloyd tried to make his transactions official, he found that he had been preempted by Puter. Not knowing that McKinley and Puter were partners, Lloyd turned to Puter for advice. Puter sent him to the "head man," Mays, who told him he did not have a case against McKinley. At this point, George Lloyd, the father who had supplied the funds for the purchases, got involved. After talking to Puter and Mays and sensing a scam, he looked for some avenue of redress. Fortunately, it was at this moment that agent Greene showed up to begin his Oregon investigation. Listening to the Lloyds retell their story, Greene, too, became suspicious. He proceeded to make a thorough investigation of the Eugene Land Office where the ring had based its operations and found evidence that Marie Ware, the US commissioner for that office and McKinley's mistress, had been involved in some of the land frauds. His search also revealed that Puter and McKinley had fraudulently obtained two large tracts of government land and that their actions warranted prosecution.

The two instances of suspected fraud that Greene stumbled upon involved two areas—Township 11 South, Range 7 East and Township 24 South, Range 1 East—soon to be incorporated within the Cascade Forest Reserve. They became known as the 11-7 and 24-1 cases. As in California, the ring realized that it might get valuable scrip if it could get title to the lands in these two townships. The lands located in the 11-7 entry were especially attractive from the ring's point of view as they were exceedingly remote. Located near the top of Mt. Jefferson in the Cascade Mountain range at an elevation of five thousand feet, the area was rough, rocky, marked with deep gorges and ravines, and covered with a dense undergrowth of brush and fir trees. The ring felt that there was little chance that the government would seek to verify claims in this area. The entire area was covered in snow for three-fourths of the year, making it impossible for anyone to make a living off the land. In fact, no one lived closer than thirty miles from the township.

Despite its isolated location, Puter and his cohorts decided to make a large number of filings there under the pretense that this was being done by homesteaders who had long been residents on the mountain. They proceeded to hire persons to fraudulently claim that they had been homesteading in the area and had been raising strawberries on their plots for the past five years. Once the claims for these fictitious settlers were patented, deeds were made out to a third party. In the 11-7 case that individual was Emma Watson, a local widow and an intimate acquaintance of Stephen Puter, who also took one of the claims for herself under the name of Emma Porter. Dan Tarpley (Daniel Webster Tarpley, actually, but known to his friends as "Lookout Dan"), a local attorney and notary public, was hired to monitor the claims and prevent any exposure of the ring. He was guaranteed a certain commission as soon as the ring acquired titles and disposed of the claims. Altogether, the ring located twelve claims of 160 acres each under the names of ten people in this manner. Only three of the ten used their own names. Puter and McKinley paid the claimants sums ranging from $150 to $800 ($3,800 for the twelve claims). The "homesteaders" were required to sign affidavits that they had not only lived continuously on the land, but that they had also built a cabin and made improvements such as a barn or other outbuildings and that they had cleared, cultivated, and fenced at least an acre of land. The requirement that affidavits and proofs had to be witnessed by two individuals who lived nearby was easily met by having the fraudulent filers serve as witnesses for each other.

But despite the careful preparations, there was trouble. A total stranger by the name of J. A. W. Heidecke, who lived in Detroit, Oregon, near the 11-7 township, approached Puter and McKinley and said that he knew that none of the homesteaders had been near their claims and demanded $50 as hush money to keep quiet about the scam. Then, when someone else filed a complaint against the entries, the commissioner of the General Land Office sent Special Agent C. E. Loomis to investigate. Puter, forewarned by Lookout Dan Tarpley, graciously offered the agent $500 to cover his "expenses" for undertaking the arduous journey to examine the 11-7 claims and promised him an additional $500 after the patents were issued. In addition to the concealed bribe, Puter also supplied Loomis with a guide. For this task he turned to blackmailer Heidecke, who agreed to do the job for $350 and a promise from Puter to help him secure a job as a forest ranger. For his part in the ruse, Heidecke took the agent along a well-defined trail that led past cabins of other settlers who lived in that part of the state, but who resided outside the 11-7 claim area. But it appeared that Loomis had overdone his favorable report, for it failed to satisfy the General Land Office.

As a follow-up measure, the GLO sent Salmon B. Ormsby, superintendent of the Cascade Forest Reserve, to look into the matter. By the time Ormsby was ready for his inspection it was the middle of January and the entire township was covered with six feet of snow. The second inspection was staged as a repeat of the first, with Ormsby receiving $1,000 for his trouble. But for some reason, the patents were delayed. Uncertain of his next step, Puter conferred with ringleader Mays, who advised him to go to Washington, DC, and see Senator Mitchell, whom Mays thought might be able to assist in the matter. He also suggested that Puter make the trip with Mrs. Watson so that a case could be made that she, as a poor widow, had borrowed money to purchase the claims and now faced the possibility of losing her investment. He felt that Senator Mitchell might do a favor for a lady.

Senator John H. Mitchell, who would become the central figure in the Oregon land fraud trials, was an interesting character. Born in Washington County, Pennsylvania, in 1835, his real name was John Mitchell Hipple. After graduating from college, he worked as a schoolteacher, and in the mid-1850s got one of his students, fifteen-year-old Sadie Hoon,

This drawing of Senator John Mitchell of Oregon by cartoonist Thomas Nast shows the senator with his long, chest-length beard, symbolic of an older generation of politicians.
COURTESY OF THE LIBRARY OF CONGRESS, PRINTS & PHOTOGRAPHS DIVISION, ALFRED BENDINER MEMORIAL COLLECTION

pregnant and then married her. The couple would eventually have three children. Mitchell began practicing law in 1857 and seemed to be on his way to a successful career as a barrister. Then he disappeared. Taking his youngest daughter and his mistress, Maria Brinker, he borrowed $4,000 from the law firm for which he worked and set out for California, leaving his wife and his other two children to fend for themselves. Then, in 1860, he abandoned his mistress and moved to Portland, Oregon, with his daughter. Finding the frontier city to be a good place to escape his checkered past, Mitchell changed his name to John Hipple Mitchell. Soon, Mitchell married Martha Price, the daughter of a blacksmith in Oregon City, but failed to bother with obtaining a divorce from his wife Sadie. A rising star in the legal profession, Mitchell met stagecoach and railroad tycoon Ben Holiday and became his personal attorney. He was now on his way to becoming Portland's leading railroad and timber lawyer.

Mitchell soon concluded that business and politics could mix well together and got himself elected to the state senate. Ten years later he parlayed that into election to the US Senate even though his political opponents had discovered that he had abandoned his family, was living under an assumed name, and was a bigamist! But the legislature picked the state's US senators at that time, and his supporters did not seem to care about his past. What followed was a thirty-year run of influence peddling, disguised by an innate ability to ingratiate himself with his constituents as someone who worked tirelessly to promote the interests of his state. By the early twentieth century, Senator Mitchell had established himself as a power broker in Washington, DC.

With a letter of introduction from Franklin Mays, Puter and Mrs. Watson traveled to Washington early in 1902. Upon their arrival, Senator Mitchell introduced them to Commissioner Binger Hermann of the General Land Office who told them that the reports on the claims had been favorable, but that it would be several months before the final patent could be issued. A short time after that, however, Hermann informed Puter that he had received a report that all of the claims were fraudulent and suggested that Puter should return to Oregon and obtain additional affidavits. In a panic, Puter turned again to Senator Mitchell. Meeting Mitchell at his room in the Dewey Hotel, Puter passed him two $1,000 bills in return for his help. The following day, Mitchell informed Puter that he had fixed things with Commissioner Hermann. A day after that, the office issued patents to all twelve claims.

The end game in the elaborate scheme was the resale of the claims to a timber broker by the name of Frederick A. Kribs. Kribs was acting as financial agent for C. A. Smith, a millionaire Minneapolis lumberman. Upon being informed that Puter had gained clear title to the twelve claims, Kribs made out a deed that he then turned over to Mrs. Watson. She took the deed to a notary public to officially acknowledge the transfer of the properties to Kribs. Upon receipt of the signed deed and the abstract of title, Kribs wrote out a check for $10,080 to Mrs. Watson, which amounted to $5.25 per acre. After depositing the check into her account, Mrs. Watson deducted the amount already advanced toward the purchase of the claims, plus the amount that she was to receive for the sale of her own personal claim, and handed over the balance to Puter.

Despite the difficulties encountered in the 11-7 case, the ring was eager to repeat their operation as soon as the 24-1 township was opened to entry. The 24-1 township was situated along the headwaters of the Middle Fork of the Willamette River at an altitude of four thousand feet and miles away from any settlement. As in the 11-7 scheme, the ring assumed that no one would know whether the homesteaders to be located there were real homesteaders or not. This time, however, the ring decided to dispense with "actual" settlers entirely (regarded as an unnecessary expense) and merely substitute the names of fictitious settlers in their place. This is where Marie Ware proved to be so valuable. As US commissioner for the land office in Eugene, Oregon, she agreed to expedite the phantom claims for a fee of $100 per claim. As before, the deeds were put in the name of Emma Watson. Six of these claims were patented, but three of the claims were those that McKinley had sold to Clyde Lloyd in a moment of panic.

After listening to the Lloyds tell their story, Special Agent Greene felt that the government had sufficient evidence for an indictment. The case was turned over to US attorney for Oregon John H. Hall who issued indictments against Ware, McKinley, Puter, Tarpley, and several lesser members of the ring for their parts in the 11-7 deal on October 27, 1903.

A second indictment, issued on March 17, 1904, added those who had posed as entrymen. Puter and his colleagues were indicted for the conspiracy to steal public lands in the 24-1 scam as well. Claiming that his court calendar was crowded with other pending cases, Hall then wired Attorney General Philander C. Knox requesting an assistant US attorney to help in the prosecution of the alleged land-grabbers. He asked that Knox appoint D. J. Malarkey, a prominent Oregon Republican, a suggestion strongly endorsed by Oregon Senators Mitchell and Fulton. But Knox, like Secretary Hitchcock, had become suspicious of affairs in Oregon, especially after Binger Hermann, who had been dismissed from the GLO, returned to Oregon and won election to the US House of Representatives (where Speaker Joseph Cannon appointed him to the Public Lands Committee!). As a result, Knox decided to appoint someone who was not connected to Oregon politics and chose San Francisco attorney Francis J. Heney. As if to emphasize his concern, he appointed Heney as special assistant attorney general and wired Hall that Heney was to be in charge of the prosecutions.

Heney was a good choice for the job. As one writer noted, "In an era of tough westerners, Heney was one of the toughest, though with his slicked-down hair parted in the middle, his clean-shaven face, and his rimless eyeglasses he hardly looked a match for the mustachioed land pirates he was going up against."[4] Heney's parents had moved to San Francisco when he was a boy and settled in the city's rough immigrant section south of Market Street. Growing up in an area known as "South of the Slot," Heney was something of a wild youth and regularly engaged in street fighting and even joined a street gang. But he was also ambitious. When his father pressured him to quit school and work in the family furniture and carpet store, he chose an independent course and completed his education and became a schoolteacher. He taught school for a term in northern California but decided to return to San Francisco and enroll at the University of California. But old habits die hard and he was expelled in his freshman year for fighting with another student. Having lost his direction, Heney wandered. He taught school again, worked in mines and mills, drank, and gambled. He eventually drifted to Silver City, Idaho, and took a job as a law clerk. This experience convinced him that he wanted to be a lawyer. Returning to San Francisco, he enrolled in the Hastings Law School (a college education was not a prerequisite for law school at the time) and, in 1883 at the age of twenty-four, was allowed to practice law by the state supreme court. But health issues intervened. Drilling rock on a wet plank in an Idaho mine had given him chronic sciatica. Seeking relief in a drier climate, Heney moved to his brother's ranch in the San Pedro Valley near Tucson, Arizona, and became a cowboy. He herded cattle, ran a small trading post in partnership with his brother, and even participated in the final battles against the Apache leader Geronimo. He eventually decided to return to the law and, after moving to Tucson in 1888, began a successful law practice.

As Heney's law practice flourished, he became active in Arizona territorial politics. Taking advantage of a split in the local Democratic Party, he became a prominent politician and was chosen as one of the territorial delegates to the Democratic National Convention in 1892. As a member of the Territorial Executive Committee, he had a voice in every important decision made by the Democratic Party. When President Grover Cleveland began his second Democratic administration in 1893, Heney gained appointment as attorney general of Arizona Territory and had hopes of being sent to the US Senate if Arizona should become a state. But Heney became a victim of his own integrity. He brought charges of corruption against the governor, but when President Cleveland delayed in removing that political appointee, Heney resigned from office. Disgusted with Arizona politics, he decided to quit the territory that had once held tremendous professional promise. He returned to San Francisco where he established a civil law practice. For the next seven years Heney worked diligently to build up his practice and by 1903 was earning about $30,000 a year. Heney had actually declined an earlier offer from Attorney General Knox to become an assistant attorney general because of his busy practice. But when Knox asked him to take over the prosecution of the Oregon trials in November 1903, he felt he should not decline for a second time and accepted the offer. In agreeing to prosecute several cases, Heney figured he could do the job in about three weeks and return to California. The ongoing Oregon land fraud trials would end up occupying most of his time for the next three years.

Before Heney could begin his first case against the "Puter gang," he was informed that Emma Watson, a key figure in the trial, had disappeared. It was later revealed that ringleader Franklin P. Mays had intended to have the trials continually postponed and then have the indictments dropped through the influence of US Attorney John Hall. Heney's appointment foiled that plan. Nevertheless, Mays still hoped to get Mrs. Watson into hiding as she would prove to be the key figure in the case, being the one to whom the supposed entrymen had deeded their claims. Mays believed that if Mrs. Watson could be kept under cover, it would be impossible for the government to establish its case against the defendants. As a result, Mays sent Stephen Puter to convince Mrs. Watson to go into hiding.

In the interim, Heney had his first opportunity to meet US Attorney Hall and was immediately puzzled by his legal strategy. Instead of beginning his prosecution on the 11-7 deal, which Heney thought was a very strong and winnable case, Hall insisted on going ahead with the 24-1 case, which Heney thought was much weaker. Although Heney was able to reverse Hall's strategy, he was suspicious. Was such a decision motivated by Hall's desire to shield certain people? Was he, in fact, part of the Oregon ring and working to undermine the prosecution?

During the trial delay, Heney also had an opportunity to meet William Burns. Burns was just finishing up his investigation of the Benson-Hyde ring and Heney wanted to consult with him on certain aspects of that case. Heney was so impressed with the detective's keen insights into the California ring that he asked Attorney General Knox for permission to bring Burns and his team of detectives to Oregon to assist in his investigation. It was the beginning of an extraordinary partnership. Both men got along famously and worked together with particular smoothness. Heney was the boss, but his success in the courtroom depended to a great extent on the evidence that his capable investigator was able to uncover. Their temperaments were something of a balance as well. Heney tended to be mercurial—easily angered, prone to choleric outbursts, and, at times, reckless in his statements and actions. Defense attorneys in the famous San Francisco graft prosecutions would later find that it was easy to get under his skin. Burns, on the other hand, was more controlled and often acted as a brake on the more emotional Heney. Burns was also more insightful in a way. A student of the underworld, he understood crooks and their devious ways better than Heney. And he could spot a liar a mile away.

As part of ringleader Mays's strategy to try and have the trial postponed indefinitely, Puter convinced Mrs. Watson to travel to Chicago where he would contact her to plan their next move. Puter eventually learned through a friend of Mrs. Watson that she had taken a room in a boardinghouse on North Dearborn Street. When he arrived in Chicago, however, Puter made a mistake. Instead of going to see Mrs. Watson first, he decided to stop at the post office and check on his forwarded mail. When Puter, who had announced his name to the clerk to receive his mail, exited the building, he noticed that he was being followed. Unbeknownst to Puter, a secret service agent had been stationed at the post office to monitor the general delivery window. When Puter was able to give his "tail" the "slip," the home office quickly sent additional agents to the Windy City to assist with further surveillance. Agents were eventually able to track Puter to the specific block on North Dearborn Street and then, by checking each private hotel and boardinghouse on the block, were able to locate and apprehend Mrs. Watson. Newspapers quickly hyped the arrest with headlines that shouted, "All about the sensational capture of Mrs. Watson!" and "Full particulars of the capture of the land fraud queen!" In the midst of all the ballyhoo, Mrs. Watson was placed on a train to Oregon under the watchful eye of a deputy US marshal.

The long-delayed and by now sensationalized trial in the 11-7 case finally got underway at the federal courthouse in Portland, Oregon, on November 21, 1904. All the defendants were charged with conspiracy to defraud the government in the acquisition of land. Heney began by establishing that Puter and Mrs. Watson had lived together and had traveled together under various assumed names in order to show that they had conspired together. After having established this initial conspiracy, Heney then proceeded to connect the other members of the ring (with the exception of Franklin Mays who had been shielded by Hall) to the conspiracy by reliable testimony. The climax of Heney's questioning came when J. A. W. Heidecke, the guide who had conducted Forest Superintendent Ormsby on a fool's errand into the mountains, was called as a witness. Nervous and extremely agitated on the stand, the guide revealed how he became involved in the scheme, how he had tried to break free only to be pulled back in, and how he had eventually been exposed.

During the trial it became apparent that the defendants had connections to some prominent individuals. Former commissioner Binger Hermann was one. Hermann was a witness at the trial, but when called to testify he could not recall ever having seen a letter addressed to him when he was commissioner of the General Land Office from Senator Mitchell, although he admitted that he recognized the senator's signature. The letter in question was one that Mitchell had written asking him to expedite the twelve homestead claims. Nor could he remember ever having met Emma Watson, the poor widow who had personally appealed to him for a speedy resolution of her claim. To try and catch Hermann in a lie, Heney immediately subpoenaed Mitchell, but he refused to comply on the grounds of senatorial privilege.

The trial ended on December 7 after the defense declined to produce a single witness. The jury then returned guilty verdicts for all the defendants except Marie Ware, who was released. Although she had been involved in the 24-1 swindle, she had nothing to do with the 11-7 case. Those convicted were not sentenced at the time so that they might testify in subsequent cases. Other conspiracy trials would follow in quick succession, while the grand jury, which would remain in session from December 1904 to April 1905, continued to gather evidence. The grand jury ultimately returned no fewer than twenty-six indictments, affecting approximately one hundred individuals, many of whom were prominent Oregonians. Indictments in the cases would continue to be prosecuted as late as 1910. Even as the November trial progressed, the grand jury heard more evidence that Senator Mitchell and other prominent individuals were implicated in the land frauds. Heney and Burns also became increasingly suspicious of attorney Hall's performance before the grand jury. Then, just before the start of the second trial, the prosecution asked for a postponement. Detective Burns had managed to get a confession

from Stephen Puter and seemed close to gaining one from Forest Superintendent Ormsby as well.

Heney and Burns believed that if there was a broader conspiracy,
Stephen Puter was the figure to reveal it. And Puter was angry. Senator
Mitchell had castigated him in the press after his conviction in the 11-7
case, and his "friends" began to avoid him so as not to draw suspicion to
themselves. When Puter asked Mays and Kribs to post bail money for
him, they turned him down. After giving Puter ample time to reflect on
his plight, Burns visited him in his jail cell and offered to cut him a deal
if he would agree to testify. Puter was initially reluctant to squeal on his
friends, but Burns asked him to consider if his associates were really his
friends. The thrust of what Burns had to say was that Puter's so-called
friends were now looking out for themselves. The implication was that
Puter had been made the fall guy. Maybe it was time he started to look
out for himself. When the naturally garrulous Puter finally decided
to confess, he revealed the whole story, including his $2,000 bribe to
Senator Mitchell and all the other bribes that had been given to public
officials to facilitate the land frauds up to the time that Special Agent
Greene arrived in Oregon to investigate. In addition, he turned over
ledger books and diaries that implicated nearly every important figure in
the Oregon Republican Party.

Burns was eventually able to get Salmon Ormsby to come clean as
well. The superintendent of the Cascade Forest Reserve confessed that
he had conspired with then commissioner Binger Hermann to create
the Blue Mountain Forest Reserve. It seems that Hermann had directed
him to contact Frederick Mays (the attorney and state senator connected
with the Puter ring) who told him that a great deal of money had been
invested in land in the area. Mays then supplied him with the money,
maps, and information needed to create the new reserve. When it looked
like Ormsby might be indicted for his part in the scheme, Senator
Mitchell had contacted US Attorney John Hall, and the case had been
dropped. For his willing participation in the conspiracy, Ormsby had
been given two sections of land which he later sold for $2,000.

With the confessions of Puter and Ormsby, Heney now felt that
he had sufficient evidence to prosecute the more prominent individuals

involved in the Oregon land frauds. On January 1, 1905, he obtained an indictment against Senator John Mitchell. This time Mitchell hurried back from Washington to appear before the grand jury to deny all the charges against him. Outraged by the apparent indignity, Mitchell issued an angry public statement: "I have served in the US Senate nearly 22 years, and I defy any man to charge me successfully with conduct that is otherwise than honorable, and I am sure I cannot be connected in any manner with any land frauds except by the grossest perjury of self-confessed and convicted thieves and perjurers."[5] He testified that he had agreed to help Puter with his claim before the land office just as he had done for a thousand citizens of Oregon. He then related his own narrative of his dealings with Puter in regard to the 11-7 claims. The senator's account paralleled that given by Puter except on the crucial question of whether or not he had accepted a bribe. The question quickly became one in which the word of a long-standing US senator had been counterpoised with that of a convicted criminal who had been induced to come forward only after receiving a promise of leniency by the prosecution. Mitchell was essentially saying that he had been framed. He then availed himself of the opportunity to charge Interior Secretary Hitchcock and prosecutor Heney with conducting "a most damnable and cowardly conspiracy" motivated partly by revenge and party politics. "This man Heney," he stated, "is a California Democrat, who is trying to blacken and destroy the character of leading Oregon Republicans."[6]

On February 1, 1905, Heney replaced his original indictment with another one charging Mitchell with having used his influence with Commissioner Binger Hermann to expedite seventy fraudulent claims for Frederick A. Kribs, the timber broker working for wealthy Minneapolis lumberman, C. A. Smith. For his services, Mitchell allegedly received fees totaling $1,750 ($25 for each claim). The fees had allegedly been paid to Mitchell's law firm, Mitchell and Tanner. (Detective Burns was later able to trace the Kribs money through the partnership account into Mitchell's personal account.) With Puter's help, Burns had been able to obtain a confession from Kribs, who then told his story before the grand jury. Strengthening the government's position was the fact that Kribs had paid the fees by check and the prosecution had the checks as evidence against Mitchell. This new charge brought the partner, Judge Albert H. Tanner, into the case. Placed before the grand jury, Tanner produced a partnership agreement with Senator Mitchell that he claimed had been drawn up in 1901. According to the arrangement, he and Mitchell had agreed that the senator was not to receive any share of the profits from the firm's legal representation before any governmental agency (including the General Land Office) in Washington, DC. If valid, the contract would exonerate Senator Mitchell.

Heney and Burns suspected that the agreement had only recently been typed and then predated to provide cover for Senator Mitchell in the case. As a result, Detective Burns immediately put his men to work tracing the manufacture of the paper on which the contract was written. In the meantime, the prosecution noticed that three words—"legitimate," "salary," and "constituent"—had been misspelled in the agreement. They were also aware, as a result of Tanner's own admission on the stand, that there had been a change of stenographers at the firm during the previous six months. When questioned on the stand, Tanner's son, the new stenographer, had denied that he had written and predated the contract. But when asked to write out a sample sentence, he repeated the same spelling errors that had appeared in the agreement that was supposedly written years before he was hired. At that point the prosecution produced proof, based on the watermark on the paper on which the contract was written, that the paper had not been manufactured until after the date of the contract and that the color of the ribbon of the typewriter on which it had been written had not been in existence before 1903. Despite this new evidence, Tanner and his son remained adamant. The prosecution then called Harry C. Robertson, Mitchell's private secretary, to testify. He confirmed that the partnership agreement was not genuine. He also revealed that Mitchell had written a letter to Tanner providing a series of instructions relating to Tanner's upcoming testimony. At the end of the letter appeared the phrase "burn this without fail." At this point in the proceedings, Tanner was indicted for perjury, to which he pleaded guilty. He then agreed to cooperate fully with the prosecution in return for the promise that his son would not face criminal prosecution. Tanner admitted that the agreement was a sham, drawn up to protect Mitchell from possible bribery charges. He also produced the infamous "burn this" letter from Mitchell directing him how to testify.

Mitchell had been warmly greeted by his senate colleagues when he first returned from Oregon in January 1905, and had even given a self-righteous speech from the floor of the chamber proclaiming his innocence. The Tanner confession in February changed that. Although his senate colleagues made no effort to expel him from that body, they turned away from him. When Mitchell's trial began in late June, the disgraced senator did not even take the witness stand in his own defense. His attorney tried to make the argument that the government's case rested on the testimony of perjurers and that his client was a victim of unnamed plotters, but it was a weak defense. Trying for sympathy and perhaps a lenient sentence, he emphasized the seventy-year-old senator's long public career, the appropriations he had won for his state, and the favors he had done for thousands of his constituents. In the end, it just seemed like a tragic demise for a man who had been revered by so many. Mitchell was formally convicted on July 3, 1905.

The conviction of Senator Mitchell dramatically exposed the old patterns of fraud on the remaining public lands and convinced a national audience that some revision of federal land policy was necessary. It also exposed the conflict between private enterprise and the public interest that had developed in Oregon. Stephen Puter, who wrote a thorough account of all the Oregon land fraud cases that he published as *Looters of the Public Domain*, considered the trial to be one of the most sensational that had ever taken place in Oregon. According to Puter, the conviction of Senator Mitchell, an elder statesman and senate patriarch, "sounded the death knell to the reign of a corrupt oligarchy that had dominated the political destinies of Oregon for practically one-quarter of a century." As Puter described it, it was a political machine that was at the height of its power at the time Francis Heney began his crusade against the Oregon land frauds. Then, when it was "hinted that John H. Mitchell, who had so long controlled the political affairs of the State with such supreme autocratic power, was likely to become involved, the idea that any Grand Jury would be found with temerity enough to indict him, or that any trial jury would convict him for his offenses, was looked upon generally as a vivid flight of the imagination."[7] Prosecutor Heney had voiced the same sentiment during the first days of the long grand jury: "The extent of the land-fraud cases in Oregon is far greater than I imagined, even after I learned the extent of the Hyde-Benson frauds. . . . Oregon is under the domination of a corrupt political ring, which hesitates at nothing to achieve its ends."[8]

On July 25, 1905, Judge John DeHaven sentenced Mitchell to six months in the Multnomah County jail and fined him $1,000. His attorney immediately filed an appeal on the grounds that the conviction was unconstitutional in that the crime was a misdemeanor and not a felony. The legal argument was that a US senator may not be prevented from attending to his duties except for conviction of a felony. But on December 8, 1905, before the appeal could be heard by the US Supreme Court, Senator Mitchell died as a result of a diabetic coma following dental surgery.

It has been suggested that Senator Mitchell, with his long, chest-length beard, represented an older generation that did not grasp the change in public mores that was taking place as an era of progressive reform began to unfold at the start of the twentieth century. One author has argued that Mitchell never seemed to understand why he was being tried, and was reported to have complained to his private secretary, Harry Robertson, "Harry, you know they hadn't ought to prosecute me for that. All I ever got was some little checks."[9] As one commentator noted, a large portion of the public was becoming "thoroughly tired of . . . [the] irresponsibility and wholesale domination of public officials by what the 'people' considered the 'interests.'" The wanton appropriation of the country's natural resources became a flash point of this new attitude. John Thurston, Mitchell's attorney and a former US senator from Nebraska, seemed to grasp the change in an interview printed in the *New York Evening Post* after his client's conviction, but argued that the ends justified the means. "To call Senator Mitchell or [Chauncey] Depew a hoary-headed old rascal is both unjust and cruel," he stated. "Neither of them has inquired too narrowly into the technicalities of law or morals; their eyes have been fixed upon higher things, nobler aims. Each has been devoted to those mighty commercial interests which are the true soul of a commonwealth. Each in his own courageous, though somewhat careless way, has been an advance agent of prosperity."[10]

Three other cases of note were brought before the grand jury immediately following the indictment of Senator Mitchell. The first of these involved US Representative John Williamson and Dr. Van Gesner, partners in a sheep business, and Marion Biggs, commissioner of the land office in Pineville, Oregon, for conspiracy to defraud the government of public lands. The prosecution charged that Williamson and Gesner had conspired to acquire a vast tract of grazing land (about sixteen thousand acres) by inducing forty-five settlers to file dummy claims under the Timber and Stone Act, swearing that they had taken up the land (which was devoid of almost any timber) for their own use and not for speculation. Biggs was the local official before whom the fraudulent proofs were made. The prosecution further charged that there was an "understanding" at the outset that the claims (the filing fees having been paid by Williamson and Gesner) would be transferred to the sheep owners as soon as final title had been acquired. After three trials (the juries could not reach a verdict in the first two), the defendants were finally convicted, given jail sentences, and fined.

The second case, the so-called Blue Mountain Conspiracy, involved three state senators including Franklin P. Mays, the linchpin in almost every land fraud scheme under investigation. In this case the prosecution charged that the trio had purchased about forty-four thousand acres of worthless school lands through the use of illegal affidavits and applications. It was their hope that these lands would be included within the boundaries of a proposed Blue Mountain Forest Reserve, where they could be used as a base of exchange for valuable timber lands under the Forest Reserve Act. Through testimony at the trial, it was shown that Senator Mitchell played a role in the conspiracy by exercising his influence with Commissioner Binger Hermann to expedite the creation of the reserve. (Mitchell was alleged to have been guaranteed two thousand acres for his services.) In the end, the entire scheme collapsed when Congress repealed the Forest Reserve Act. All three state senators were found guilty for their part in the conspiracy in September 1906 and sentenced eight months later. At that time, the court ordered Mays, the ringleader, to pay a fine of $10,000 and serve four months in the Multnomah County jail in Portland.

The final case involved the Butte Creek Land, Livestock, and Lumber Company in Wheeler County, and brought John Hall, the US attorney for Oregon, into the spotlight. The company was accused of engrossing about twenty thousand acres of government land that was valuable primarily for grazing purposes. Surrounded by high rocky bluffs, the entire tract could be turned, with the use of connecting fences, into a giant corral. This, in fact, is what the company had done, thereby preventing other settlers from using the range. Responding to a formal complaint, Secretary Hitchcock dispatched Special Agent Edward Dixon to make a careful inquiry into the situation. It did not take Dixon long to find the company at fault. He then presented his findings to US Attorney Hall, along with the recommendation that criminal action be taken against the officials of the Butte Creek operation. Instead, Hall brought a civil suit against the company. It seemed obvious that Hall was trying to protect company officials and that he had, as was later shown, chosen not to prosecute them because of political pressure placed on him by Franklin Mays (who was also the attorney for the Butte Creek Company). There seemed to be a pattern, first sensed by Heney when he had been assigned to the fraud cases, that Hall was intimately connected to the ring and that his primary role was to shield those "higher up" in this and other land fraud schemes. Hall's consistent dereliction of duty as US attorney would eventually lead to his removal from office by President Roosevelt in January 1905 and his indictment for conspiracy to defraud the government in the Butte Creek case. Hall was finally convicted for his part in the conspiracy in February 1908.

While watching the string of indictments issue forth from the grand jury, Stephen Puter and Horace McKinley discovered that they were again under investigation for other school land transactions of an alleged fraudulent nature in Oregon. Already convicted in the 11-7 case and under indictment in the 24-1 case, both men were out on $8,000 bond while they awaited the prosecution's next move. Panicked by the prospect of additional jail time, they decided to flee. Determined that it was best if he left the country, McKinley consulted a Chicago lawyer to learn where he might be safe from extradition under treaty laws for offenses of a conspiracy nature. Apparently informed that his best choice was either China or some Latin American country, he opted for the former, forfeiting his $8,000 bond. Tabloids later reporting on his flight said that McKinley, known as something of a lothario, had fled to the Orient accompanied by "Little Egypt," a notorious belly dancer. It was later reported that McKinley had, in fact, landed in China and was operating a small hotel on the outskirts of Shanghai. Early in 1907, the Justice Department made a formal request to the Chinese government to extradite McKinley back to the United States. He was eventually arrested by Chinese officials in October 1907 and held until claimed by a US deputy marshal and escorted back to the United States. McKinley was finally sentenced on February 28, 1908, to two years in jail and fined $7,500.

Puter's attempted escape from the grasp of the courts was just as sensational. Fleeing first to New York City and then to Boston, Puter, using the name Brownell, rented a by-the-week room from a private family on Massachusetts Avenue, opposite the Fenway branch post office. Late in the afternoon of March 26, 1906, Puter, who had made the same mistake before, stopped into the post office to ask for his mail and received a light tap on his shoulder. Glancing quickly around, he realized that he had been caught by Detective William J. Burns. After an exchange of pleasantries, Burns escorted Puter down the front steps of the post office to the busy street below. Expecting to find a squad of patrolmen there to escort his prisoner to the nearby police station, Burns was surprised to find himself alone with his charge. Puter, wearing a long, heavy overcoat, carried a revolver which he kept concealed in his rear trousers pocket. Sensing that there was a mix-up, Puter decided to attempt an escape. Pulling a handkerchief from the inside pocket of his overcoat, he made it appear like he was mopping his brow. Then, fumbling for a pocket to return the item, he carelessly dropped it to the ground. As Burns's eyes followed the falling kerchief, Puter pulled the gun from his back pocket. Pointing his revolver at the famous detective, Puter backed slowly away through the crowd and made his escape. Hoping to negotiate the terms of his return to custody with Francis Heney, Puter decided to return to the Pacific coast. While arranging his anticipated meeting with the prosecutor, Puter was betrayed by an associate and captured. He was eventually sentenced to two years in jail and fined $7,500. It was while in the Multnomah County jail that Puter collaborated with Horace Stevens (a former clerk in the General Land Office) to write an account of his exploits entitled *Looters of the Public Domain*. After serving seventeen months of his sentence, President Roosevelt awarded Puter a pardon upon Heney's recommendation.

By the time Francis Heney concluded his direct involvement in the Oregon land fraud cases, he had managed to secure thirty-three convictions in thirty-four indictments. The list of those convicted included a US senator, a US congressman, a US attorney, several state senators, and a former US deputy surveyor. Some of those directly involved in the frauds were not indictable due to the expiration of the statute of limitations. Others gained their freedom in return for agreeing to cooperate with the prosecution. It has been suggested that hundreds more would have been indicted if the government had made more extensive use of its resources. According to Stephen Puter, "Thousands upon thousands of acres, which included the very cream of the timber claims in Oregon and Washington, were secured by Eastern lumbermen and capitalists . . . and nearly all of these claims, to my certain knowledge, were fraudulently obtained."[11]

Ironically, the one individual who escaped conviction was Binger Hermann, the former commissioner of the General Land Office whose dismissal for incompetence started the land fraud investigations. Hermann was actually tried twice, the first time for his destruction of the files and letter books in his possession at the time of his dismissal. Hermann's attorneys were able to gain an acquittal in the trial on the grounds that the files were his own property and not that of the government. Hermann was tried for a second time in January 1910 for having been a participant in the Blue Mountain conspiracy. Although the prosecution introduced a great deal of evidence to establish the existence of a conspiracy, it had difficulty in linking Hermann to the scheme. The prosecution's prime witness against Hermann was Henry Meldrum, former US surveyor for Oregon, who testified that Hermann had advised him to invest in lands about to be included within the reserve. But Meldrum's testimony was suspect as he had already been convicted at an earlier trial and had been pardoned by President Taft so that he could testify in the Hermann case. In the end, the jury reported that it could not reach a verdict, eleven members of the jury voting for conviction and one for acquittal. The Portland *Oregonian* reported that the holdout juror was a friend of Hermann's son and "Binger's man" on the jury.[12] The Hermann case marked the end of the land fraud trials. In September 1910, Heney decided to drop any remaining charges against Hermann who was old and ill.

The California-Oregon land fraud trials were significant in several ways. Firstly, they were important in curtailing the flagrant abuses in the distribution of public lands and served as a major factor in bringing about the repeal of the lieu lands provisions of the Forest Reserve Act in 1905. Secondly, they helped shape the conservation policies of the Roosevelt administration by creating a clearer understanding of the need for land law reform. Thirdly, the trials also had an impact on national public opinion. They contributed to the popular acceptance of the idea of conservation, the understanding that conserving the remaining natural resources of the country was the only acceptable alternative to the wanton expropriation and reckless exploitation of those resources as allowed under antiquated land laws.

The trials were also important for Francis Heney's later career. While he was in Washington, DC, tending to details relating to the ongoing land fraud cases, he was approached by Fremont Older, a San Francisco newspaper editor, who had been crusading against the corrupt Union Labor government in that city. Older had been impressed by Heney's success in the Oregon trials and his growing national reputation as a prosecutor. He also remembered a speech that Heney, a resident of San Francisco, had made during the recent municipal elections (1905) and the vigor with which he had lambasted the Union Labor Party and its boss, Abraham Ruef. Older had the idea of approaching Heney to see if he would be willing to undertake the prosecution of officials in the City by the Bay for accepting bribes (graft). He broached the idea to Heney at a luncheon at the Willard Hotel in Washington, DC. Heney said that he would be willing to come, but that he would want William Burns to work with him as a detective in the bribery cases. But there were problems. Both Heney and Burns were currently employed by the government and would have to be released from their Oregon assignment, and then there was the question of money. Heney informed Older that it would take $100,000 to start any investigation. The following morning Older talked to President Roosevelt who was sympathetic to the idea but said that Heney and Burns would have to finish the Oregon cases first. Emboldened by these provisional pledges, Older returned to San Francisco to raise money. The sensational San Francisco graft trials were about to get underway.

CHAPTER FIVE

The San Francisco Graft
Prosecutions (Part I)

A City in the Throes of Change

AT 5:12 A.M. ON WEDNESDAY, APRIL 18, 1906, A LOW RUMBLING SOUND signaled disaster, and the majestic Florentine dome atop San Francisco's City Hall began to shake. This was the start of the famous San Francisco earthquake, estimated to have reached a magnitude of between 7.7 and 7.9. Buildings began to collapse throughout the city. Those constructed on the hard clay of the city's higher ground fared better than those built on "made ground" along the bay shore—land that San Franciscans had filled with sand and garbage to create building lots. One of the most severely damaged areas was south of Market Street, where the ground was flat and the soil mostly alluvial. When the quake struck, many of the buildings there shifted or sank into the liquefying soil. Buildings quickly dropped their pediments, cornices, and parapets, while other structures collapsed completely. Chimneys fell everywhere and plaster and cement dust began to hang like a pall over the city. For miles in every direction the heaving, waving earth undermined the foundations of countless buildings. Up and down the Pacific coast, houses shook and fell into piles of brick and rubble. Triggered by a sudden surge in the Pacific tectonic plate, the earthquake caused movement along the 270 miles of the fault line. People felt the earthquake in Coos Bay, Oregon, to the north; in Winnemucca, Nevada, to the east; and in Los Angeles, to the south. The temblor caused destruction as far as fifty miles to the east of the city and a hundred miles to the north and south. After roughly forty-five seconds, the shaking stopped.

Half-clad, disheveled, and frightened people rushed into the streets. Quiet, bewildered, yet watchful, they could see gaps in the pavement, fallen buildings, tilting structures, and the gray, set countenances of other fortunate survivors. As the people wondered what to do next, the first columns of smoke began to drift upward from the area south of Market Street. Fires could soon be seen burning in every direction. Fifty fire alarms were reported in the first half hour alone. One of the earliest casualties of the earthquake was the city's water system. Firemen immediately rushed to the financial district, and then stood around stunned as water hydrants yielded only a trickle of water and then stopped. The lack of water was not, as some suspected, due to the failure of three large reservoirs on the outskirts of the city that were located on or near the San Andreas Fault. Nor was the problem caused by broken conduits that transferred the water from those reservoirs to the nine distribution reservoirs and storage tanks located within the city. The problem was with the distribution mains that carried the water from these reservoirs to the thousands of service pipes. About three hundred distribution mains and twenty-three thousand connecting pipes were broken by the earthquake, and most of those were in areas where the ground was soft or had been filled.

The lack of water was not the only problem. Immediately after the quake, gas mains began to explode. Four hundred miles of gas mains ruptured and, as underground electrical conduits were often tied to the gas mains, the explosions severed the electrical cables as well. Poles carrying overhead electrical lines either toppled over or burned. Water from the broken distribution mains flooded the underground gas and electrical network making a bad problem even worse. Within an hour of the earthquake, firemen could be heard dynamiting buildings in a frantic effort to create firebreaks. But the dynamiting actually started new fires. The problem stemmed from the indiscriminate use of black powder, a form of gunpowder. When black powder exploded, it generated a combustion that ignited all woodwork with which it came into contact. In some instances, giant powder (granular dynamite) made of nitroglycerine was also used with the same destructive results. It was not until officials belatedly shifted to 75 percent dynamite in stick form that buildings were safely leveled without combustion. But the fire proved unstoppable, advancing with a hideous roar and devouring everything in its path from wooden shanties to the city's finest buildings. The Paris of the Pacific had become engulfed in a firestorm. "All night the city burned with a copper glow," remembered one observer, "and all night the dynamite of the fire fighters boomed at slow intervals, the pulse of a great city in its agony."[1]

The fire that followed the earthquake lasted for three days and blackened an area of nearly five square miles or more than five hundred blocks of the central city. The perimeter of the fire extended for over nine miles and encompassed the center of the city's commercial and residential districts, about three-fourths of San Francisco's developed landscape. The fire burned through 28,188 structures, 24,671 of which were made of wood. It destroyed the city hall, the Hall of Justice, the Hall of Records, the county jail, three emergency hospitals, thirty-one schools, nine libraries, thirty-seven national banks, the Pacific Stock Exchange, three major newspaper buildings (the *Call*, the *Chronicle*, and the *Bulletin*), two opera houses, and one of the largest imperial hotels in the world. More than two hundred thousand people were forced from their homes by the flames. Underwriters placed the assessed value of lost property at $52.5 million, a figure that did not include the thirty-nine churches and many public buildings that were not assessed for tax purposes. The official estimate of total property loss was $250 million.

On the morning of April 18, Mayor Eugene Schmitz appointed a "Committee of Fifty" to assume the functions of government that were required by the emergency. On May 3, the mayor announced that the Committee of Fifty would be replaced by a "Committee of Forty on the Reconstruction of San Francisco." A central figure on this new committee was Abraham Ruef, like Mayor Schmitz, a key figure in the Union Labor Party that controlled the municipal government in San Francisco. Ruef had managed to secure his own appointment to the important subcommittee on proposed amendments to the city charter, as well as that of prominent attorney and former state attorney general Tirey L.

Ford as chairman of the subcommittee on proposed state legislation. As chairmen of their respective committees, Ruef and Ford then tried to take advantage of the emergency to argue before a special session of the state legislature in Sacramento that all state oversight in matters relating to the relocation of streets and the modification of the terms of municipal franchises should be turned over to Mayor Schmitz and the Board of Supervisors, at least during the ensuing recovery period. Although the legislature declined to approve their request for expanded authority, the San Francisco *Bulletin* was sufficiently alarmed by the action to assert that the city had narrowly escaped "a worse evil than the earthquake and fire." It went on to charge that the scheme had demonstrated remarkable "audacity . . . by a crafty brain [Ruef]," and that if it had succeeded, "a place on the Board of Supervisors would be worth a million dollars a year to a boodler."[2] The action raised the suspicions of many who had come to regard the Union Labor Party as nothing more than a den of thieves, and that individuals connected to it might try to take advantage of the chaotic situation for personal gain. But to understand the origins of that feeling of distrust, one needs to look at events in San Francisco almost five years before the earthquake and fire.

In August and September 1901, the city of San Francisco became ensnared in what was called the great Teamsters' Waterfront strike. It began when the Brotherhood of Teamsters refused to allow its members to deliver goods to a nonunion express company. The union charged that to do so would violate its current arrangement with the Draymen's Association by which the association agreed not to employ any teamsters that did not belong to the brotherhood, while members of the union agreed to only carry the trade of firms that were members of the association. The Draymen's Association quickly turned the management of the strike over to the Employers' Association, a central body whose membership included nearly all of the wholesale merchants and manufacturers as well as many of the larger retail merchants in the city.

At that point the strike came to embrace a larger issue—whether or not employers would recognize the "closed shop" and hire only union workers. Refusing to accept labor's demand for the closed shop, employers began to look for nonunion workers to take the places of the striking teamsters. Some employers mounted their own wagons and drove their own teams, others hired discharged army teamsters who had recently returned from the military campaign in the Philippines. Still others began to recruit scabs from the agricultural districts outside the city. As employers frantically searched for replacement drivers, the strike began to take a toll on the city. The major factories in the city closed their operations and laid off their workers. Porters and packers lost their jobs when they refused to help nonunion drivers load their delivery wagons. Union bottlers suffered a similar fate when their union officials refused to allow them to work for employers whose beer was hauled by nonunion drivers. The California Wine Association laid off its coopers, stating that there would be no work as long as teamsters could not be found to haul barrels. Furniture dealers, hardware merchants, and all the large retail houses were similarly affected by the strike.

As the strike dragged on, the number of replacement workers entering the city increased, as did the level of violence. The hoots and jeers of the crowds of idle workers soon gave way to stone throwing and fistfights. When scabs seeking to replace striking teamsters became too intimidated, employers turned to the municipal administration for protection and convinced Mayor James D. Phelan to order the chief of police to assign an officer to accompany each nonunion driver. In the process of protecting strikebreakers, labor pickets were clubbed and arrested. Outraged by these actions, labor leaders appealed to the mayor to withdraw the police from the wagons and the waterfront where dockworkers had joined the strike. But Phelan—in an action that would sidetrack his political career for more than a decade—refused to meet their request on the grounds that it was his duty to preserve public order. Sympathy strikes only compounded the tense situation and almost completely shut down normal shipping activity. It was reported that the strike tied up nearly two hundred ships in the harbor. Workers simply deserted their ships, leaving no one to take on or discharge cargoes. At its height, the strike forced twenty thousand men out of work. The wharfs became quiet and street traffic ceased. It was estimated that at least 60 percent of the city's business had ground to a standstill.

Unwilling to give in to organized labor's demand for a closed shop, employers began to advertise in outlying city newspapers offering special inducements to experienced drivers and sent agents into the countryside to recruit them. Consequently, farmers in the region found it increasingly difficult to transport their wheat, which, in turn, triggered a migration of farmers and farmhands into the city hoping to load and move their crops. These actions only served to escalate the violence. When groups of strikebreakers arrived in the city by rail, they were met by angry workers determined to turn them away. But soon, despite the efforts of labor pickets, the influx of replacement workers began to have an effect. By late September the waterfront had recovered to something approaching normal operation. Although strike leaders urged their men to maintain order, ruffians and criminals took advantage of the prevailing conditions to increase their rate of burglary and petty crime. In response, Mayor Phelan increased the police force while many employers began to hire their own guards and private detectives for protection. When officers were removed from the wagons because of the increased need for their services on the streets, employers hired discharged soldiers to take their places and had them sworn in as special officers.

The climax of the strike came on the night of September 29, 1901, when an armed mob attacked a small body of special officers on a major business street in the city. A pitched battle ensued in which a number of individuals were shot before a contingent of regular police arrived as reinforcements. Something resembling a reign of terror ensued. People barricaded their houses. Many stayed home at night and then walked the streets armed with weapons by day. But the struggle was actually nearing an end. Although many workers had acquired some savings during generally prosperous times, they could not afford to stay out of work forever. Finally, on October 2, California Governor Henry T. Gage arrived in the city to negotiate an end to the strike. Although the terms of the settlement were never made public, the unions and the principle of the closed shop had been defeated.

In August, long before the strike reached its crisis point, union officials had begun to discuss other ways in which workers might be able to achieve what they believed to be their rights. As the strike unfolded, many laboring men and their sympathizers became convinced that the operation of government in the city was largely at the command of the

Employers' Association. Such a feeling began to push many in the labor movement toward political action. "If the strike lasts long," stated one prominent unionist, "the men will take part in politics and work changes in the city government." To that end, labor officials began to take steps to have a labor ticket placed on the ballot in the municipal elections that fall under the banner of the Union Labor Party and looked to elect a mayor who would not use the police against them. As the secretary of the

San Francisco Mayor Eugene Schmitz (shown here making his rounds) demonstrated surprising leadership after the earthquake and fire that destroyed the city in 1906.
COURTESY OF THE LIBRARY OF CONGRESS, PRINTS & PHOTOGRAPHS DIVISION

machinists' union noted, "This is just the beginning for we are determined that the workingmen shall run this government."[3]

The man chosen to be the mayoral candidate of the new Union Labor Party was Eugene "Handsome Gene" Schmitz. Born in San Francisco, he had roots that were German and Irish (the two largest ethnic blocs in the city). A man of culture, Schmitz was an accomplished violinist and had gained some local notoriety as a composer. He was a commanding figure, a tall, broad-shouldered, handsome man with a well-trimmed Vandyke beard, luxuriant mustache, and a thick crop of curly black hair who carried himself with an easy and gracious manner. He also had a platform presence that he had acquired as director of the Columbia Theater orchestra, and his theatrical experience aided him greatly as a public speaker. His only connection to the labor movement came from his membership in the musicians' union. The new party never had the unanimous support of the various labor unions or of the rank-and-file union members. Many of the labor leaders thought that labor should stay out of politics, but they also believed that the situation offered no other alternative. Most believed that the new party was an expedient of the moment, not the beginning of a new and lasting political organization. Once started, however, the movement quickly moved beyond their control.

From its inception, the Union Labor Party had the support of interests outside the labor movement. Much of this support came from citizens who had simply grown dissatisfied with the dominant political parties. It was a very fluid situation that presented an opportunity for a political manipulator. That man was Abraham Ruef. A lawyer rather than a member of a labor union, Ruef had the political vision to see the possibilities that a third-party movement might offer. He knew that the labor leaders could not control what they had created, but he reasoned he could. He managed the new party's 1901 campaign and even supplied most of the money ($16,000) used to fund the campaign. Ruef and Schmitz had been friends for fifteen years. Ruef was Schmitz's personal attorney, as well as the attorney for his labor union. It was his genius that made Eugene Schmitz the mayor of San Francisco, showed him the ropes of municipal affairs, and then saw to his reelection in 1903 and again in 1905.

Abraham Ruef graduated from the University of California at the age of eighteen as valedictorian of the class of 1883. Something of a Renaissance man, he had majored in classical languages, could speak several modern languages fluently, and had an avid intellectual interest in philosophy, art, and music. He was a wiry little man, about five feet, eight inches tall, with shifty black eyes, curly dark hair, and a thick mustache that he probably adopted to disguise his youthfulness. He possessed a fine wit, an affable and polished manner, and a reservoir of energy to go along with tremendous political ambition and boundless avarice. After graduating from the Hastings College of Law, he was admitted to the bar at the age of twenty-one. Ruef started his legal career with visions of becoming something of a civic reformer and had actually formed a club to study civic problems with two former law students. But Ruef's early idealism was not to last, and he soon fell in with Martin Kelly and Phil Crimmins, two powerful political bosses. Ruef worked as an underling for their political machine for ten years and secured excellent training for his future career in the process. He found that his law practice grew with his political importance, and he used his profits to invest in real estate. Immersed in the school of ward politics, he quickly mastered the art of patronage and the various methods that could be used to garner votes.

Ruef's big opportunity came in 1901 when the legislature enacted a new primary law in an attempt to throw off the control of the bosses. Ruef quickly seized upon the new law as a means to organize a "reform" movement and called his new organization the Republican Primary League. He quickly secured a large following and started to become something of a power broker. It was during this time that he began meeting men of political and social importance in the state such as William F. Herrin, chief counsel of the powerful Southern Pacific Railroad, always presenting himself as a valuable political ally. But Ruef was still a minor player. This soon changed; labor unrest in San Francisco and the beginning of the Union Labor Party movement afforded him an opportunity. Out of that turmoil, Ruef managed to facilitate a merger of his Republican Primary League with the Union Labor Party. His management of the campaign and the election of Schmitz made him a kingpin. As an acknowledgment of Ruef's services during the campaign, Mayor Schmitz issued a public letter saying that he was privileged to call Ruef his "friendly" counselor. That recognition certified that Abraham Ruef was now the political representative of the Union Labor Party administration in San Francisco. He was now the new "boss."

Boss-directed or machine-driven government in San Francisco, as in other major cities, required money as well as votes. Some of the most lucrative sources of revenue for any political machine were the various public service corporations, which, in turn, depended on the goodwill and cooperation of politicians. In the city of San Francisco, the legislative body invested with the authority to grant franchises and privileges to public service entities like street railway or public utility companies, and to set the rates charged to consumers by gas and water companies, was the Board of Supervisors. It was a widely held belief in the city that bribery of the supervisors was common practice. If a boss accepted money from a public service corporation, he could merely claim that it was a campaign contribution. If he was an attorney, he could accept the money under the guise of attorney's fees. Conspiracy to pass money on to individuals who were public officials, however, was illegal. But it was always extremely difficult to prove.

It took a while before the new municipal government of San Francisco fell completely under the thumb of Boss Ruef. Under the existing election system, the mayor and eighteen members of the Board of Supervisors were elected every two years. In 1901 and again in 1903, the Union Labor Party failed to capture a majority of the Board of Supervisors even though Mayor Schmitz won easily in three-party contests. Gradually, the opinion started to mount among reformers that management of some of the departments was unsatisfactory if not corrupt. As a result, in 1905, the Democrats and Republicans agreed to "fuse" their tickets in an effort to unseat Schmitz and defeat the other Union Labor candidates. But the leaders of the two parties had trouble agreeing on a mayoral candidate and finally settled on John S. Partridge, an attorney of good reputation but someone not well known to most voters. Ruef characterized Partridge as being "pale and spare" and "devoid of external magnetism," a weak candidate when set against a dynamic personality like "Handsome Gene" Schmitz.[4]

During the bitterly contested campaign, the opposition accused the Union Labor Party of being corrupt and, to stress that point, even brought hometown attorney Francis Heney, currently riding the crest of national celebrity due to his recent triumphs in the Oregon land fraud cases, to the city to deliver a public address. In his speech, given at the Mechanics' Pavilion on the closing night of the campaign before the largest political gathering ever assembled in the city, Heney said that he knew Ruef was corrupt and that, if given the opportunity, he could prove it. "If you elect these people [the Union Labor slate]," said Heney, "the graft of this city will become so great that the citizens of San Francisco will ask me to come back and prosecute him [Ruef]."[5] But the voters did not seem sufficiently alarmed to heed Heney's advice. One-third of the registered voters did not even bother to cast a ballot in the election. Those who did, however, gave Schmitz and Ruef a stunning victory. Mayor Schmitz tallied 40,191 votes to only 28,687 for Partridge.

In her personal account of the San Francisco graft trials published in *McClure's* magazine after the close of the investigations in 1909, Cora Older [the wife of newspaper editor Fremont Older] remembered the election night well.

> *About half-past five I went to the* Bulletin *editorial rooms. There I encountered none of the currents of contest, the heat of struggle that are usually sensed in a newspaper office when election returns are coming in. . . . Arthur McEwen [a brilliant reporter for the paper] was with Mr. Older in his office.*
>
> *'Have you heard anything?' I asked. . . .*
> *He pointed to the papers on his desk.*
> *'Look at those returns from the Western Addition!'*
> *This portion of the town was the residence section of the arch-respectable, the wealthy; it had gone overwhelmingly for the boss's candidate. Schmitz was no longer the Mayor of the poor. He belonged to the rich; they could buy him. . . .*

Someone came to say that Ruef supervisors had been elected.
'That's good,' said Mr. Older bitterly; 'they'll loot the town. Now
the people will get the kind of government they deserve; the worst the
city has ever known.'[6]

To the surprise of everyone including Ruef, the hastily and carelessly selected Union Labor Party ticket won every contested office, including the election of all eighteen supervisors.

Ruef, who was more concerned about offering a slate of candidates that would appeal to organized labor, did not spend much time evaluating their qualifications. Interestingly, not one of the new members of the Board of Supervisors was a prominent labor leader. One member was a piano polisher, while others included a bakery delivery driver, an electrician, a carpenter, a printer, a shoemaker, a hack driver, a clerk, an orchestra musician, and a blacksmith. Eight of the eighteen had no connection to labor unions whatsoever. They included an attorney, a dentist, a painter, a wholesale grocery salesman, a plumbing contractor, a drayman, a saloonkeeper, and a grocer. The key member on the Board of Supervisors was James L. Gallagher, a shrewd, forceful, and persuasive former city attorney, who acted as liaison between Ruef and the other supervisors. He would also serve as Ruef's "paymaster." In responding to the overall look of the new board, one despondent journalist commented that voters had elected "the most ignorant, venal, and generally disreputable lot of men that ever disgraced an American city."[7] Politician Gavin McNab wittily commented that all the burglar alarms in the city rang of their own accord when the election of the whole Union Labor ticket was announced.

Some attributed the surprising Union Labor victory to bickering in the ranks of their opponents, while others suggested that the Union Laborites made excellent use of propaganda in linking the fusionist movement to the Citizens' Alliance, a staunchly anti-labor organization that unabashedly championed the open shop. Further complicating matters for the opposition in the election was the introduction of voting machines for the first time. Many citizens who wanted to vote for Schmitz but were not too excited about his little-known running mates were afraid to risk invalidating their ballots by trying to vote a split ticket on the new, unfamiliar machines. But regardless of the factors involved, Boss Ruef, political advisor to the mayor and political agent for the Union Labor Party, now controlled every department of the municipal government in San Francisco.

But Ruef had created a problem for himself. Many of the newly elected supervisors had no real idea of the responsibilities attached to their new offices, except for the popularly held belief that supervisors regularly received bribes and had done so in the city for half a century. It soon became obvious to Ruef that most of the eighteen members of the new Board of Supervisors were motivated simply by greed and would easily succumb to the temptation of petty gain. A number of the supervisors had heard that Ruef received large "fees" from public utility corporations, and they wanted him to share his boodle. Ruef tried to explain to them that it was legal for him, as an attorney, to accept fees, but that it was illegal and reckless for them, as public officials, to do the same. That would be bribery. The board, however, failed to grasp the distinction, and Ruef was ultimately forced to share his fees with them. In return, they had to promise not to accept any bribes from parties that did not conduct their business through the boss. It was a promise that the ill-conceived board would not be able to keep.

Ruef had been receiving retainers as confidential attorney for a number of public utility corporations that hoped to obtain or maintain privileges from the city. The Pacific Gas and Electric Company, for example, paid Ruef $20,000 to persuade the Board of Supervisors to increase the existing gas rate from $0.75 to $0.85, an action that was worth $600,000 a year in additional profit to the company. Sharing his fee, Ruef gave $13,500 to the supervisors and $3,000 to Mayor Schmitz. The newly established Home Telephone Company, headed by Ohio capitalist Abram K. Detwiler, held the patent for the new dial service. After meeting with Ruef, Detwiler offered him an "attorney's fee" of $125,000 to obtain a franchise that would allow his company to establish a telephone system in competition with the existing Pacific States Telephone and Telegraph Company. In this instance, however, there was a problem. Eleven of the supervisors decided on their own to accept

$5,000 bribes from Theodore V. Halsey, "lobbyist" for the Pacific States Company, to vote against granting Home Telephone a franchise. They mistakenly assumed that Ruef would continue to do business with the established company as Ruef was already acting as an attorney for them and accepting a monthly retainer of $1,200. The mix-up led to an argument between Ruef and the board. Finally, after a great deal of debate, it was agreed that the board would vote for the Home Telephone franchise as Ruef wished. Those who had already accepted money would receive less than their normal cut from the Home Company and would have to give half of the Pacific States money back. In the end, Ruef kept $33,000 for himself, gave $30,000 to Mayor Schmitz, and passed $62,000 to the Board of Supervisors to be apportioned among themselves. The Pacific States Company found itself in the awkward position of having paid bribes to block a franchise only to see it granted to its competitor. In a sense, Ruef had arranged to punish the company for trying to bribe a majority of his untrustworthy supervisors away from him.

Another one of Ruef's affairs involved the Parkside Realty Company. Parkside was a large planned real estate subdivision in the Sunset District of the far-western part of the city, an area that was then largely barren sand dunes. The promoters of the Parkside development believed that the sale of lots in this area could return profits of $4 to $5 million on an initial investment of approximately $2 million. To realize this potential windfall, however, they would need to obtain a franchise for a trolley line that would connect the area with the more established parts of the city. For that they would need the approval of the Board of Supervisors.

The Parkside Realty Company had been organized in July 1905, and as quietly as possible had purchased a large number of lots from previous owners, one of whom happened to be Abraham Ruef. Their collective purchases comprised a tract of about four hundred acres or an area about five blocks wide and twenty blocks long. Within that area the promoters hoped to sell five thousand twenty-five-foot lots to lower income families. The area was about one mile south of Golden Gate Park. The nearest car line was owned by the United Railroads Company and was part of its main streetcar system. Because that line ran along the southern boundary of the park, the Parkside promoters hoped to connect their properties with this line by building a connecting line along 20th Avenue. Looking to move forward as quickly as possible with their venture, the directors of the company arranged an interview with Mayor Schmitz. They told the mayor that the new subdivision would contribute greatly to the development of the city, create jobs, and expand the tax rolls, and stressed the importance of the trolley franchise to the completion of the project. After inspecting the site, Schmitz assured the directors that he supported the idea and thought the franchise could be secured. Based on the mayor's assurances, the promoters proceeded to grade and pave the streets and install the sewer and utility systems.

Schmitz pitched the Parkside proposal to the Board of Supervisors in January 1906 and informed them that he had already promised the promoters that he would support the project. But when the mayor informed the supervisors that the investors hoped to reap at least $3 million in profits, they became suspicious of the mayor's motives, especially after he had presumed to speak for the board before consulting it. Hoping to learn more about a suspected "arrangement" between the mayor and the investors, the board decided to defer action on the matter. Ruef did not believe that the board would be willing to grant a franchise without being compensated for it. When the board failed to take immediate action, J. E. Green, president of the Parkside Company, concluded that he needed to work through Ruef. Green then asked Gustav (Gus) Umbsen to act as an intermediary. Umbsen was not an official with the Parkside Company, but his own real estate firm was the exclusive agency for the sale of Parkside lots at a 10 percent commission. Following what had become the standard pattern, Umbsen asked Ruef if he would accept employment as an attorney for the Parkside Company. When Ruef said that he would, Umbsen then offered him a fee of $30,000 for two years. Although Umbsen was the middleman, it was Green, in his capacity as general manager, who came up with the money and cleverly disguised it on the company's books. When Ruef announced that he had been retained as an attorney for the company, the supervisors proceeded to grant the desired trolley franchise. At that time Umbsen paid Ruef $15,000, retaining the final $15,000 payment until all arrangements had been finalized. Ruef had intimated to Supervisor Gallagher that each of the members of the board would be paid $1,000 and that Gallagher himself could expect somewhat more than that. But Ruef never actually paid any money to the members of the board because the graft prosecution prevented the Parkside business from being completed while they were still in office.

One other corporation that was to become a major target of the graft investigations was the United Railroads Company. Heading the company was Patrick Henry Calhoun who happened to be a grandson of the Southern firebrand John C. Calhoun. Tall, portly, comfortable in appearance, with the manner of a southern gentleman, Calhoun possessed a penetrating set of cold, steely blue eyes, a drooping white mustache, and a downturned mouth that made him appear somewhat stern and humorless. Rising on his own merits, Patrick Calhoun had become by the 1880s perhaps the most successful corporate attorney in the South. Over the years, he enhanced his reputation as a Wall Street corporation lawyer and as a major investor in mining, manufacturing, cotton, oil, lumber, and real estate. He was also instrumental in organizing the Southern Railroad system on behalf of J. P. Morgan and Company. It was this latter experience that got him interested in municipal railway systems. In pursuit of that interest, he acquired and reorganized street railways in Pittsburgh, Baltimore, St. Louis, and San Francisco. After acquiring street railway properties in San Francisco, Calhoun moved to the city in early 1906 to assume duties as president of the United Railroads of San Francisco.

United Railroads controlled nearly all the streetcar lines in the city, about half of which had been converted from cable cars to overhead electric trolleys. Calhoun wanted to complete the conversion to trolleys, because they were cheaper to operate and United Railroads was already overcapitalized. But many civic-minded individuals like former mayor James D. Phelan and banker Rudolph Spreckels favored an underground electric conduit system as being more aesthetically pleasing, not as dangerous, and less of an impediment to firemen fighting fires. But Calhoun found underground conduits to be cost prohibitive and refused to consider them as an option. Looking to gain the favor of influential people in the city, United Railroads, through its chief counsel Tirey Ford, sought to win the goodwill of Boss Ruef and employed him as an attorney at a retainer of $1,000 a month. When the company's trolley-conversion plan seemed stalled, Ford approached Ruef and agreed to pay him a fee of $200,000 if he could persuade the Board of Supervisors to grant the corporation the privilege of converting its remaining cable lines to overhead trolleys. As there was an urgent need to rebuild the inner-city transportation grid after the destruction caused by the earthquake and fire, the supervisors quickly passed the necessary ordinance and Mayor Schmitz signed it. It was said that the franchise was easily worth $2 million to the city if sold at its true value. For their efforts, Ruef paid the supervisors $85,000, gave $50,000 to Mayor Schmitz, and kept $65,000 for himself.

Another important concern to the growing municipality was its water supply. The Spring Valley Water Company currently had a monopoly of this necessity, drawing its supply from nearby lakes and reservoirs. But by the turn of the century, most San Franciscans believed that the Spring Valley facilities would never be adequate to meet future demand. As a result, there was a growing popular sentiment that the city should plan to bring additional water from the Sierras. This feeling opened the door to the most grandiose of all Ruef's schemes for profit and involved the Bay Cities Water Company. Although never completed, this projected plan was designed to meet the water supply needs, especially after the earthquake and fire, of a rebuilding and expanding metropolis. The city of San Francisco had been negotiating with the federal government for the rights to store and use water from the Tuolumne River in the northern part of Yosemite National Park by building a dam at the end of the Hetch Hetchy Valley. Because access to that supply involved commercial development inside a national park, approval from the Department of the Interior appeared unlikely. In fact, Interior Secretary Ethan Allen Hitchcock refused to grant the city's application without a special act of Congress as the existing law required him to preserve "the natural curiosities" of the park "in their natural condition." As an alternative plan, William S. Tevis, a wealthy San Francisco entrepreneur, had organized the Bay Cities Water Company and had begun to acquire water rights to the American River near Lake Tahoe. The company held the options to purchase lands and rights-of-way on which it proposed to build a water system which it would sell to the city for $10.5 million. It was estimated that the capital needed to purchase lands and rights-of-way and make improvements would total $7.5 million. From the projected $3 million profit, Tevis promised Ruef a cool $1 million as an attorney's fee to see the project through the necessary administrative channels. Ruef had only begun to work on the project as the company's confidential attorney when later events derailed it.

During the spring and summer of 1906, both Schmitz and Ruef seemed to be basking in the glow of public approval. Mayor Schmitz had shown surprising leadership after the earthquake and fire, and the vigorous posture he assumed in leading the recovery and rebuilding efforts made him something of a national celebrity. At that time there was still no evidence of bribery and even the rumors of illicit dealings involving the telephone and trolley ordinances that appeared in a couple of local newspapers had little impact on public opinion. Meanwhile, Ruef had continued to expand his power, managing the election of almost all the San Francisco delegates to the Republican state convention and then holding the balance of power between rival factions at the convention. By throwing his support behind James N. Gillett, the candidate endorsed by the powerful Southern Pacific Railroad and the eventual governor, Ruef won the praise of William F. Herrin, chief counsel and state political boss for the Southern Pacific. A flashlight picture taken at a special dinner given for the state leaders of the Republican Party during the Santa Cruz convention shows Governor Gillett standing behind Ruef with his hand resting comfortably on Ruef's shoulder. It would be reproduced much later on billboards all over the state as "The Shame of California" during the campaign in which California progressives were able to topple the Southern Pacific machine in 1910. Ruef, now a key figure in the California Republican Party, had reached the height of his power. On September 11, 1906, just days after the convention, the San Francisco *Call* ran a sensational story in which it alleged that William F. Herrin had paid Ruef $20,000 for delivering the San Francisco votes to the Southern Pacific machine candidate for governor at the convention. It began to look to some that anything involving politics was up for sale.

There was a small group of individuals in San Francisco who did not like the way things were shaping up politically. One of those was Fremont

Older, editor of the San Francisco *Bulletin*. Tall, lanky, balding, and sporting what might have been called at the time a Western-style mustache, Older had decided on a career in journalism as a thirteen-year-old youth in Wisconsin after reading a biography of the famous newspaper editor Horace Greeley. Leaving school at an early age, Older went to work on a small, rural newspaper as an apprentice printer setting type, correcting proofs, and writing notices. Arriving in San Francisco in 1873 at the age of seventeen, Older got his first job on the San Francisco *Call* as a typesetter. Working his way up through the ranks, he had established a reputation by the early 1890s as a first-class reporter and editor. The purchase of the ailing San Francisco *Bulletin* by R. A. Crothers in 1895 gave Older the opportunity to become a managing editor based on his reputation as a circulation builder. Something of a "yellow" journalist in the 1890s, Older became interested in municipal reform, a cause that he increasingly felt was necessary to combat the rise in vice and corruption as well as the general disorderly condition that seemed to plague the city. Embarking on a campaign for clean government, Older was instrumental in getting James D. Phelan elected as reform mayor in 1896. When the Teamsters' Strike of 1901 forced the ouster of Phelan's reform administration and appeared to usher in a return to the days of vice and corruption under the guise of the Union Labor Party, Older stood ready to fight against it.

Older editorially opposed Ruef and Schmitz from the beginning of their partnership in 1901 and looked for a way to unseat them. To that end, he played a key role in the fusion movement in the election of 1905 and had been devastated by its stunning defeat. It was immediately following that election that Older came up with the idea of having Francis J. Heney conduct an investigation of municipal governance in San Francisco similar to what he had recently done with spectacular results in the Oregon land fraud trials. Older traveled to Washington, DC, in December 1905, and met Heney for the first time.

You said in your speech last fall [he explained to the famous prosecutor], that if ever we wanted you in San Francisco to go after Ruef and Schmitz, you'd come. Although no one knows I've taken this trip to see you, I believe from a conversation I had last summer with Rudolph

*Spreckels that he's as much interested in cleaning out San Francisco
as I am. I think he and James D. Phelan will give money for a big
investigation, if you'll come out and conduct it.*

*I'll be ready, [said Heney] just as soon as I get these Oregon land-
fraud cases off my hands, but I want William J. Burns to go with
me. I am only a lawyer; Burns has marvelous capacity for digging up
evidence. Besides, he's absolutely honest.*

*How much money do you think an investigation like the one
necessary would cost? [asked Mr. Older].*

*We should need to be able to count on a hundred thousand dollars,
[said Heney].*[8]

The following morning Older met with President Theodore Roosevelt
who said he was in sympathy with what Older was trying to do and
would do all in his power to help, but he could not see a way clear to
release Heney and Burns at that time. Perhaps something could be done
after their duties in Oregon were completed. As Older recalled, with
these partial assurances, he returned to San Francisco.

Two stumbling blocks remained, however. Heney had agreed to
come if Older could raise $100,000 to cover the anticipated expenses of
a special investigation and prosecution. Upon his return to San Francisco,
Older turned to civic-minded businessman-banker Rudolph Spreckels (the son of Claus Spreckels, who had founded the Spreckels sugar
empire). When Older proposed that such an investigation would not
only rid the city of its bribe givers and bribe takers but might also reach
the powerful Southern Pacific state political machine, Spreckels agreed
to set up a fund of $100,000 of his own money to finance their efforts.

Having obtained financial backing for the investigation, Older was
eager to begin. To speed up Roosevelt's anticipated release of Heney and
Burns, Older cleverly directed several reporters from his paper, the *Bulletin*, to investigate the rumors that Chinese women were being imported
into San Francisco's Chinatown as part of a white slave market to work
as prostitutes. Their investigation produced proof that sex trafficking did
occur and that this was in violation of federal immigration laws. Older's
men discovered that such women, worth $3,000 in this trade, were being

imported under the ruse that they were actually the wives of American citizens of Chinese ancestry. All that was necessary was to find a corrupt notary who would sign a fraudulent marriage affidavit for a Chinese girl and her "husband." Armed with this evidence, Older then returned to Washington in February 1906 for a second conference with President Roosevelt. Shocked by the report, Roosevelt forwarded the information to Heney and Burns in Oregon and asked them to look into the matter. When they were able to confirm the evidence uncovered by Older's men, Roosevelt released Burns to work on the San Francisco investigation, with the understanding that Heney would follow as soon as his Oregon trial work was completed.

The other hurdle involved Heney's demand that the district attorney of San Francisco would have to be on board and willing to cooperate with the investigation. That individual was William H. Langdon, who had been elected along with Ruef's Union Labor ticket. But Langdon was actually an honest and principled individual. Ruef would never have selected him for a place on the ticket if he had truly thought he had any chance of being elected. Langdon was a schoolteacher who had studied law, but he had been unable to build up a successful legal practice. He had entered politics, won election as superintendent of schools, and had established a good job approval rating in that office. Ruef offered him the nomination for district attorney in the hope that the superintendent's reputation and popularity (he was known by twelve hundred teachers, their families, and their acquaintances) would add a few thousand votes to Schmitz's total. Langdon, for his part, accepted the nomination not because he thought he could win, but in the hope that his visibility during the campaign might serve to advertise and promote his position as a lawyer and attract needed clientele. Langdon had not encumbered himself with promises to Ruef or Schmitz during the campaign. In fact, shortly after assuming office, Langdon had earned the enmity of the boss and the mayor by cutting off an avenue of the administration's revenue by closing down gambling houses operating under police protection and curtailing the use of illegal nickel slot machines in the city. As a result, when Older, Heney, and Spreckels approached him, he agreed to supervise their investigation from his office.

Before Heney could officially wrap up his affairs in Oregon, San Francisco was rocked by the earthquake. Surprisingly, Mayor Schmitz rose to the occasion during the aftermath of the quake and fire—issuing orders and deploying the militia and police in an effective and inspiring fashion. He also appointed the Committee of Fifty to deal with the immediate emergency. The committee included the city's most able lawyers and business and civic leaders. Members of the Ruef-Schmitz-controlled Board of Supervisors were omitted from its ranks, while outspoken critics of the administration like Francis Heney, who had a law office and extensive law library in the city that were completely destroyed by the fire, ex-mayor James D. Phelan, and Rudolph Spreckels were included. Ruef was not on the original list but was added by the mayor soon afterward as if his omission had been an oversight. Initially, everyone worked together toward one common goal, and a spirit of camaraderie prevailed. Soon, however, this spirit began to wane and earlier suspicions began to resurface. Ruef, who had been assigned only a minor role on the Committee of Fifty, felt slighted by his subordinate position. To remedy that problem, he convinced Mayor Schmitz to replace the Committee of Fifty with a new Committee of Forty. Missing from the ranks of the second committee were strong critics of the administration like Francis Heney. Spreckels retained his position for a time, but eventually resigned in protest over Ruef's domination of the new body. It was during the emergency that the public service corporations increased their illegal activities with the city government.

The San Francisco graft investigation formally got underway on October 20, 1906, when District Attorney Langdon publicly announced that he was appointing Francis Heney as deputy assistant district attorney assigned to the special duty of conducting the investigation of corruption in the municipal administration. He also informed the public that millionaire Rudolph Spreckels had arranged a private fund to cover the costs of the investigation, and that Detective William J. Burns, on a leave from the federal government, would lead a team of investigators. In fact, Burns and his associates had been quietly at work in the city for several months gathering evidence. Eager to begin, Heney and Burns immediately established a headquarters in what was later known as the

"Red House" on Franklin Street. Heney's legal team included attorneys Charles W. Cobb and Joseph J. Dwyer as his assistants, while Burns brought with him a small cadre of assistant detectives that would eventually form the core of a strong detective force. And the fall of 1906 was a good time to start an anti-corruption movement. After the earthquake and fire, civil law and order had begun to erode in the city. Police seemed to be increasingly unable to control the hoodlum element, and a rebuilt Barbary Coast (the red-light district) seemed even lustier than before. Reports of looting, mugging, rape, and murder now appeared as daily occurrences. Among the more respectable elements of the city there was talk of the need to revive vigilante action.

The announcement of the graft investigation alarmed Ruef and provoked him into attempting a bizarre ploy. Mayor Schmitz had left the city on October 1 for a trip to Europe, purportedly to persuade various German insurance companies to drop their claims that they were not fully liable for fire losses that had resulted from the San Francisco earthquake. His absence meant that Supervisor Gallagher would be the acting mayor until Schmitz's return. After consulting with Gallagher, Ruef had his confidant on the Board of Supervisors abruptly announce that he was suspending District Attorney Langdon from office. His formal order of removal charged the district attorney with a dozen cases of neglect, dereliction, and violation of duty and of using his office for ulterior purposes. He then announced, to the shock and surprise of everyone, that he was appointing Abraham Ruef to be the new district attorney in charge of the graft investigation! The announcement was quickly followed by an endorsement of Gallagher's action by the full Board of Supervisors. This attempted burglary of office set off a firestorm of protest among the city's press. The *Call* denounced Ruef as "District Attorney by usurpation; a prosecuting officer to save himself from prosecution." The *Chronicle* concluded that "as long as they [the Ruef-Schmitz ring] felt safe from prosecution, they jauntily declared that they would like to see the accusations fully justified, but the instant they began to realize the possibility of being sent to San Quentin, they turned tail and resorted to a trick which everyman ... will recognize as a confession of guilt." The *Examiner* called the removal of Langdon the "last stand of criminals hunted and driven to bay." "They have," said the *Examiner*, "come to a point where they will stop at nothing." Joining the assault, the *Bulletin* devoted its entire editorial page to Ruef's attempted coup under the heading, "Ruef's Illegal Action is Confession of Guilt."[9] For the first time, it seemed like San Franciscans had finally been aroused to the fact that there was something to investigate.

Superior Court Judge James M. Seawell issued a writ prohibiting Ruef from assuming office. But it would be up to Judge Thomas P. Graham to determine whether Ruef or Langdon would be recognized as district attorney. On the day of the anticipated decision, five thousand people gathered before the Jewish synagogue where court was being held. Some had guns, others carried ropes in their pockets. When it was finally announced that Judge Graham had recognized Langdon and that the mayor did not have the authority to remove a county official, there was a tremendous cheer of triumph. As Langdon, Heney, Spreckels, Burns, and Older exited the building it was as if the graft prosecution was being introduced to the city for the first time. Ruef, guarded by police, appeared last. When he did, a young physician in the crowd took a swing at the boss. When he did, the throng surged forward. Cora Older remembered the scene: "There was the voice one reads of, but rarely hears; when you have heard it you try to forget it; the voice of human beings so filled with hatred that they growl for blood."[10] Ruef was saved by the police, but his troubles had only just begun. It was obvious to all involved that the upcoming investigation would be a long-fought, bitterly contested, no-holds-barred affair.

When prosecutor Heney and Detective Burns formally began their investigation, the only evidence against Boss Ruef and Mayor Schmitz concerned the so-called French Restaurant affair. The French restaurants were a unique San Francisco institution and regarded by most people at the time as part of the gay and lively life of the city. In these fashionable establishments like Marchand's, Delmonico's, the Poodle Dog, and the Pup, customers could find on the first floor a public dining room serving excellent food at reasonable prices to respectable diners. The second-floor rooms of these restaurants, however, were reserved for private dinner parties and had sofas, while the third-floor rooms were more like private supper bedrooms and reserved for assignations. Although the vice attachments to these restaurants were against the law, everybody knew about them and few seemed to complain. Most San Franciscans regarded the French restaurants as an "attraction," and scenes about them had appeared on the local stage. These popular restaurants did a good business but did have to rely on the city for one thing—the quarterly renewal of their liquor licenses. These licenses were awarded by the Board of Police Commissioners appointed by the mayor. In 1904, Mayor Schmitz directed the police commission to hold up renewals. As a result, the French restaurants, for which the sale of fine wine with dinner was an indispensable commodity, faced the loss of their business. Feeling the financial pinch, the owner of one of these establishments asked Ruef to intercede. Ruef suggested that the affected restaurants form an "association" and hire him as their attorney at an annual salary of $5,000 a year. Seeing no alternative, the owners did as Ruef suggested, and the mayor directed the police commission to renew their liquor licenses.

Freemont Older learned about the license renewal holdup while having lunch at Marchand's and talking with the owner, who was elated that he was able to sell wine again. Older charged that Ruef and Schmitz were guilty of a criminal conspiracy to extort money from the French restaurateurs. But the grand jury refused to take any action in the matter, stating that they doubted that any illegality had been committed. When the graft prosecution began in October, Heney impaneled a new grand jury and commanded the French restaurant owners to testify before it. Ruef and Schmitz were subsequently indicted for extortion. Ruef denounced the indictment as "absurd," and insisted that he had merely accepted legal fees for services rendered.

The bold stance that Older and the *Bulletin* assumed against the Schmitz-Ruef regime was not taken without consequences. Libel suits were brought against the paper. R. A. Crothers, the owner of the paper, was assaulted as he left the *Bulletin* office by an assailant who struck him over the head with a piece of metal pipe. The blow might have crushed his skull had it not been for the derby hat he was wearing that cushioned the blow. A band of thugs who called themselves newsboys, allegedly hired by Ruef and directed by elements in the Tenderloin District, organized into a "union" and went on strike against the paper. Carriers were assaulted, merchants were struck with stones and bricks for buying the paper, windows were broken in the *Bulletin* office, copies of the newspaper were ripped from the hands of customers who had purchased it, and horses were unhitched from delivery wagons. A howling mob followed Fremont Older to the door of his hotel and threw sticks and stones at him. All the while the police stood by and did nothing to stem the lawlessness.

The day before Ruef was scheduled to appear in court, however, he jumped his bail and disappeared. Regular police officers searched for him but could not determine his whereabouts. Heney then filed an affidavit charging that the sheriff owed his appointment to Ruef and was prejudiced in his favor. Judge Frank Dunne then disqualified Sheriff Thomas F. O'Neil and named the next officer in authority, Coroner William J. Walsh, as elisor (a special officer appointed by the court to perform a duty) to arrest Ruef and bring him to court. When the coroner had no better luck than the sheriff, Heney filed a second affidavit. This time Judge Dunne disqualified the coroner and appointed William J. Biggy, who would afterward become the chief of police of San Francisco, as elisor and charged him to arrest fugitive Ruef. Finally, with the help of Detective William Burns, they found Ruef hiding in the Trocadero roadhouse on the outskirts of the city and placed him under arrest. This then created the problem of what to do with the prisoner. To put him in the city prison meant turning him over to the Ruef-controlled police department headed by Chief Jeremiah T. Dinan. To put him in the county jail meant turning him over to Sheriff O'Neil, who had just recently been disqualified. As a result, elisor Biggy was instructed to hold the prisoner at the Little St. Francis Hotel, a temporary structure erected after the fire near Union Square, until his trial could begin. But Ruef had made a mistake in his ill-conceived flight from trial. He was now caught in a situation (house arrest) where he could no longer consult with his men (the Board of Supervisors) and offer them advice and give them reassurance.

With no news in the headlines aside from the rather minor French restaurant extortion charges, and with the public becoming increasingly doubtful that the heralded probe of municipal corruption would ever get to the root of "big graft," Detective William Burns scored a coup. Burns had approached Golden Moritz Roy, a businessman who was active in local politics and who felt that his campaign work on behalf of Mayor Schmitz had not been sufficiently rewarded. As a result, he bore the mayor a grudge. Burns hoped to exploit Roy's dissatisfaction to gain some inside information on Ruef and Schmitz. When he met Golden M. Roy, however, Burns recognized him as Moritz Roy Golden who had fled the state of Oklahoma ten years before after forging the name of the secretary of the interior on a letter confirming his appointment as an Indian agent. Enlisting the help of Fremont Older, he had the editor mock up a page proof in the *Bulletin* office describing Roy's former life. They then sent for Roy, showed him the proof, and threatened to have it published unless Roy agreed to cooperate with the prosecution. Roy was stunned. Since he had left Oklahoma, he had changed his name and made a success in business, owning wholly or in part a jewelry store, a restaurant called the Café Francisco, and a skating rink. He had also gotten married and had a wife and children who knew nothing of his checkered past. He had no choice other than to cooperate. With the assistance of Roy, Burns was able to trap three of the supervisors. Burns had Roy approach Thomas Lonergan, one of the supervisors, and ask him to help defeat an ordinance regulating skating rinks that was pending before the Board of Supervisors. Lonergan was a driver for a pie bakery and it was said that of all the board, he was the one most greedy for bribes. He agreed to meet Roy at his skating rink office while Detective Burns and two associates concealed themselves in an adjoining room. From their hiding place they were able to hear and see Roy offer and Lonergan accept a $500 bribe to defeat the skating ordinance. A similar trap was set for Supervisors Edward Walsh and Dr. Charles Boxton, who also accepted bribes of $500 for their "no" votes on the skating rink ordinance.

Before Burns was through, he set a trap to catch Lonergan for a second time. On this occasion, he had Roy invite the unsuspecting supervisor to his home while he and his men waited in a darkened dining room with the folding doors left slightly ajar. This time Lonergan accepted another $500 bribe to support a faked ordinance to regulate the storage of petroleum inside the city limits. Caught in the act for a second time,

Lonergan agreed to tell what he knew of graft in the Schmitz-Ruef administration. Heney and Langdon were sent for and joined the gathering at Roy's home to hear Lonergan's story. He stated that Supervisor James Gallagher had acted as the go-between from Ruef to the supervisors. Lonergan stated that he had received from Gallagher $475 to influence his vote on an ordinance granting permits to prizefight promoters, $750 to influence his vote on an ordinance to raise gas rates, $3,500 in the matter of granting a franchise to the Home Telephone Company, and $4,000 for his vote granting a permit to the United Railroads Company to establish an overhead trolley system. In addition, Lonergan confessed to receiving $5,000 from the Pacific States Telephone Company to vote against granting a franchise to its rival. But even with the confessions of Lonergan, Walsh, and Boxton, the prosecution was in a weak position. It would still be difficult to prove that Gallagher had offered bribes to them when the remaining fifteen supervisors would certainly swear that they voted for the measures without any financial inducement, and the measures could have been passed or defeated without the votes of the three trapped supervisors. They needed to have Gallagher's testimony and that of a majority of the members of the Board of Supervisors to have any chance at a conviction. And it was only through Gallagher that there was any direct connection to Ruef. Repeating the strategy that had worked in Oregon, the prosecution then offered immunity to all of the supervisors provided they would give sworn testimony concerning the crimes in which they were complicit. Ultimately, all the supervisors agreed to accept the deal and on March 16, 1907, dictated their full confessions to the prosecution.

As an interesting aside to the agreement, none of the supervisors were required to immediately resign their positions. The thinking of Heney, Langdon, and Burns was that as long as the supervisors remained in office, they could be controlled by them. But if they resigned, Mayor Schmitz could easily appoint new supervisors and Schmitz and Ruef would be able to maintain control of the board. Not everyone in the city, however, would understand the strange situation in which confessed crooks would be allowed to remain in office. The supervisors repeated their stories before the grand jury on March 18. Immediately after testifying, they granted interviews to the newspapers in which they repeated the substance of what they had said. With the next day's editions, the details of the briberies became public knowledge. Two days later the grand jury returned sixty-five indictments against Abraham Ruef for bribing supervisors in the prize fight, gas rate, Home Telephone, and United Railroads ordinances. Additional indictments were returned against Theodore Halsey, the bribing agent of the Pacific States Telephone Company, and Louis Glass, the executive officer of the company who was responsible for ordering Halsey to make the bribery payments.

In only one of the major briberies, however, could the supervisors testify that money had been paid to them directly by any public utility corporation. That corporation was the Pacific States Telephone Company and, as mentioned, two of its officials were indicted. But in each of the other instances in which money had been paid to the supervisors, the money had come from Ruef and not directly from the corporation seeking preferment. The only way to convict the original bribe givers of conspiring with Ruef to bribe the supervisors was to have Ruef testify against them. To that end Heney entered into negotiations with Ruef, offering him partial immunity in return for entering a guilty plea in the French restaurant extortion case, providing a complete confession of his role in the other bribery cases, and giving testimony sufficient to convict the higher-ups. Ruef reluctantly agreed to accept the deal and to testify before the grand jury. Ruef's admission of guilt made the headlines in all the San Francisco newspapers and had now become a topic of national interest. The *Call* commented that the story "interested the largest number of outside readers that have ever been interested in a San Francisco occurrence, with the exception of the earthquake and fire."[11] It remained to be seen whether San Franciscans could stay united in the effort to rid their city of bribery and corruption.

CHAPTER SIX

The San Francisco Graft
Prosecutions (Part II)

A City Goes on Trial

WHEN THE TRIAL OF MAYOR SCHMITZ FOR HIS ROLE IN THE LICENSE renewal holdup finally began, Ruef testified that he paid Schmitz half the money he had received from the French restaurant owners. His testimony was enough to convince the jury, which, after only one ballot, found the mayor guilty of extortion on June 13, 1907. Convicted of a felony, Schmitz was then remanded to the county jail while he awaited sentencing. What followed was a remarkable episode in political maneuvering. The law stated that if the mayor was convicted of a felony, he automatically vacated his office. Under the charter, the choice of a successor then devolved upon the Board of Supervisors. But because the supervisors had all confessed to a crime and were only allowed to continue in office at the discretion of District Attorney Langdon, the selection of a new mayor rested with his office as well. The selection immediately became a subject of controversy especially between the conflicting interests of business and labor in the city. In order to allow time for a thoughtful resolution of this dilemma, the prosecution resorted to a stopgap measure. Because Schmitz was in jail awaiting sentencing, they declared that the office was not immediately vacant. Reasoning that the mayor was at least for the time being "unable to perform the duties of his office," they followed the charter and allowed the supervisors to choose one of their own for the temporary position of acting mayor. For this dubious honor, they selected Supervisor Gallagher. Schmitz, clinging to the theory that he was still the mayor, sent an order to his loyal Police Chief Jeremiah Dinan to have a policeman stationed outside the mayor's office to prevent Gallagher from entering. The next morning agents of the district attorney's office had to forcibly remove the guard so that Gallagher could begin his duties.

On July 8, Judge Dunne sentenced Schmitz to five years in the state penitentiary at San Quentin. Due to the formal sentencing of Schmitz, his office was now officially vacant. But the prosecution still had not come up with someone to instruct the supervisors to elect as Schmitz's successor. As a result, the prosecution resorted to a second rather bizarre expedient and named Charles Boxton, another of the guilty supervisors who had turned state's evidence to escape punishment, to be the "elected" mayor with the understanding that he would immediately resign once a suitable substitute could be found. At this point, the *Examiner*, undoubtedly speaking for a confused public, acerbically commented: "Having put our bribe-taking Mayor in jail, and having put in his place a taker of smaller bribes, we have now substituted for Gallagher, Boxton, who differs from Gallagher principally in having sold his vote for still less of the bribing corporations' money."[1] At this juncture, Schmitz once again tried to reassert his claim to office. This time a crowd of his supporters stationed themselves outside the door of the mayor's office to prevent Boxton from entering. Rather than confront the crowd, Boxton announced that he would carry out his duties from another location. At one point in all the confusion, the city auditor refused to approve a claim on the treasury that required the mayor's signature until it had been signed by three "mayors"—Schmitz, Gallagher, and Boxton.

The man finally chosen by the prosecution to be the new mayor was Dr. Edward Taylor, who was widely respected in the city as both a physician and an attorney. He had served for many years as president of the Cooper Medical College and, at the time of his appointment, was dean of the Hastings College of Law. On July 16, after serving as acting mayor for only one week, Boxton resigned and the supervisors elected Taylor to take his place. Having settled the mayoral issue, the prosecution could now order the resignations of the supervisors who had confessed to bribery. After a little more than four months, the "boodle" board was no more. New supervisors would be selected by Mayor Taylor.

Up to this point, the prosecution had received general praise and only moderate criticism from the newspapers. And despite its clumsiness in handling the transition in the municipal administration, the prosecution had accomplished a great deal. It had broken the corrupt political machine. The boss had been forced to plead guilty to extortion, and the mayor had been removed from office for his part in the same crime. The prosecution had also forced the "ring" (the supervisors) to confess to accepting bribes and had removed them from office as well. But the victories achieved had been against bribe-taking politicians, not the higher ups. To justify the grants of immunity, the prosecution would now have to go after the bribe givers, the men of wealth, power, prestige, and influence.

The first prominent corporate official to come to trial was Louis Glass, the socially well-connected and very popular executive vice president of the Pacific States Telephone Company. Glass, along with Theodore Halsey, had been indicted for bribing ten supervisors to prevent the Home Telephone Company from obtaining a competitive franchise. After examining a number of company officials, the grand jury concluded that Glass was the official who had authorized the payment of money to Halsey. Supported by the testimony of a number of supervisors, the evidence against Glass and Halsey looked rock-solid. But Glass chose to fight his indictment in court and hired Delphin M. Delmas, a San Francisco attorney who was currently riding a wave of national publicity for his part in what some tabloids had called "The Trial of the Century." Delmas had been chief counsel for the defense in the first trial of millionaire playboy Harry K. Thaw. Thaw had murdered noted architect Stanford White, the alleged lover of his wife, model/chorus girl Evelyn Nesbit. Although the murder had been committed before hundreds of onlookers at the Rooftop Garden Theater of Madison Square Garden in New York City, the jury had been unable to reach a verdict. Many San Franciscans had celebrated this dubious verdict as a triumph for Delmas over the formidable New York District Attorney William Travers Jerome. Many were intrigued to see if Delmas could achieve the same result for Louis Glass.

In hoping to establish a conspiratorial connection between Glass and Halsey, the prosecution turned to the testimony of company auditor Emil J. Zimmer, who had previously testified that he had paid money to Halsey upon instructions from Glass. But when placed on the stand, Zimmer refused to corroborate his previous testimony. Without Zimmer's testimony, there remained only circumstantial evidence connecting Glass with the bribery. After deliberating for forty-seven hours, the jury declared that it could not reach a verdict. Glass was immediately retried before a new jury. In the retrial, Heney excluded the testimony of Zimmer and produced a time line showing that Glass was the only official who could have approved the payment to Halsey based on the dates of the checks cashed by the supervisors. This time the jury needed only twenty-five minutes to find Glass guilty. Five days later, Judge William Lawlor sentenced Glass to five years in the San Quentin penitentiary. He was taken to the county jail while he awaited the outcome of his appeal.

During the second trial of Louis Glass, the trial of Theodore Halsey got underway. But before jury selection could be completed, Halsey was stricken with appendicitis. As Halsey had difficulty recovering from his operation, his trial was indefinitely postponed. It might be remembered that the bribes paid by the Pacific States Telephone Company to deny their competitor a franchise had been unsuccessful, while the bribes paid by the Home Telephone Company to obtain a franchise had successfully achieved their objective. But it was the Pacific States officials who were being prosecuted while the Home Telephone officials were not. The reason for this was that Home Telephone president Abram Detwiler had disappeared from his home in Toledo, Ohio, at the time of his indictment and could not be found. Admitting defeat, Heney announced to the press that Detwiler had apparently paid the money to Ruef out of his own pocket rather than from corporate funds. As a result, there was no way to trace the bribe money.

The conviction of Louis Glass, and the prosecution's eagerness to press ahead with cases against Tirey Ford, Patrick Calhoun, and other business leaders triggered a backlash. As long as Ruef and Schmitz were under indictment, the business class in San Francisco had stood behind the prosecution and praised it for ridding the city of corrupt Union

Labor politicians. But when the investigation started to set its sights on the "best people," the mood changed. The shift underscored the fact that it was easier for reformers to convict corrupt public officials for their relationship to organized vice, as in the French Restaurant matter, than for their connection to organized corporate bribery. The search for the former involved a segment of society that possessed little influence, while the hunt for the latter embarrassed very prominent figures and alienated the establishment from their cause. As such, the investigation suddenly became "bad for the city's reputation," and "it was hurting business." Newspaper support trended the same way. Major papers like the *Chronicle* and the *Examiner* swung to the opposition, while only Freemont Older's *Bulletin* and the *Call*, owned by Rudolph Spreckels's brother John, continued to lend their support. As a further indication of the growing animosity in a city that had begun to fracture along class lines, the daily *Globe* started in business in order to compete with the reform-minded *Bulletin*, its funds furnished by Patrick Calhoun.

The next major trial involved Tirey Ford, chief counsel of the United Railroads, for paying $200,000 to Ruef, who then gave the supervisors $85,000 for their votes in favor of an ordinance permitting the company to convert its remaining cable lines to overhead trolleys. Both Calhoun and Ford had declined to answer questions when called before the grand jury, and Calhoun had commented at the time that: "We know that they [the prosecution] cannot produce any truthful evidence connecting . . . any officer of the United Railroads with this alleged crime."[2] Calhoun also boldly mounted a public counterattack, accusing Rudolph Spreckels and James D. Phelan, two ardent supporters of the bribery investigation as well as directors of the rival Municipal Street Railways Company of San Francisco, of trying to injure the United Railroads for the sake of their own corporate profits. Then, in the midst of what looked to be the beginning of a titanic contest in court, the entire situation was complicated by the beginning of one of the most fiercely contested streetcar strikes to ever engulf a major city.

On May 5, 1907, the car men's union struck against Patrick Calhoun's United Railroads demanding wage and hour concessions. The walkout of the workers paralyzed a city already "fractured by an earthquake, blackened by fire, overrun by the homeless, afflicted by deadly diseases, split by racial hatreds, . . . and torn asunder along social, religious, and political affiliations" by what some were coming to regard as a "municipal vendetta."[3] The walkout quickly escalated into one of the most violent strikes ever to take place on the Pacific coast. Fremont Older believed that Calhoun deliberately provoked the union in order to distract San Franciscans from the ongoing graft investigation in general and his own personal indictment in particular to rally the anti-labor establishment behind him. Within days after the union called the strike, Calhoun imported twelve hundred strikebreakers from outside the state and housed them in fortified car barns in the city. When the company was finally able to restore service, workers constructed barricades and riots broke out. There were reportedly six fatalities from gunshot wounds and 250 serious injuries. As historian Kevin Starr colorfully commented: "Throughout it all, Calhoun, surrounded by armed bodyguards, rode around San Francisco in an open automobile like a tsarist police commissioner suppressing Bolsheviks. To his own, Calhoun seemed a champion of the capitalist system. . . . To the strikers Calhoun epitomized the insufferable arrogance of ownership. To the reformers, he seemed a man willing to provoke civil insurrection in order to destroy the graft investigations and thus avoid a jail sentence."[4]

When Calhoun refused to negotiate with the union, the public knew the strike would be a long one. Throughout the summer and fall, newspapers carried daily accounts of streetcar wrecks and smashups, some of them apparently caused when strikers greased the tracks on hills. The strike did not come to an end until December when the union finally admitted defeat. Calhoun's uncompromising position during the strike made him a hero in the eyes of many San Francisco employers. In fact, outside the ranks of organized labor, public sentiment was overwhelmingly against the strikers. Even newspapers like the *Bulletin* and *Call* that openly denounced Calhoun were only lukewarm in their support of the strikers. Eventually the emotions aroused by the strike became entangled with similar feelings generated by the graft prosecution. Many now came to see the graft trials as yet another attack on private property.

Tirey Ford proved to be a difficult figure for the prosecution to attack in court. Handsome, capable, and charming, he had been one of the most popular and respected figures in California for years. His career even had a bit of the rags-to-riches quality to it. He had begun as a ranch hand in the Sacramento Valley and studied law in the office of a small-town lawyer. After serving as a county prosecutor and a state senator, he had become state attorney general, and then had attained the position of head of the law department of United Railroads. To convict him or Calhoun of the crime of bribery depended on the presentation of convincing evidence that they had entered into a conspiracy with Abraham Ruef, who was not a public official, to bribe the supervisors, who were. The prosecution needed Ruef, who was under an agreement granting him partial immunity, to testify that in accepting his attorney's fee from Ford, that Ford not only understood that Ruef would use part of it to bribe the supervisors, but that he had authorized Ruef to do so. But Ruef would not cooperate and continued to insist that in all his dealings with Ford, neither of them had ever made reference to any possibility that the money would be used for any other purpose than to compensate Ruef for his legal services.

To exploit this weakness to the fullest, Calhoun hired Earl Rogers as chief counsel to defend Ford. Rogers had a reputation in the state as a capable lawyer who excelled in cross-examination and in baiting prosecuting attorneys and had established an extraordinary record for securing acquittals in murder cases. He was also flamboyant, often appearing in court wearing a cutaway morning coat, striped trousers, patent leather shoes, and spats, "his shirt and necktie a symphony of hues that blended more or less harmoniously with his checkered waistcoat."[5] But Rogers was not above bending the rules to win a case. In this instance, he employed one Walter E. Dorland to pose as a magazine writer from the East who managed to gain an interview with Thomas Lonergan, one of the supervisors, ostensibly to write a story in which the former United Labor Party supervisors would be put in a better public light. The truth was that Dorland was not a magazine writer at all, but a detective employed by Rogers and United Railroads. And his goal was not to obtain an interview, but, instead, to lure Lonergan into a compromising situation with a "woman of the evening." Upon uncovering the plan, Detective Burns charged that it was nothing more than a frame-up designed to compromise the prosecution's key witness, and that the woman involved was to have charged Lonergan with attempting a criminal attack upon her.

In addition to the shenanigans in court, things were starting to get uglier out of court. Calhoun decided to strengthen his private detective force, which had already been beefed up because of the streetcar strike, by increasing its numbers until it approximated a small army. The action was taken, it was said, to counter the efforts of the prosecution's detective force under the direction of William J. Burns in such matters as questioning prospective jurors. Editor Fremont Older remembered the atmosphere at that time: "[T]he very air of the streets became tense. Every few feet one met a man who was working for one side or the other, and many men of prominence were constantly shadowed by both sides, and even the men who were following them were also followed and watched."[6] It was not long before the prosecution registered angry complaints against the character of some of the individuals employed by the defense. Heney asserted in open court that the detective force employed by United Railroads included such notorious characters as gunfighter Dave Nagle, "Bogie" O'Donnell, Harry Lorenstzen, known throughout central California as the "Banjo-Eyed Kid," as well as "Butch" Bell, "Bunco" Kelly, and "Kid" Nelson, all notorious hoodlums. Heney also claimed to have seen these men in the courtroom itself. The *Call*, still strongly loyal to the prosecution, charged that "[b]ehind the expert lawyers of last resort troops a motley train of gun fighters, professional plug-uglies, decoys, disreputable 'detectives,' thugs, women of the half world and the wolfish pack of gutter journalism."[7]

An even more bizarre example of the tactics being resorted to by the defense was the "kidnapping" of Fremont Older, the fiery editor of the *Bulletin*. In covering the Dorland-Lonergan story, one of Older's reporters had confused J. C. Brown, a United Railroads detective, with Luther Brown, the head of the United Railroads Detective Bureau. The reporter had proceeded to describe Luther Brown as one of the individuals involved in trying to "frame" Lonergan in a sex scandal. On the day following the publication of the story, chief counsel for the defense Earl Rogers accused Older and the *Bulletin* of criminal libel against his friend Luther Brown. Rogers and Brown then made secret arrangements to

Famous Detective William J. Burns (shown here in 1907) was instrumental in both the California-Oregon land fraud and San Francisco graft investigations.

have Older prosecuted for criminal libel in Los Angeles. A justice of the peace in Los Angeles, who owed his position to Brown, issued a warrant for Older's arrest, and two Los Angeles constables were dispatched to San Francisco to serve the warrant. Because this action had been initiated in another city, the policemen needed the approval of a San Francisco court which they obtained from Judge Carroll Cook. The obliging judge himself had been under criticism by the *Bulletin* for years.

According to the story later told by Fremont Older, he received a telephone call late in the afternoon of September 27, 1907, while at Heney's office. The caller, identifying himself as Mr. Stapleton, offered to convey some important information if Older would come and meet him at the Savoy Hotel on Van Ness Avenue only a block and a half from the Red House. On impulse, Older agreed to go. In leaving, he said to Charles Cobb, Heney's law partner: "This may be a trap. If I'm not back in fifteen minutes you'll know it is." As he walked along Van Ness Avenue, a motorcar with four passengers pulled up beside him. Two of the occupants hopped out of the car. One of the men stepped up to Older, showed him his police badge, and presented him with a warrant for his arrest on a charge of criminal libel. He then ordered Older to get into the vehicle. Older immediately asked to be taken to see his lawyer so that he might arrange bail. One of the policemen told him that they would go to Judge Cook's chambers where an order for bail could be obtained. But as the car proceeded rapidly in the direction of the suburbs, Older realized that he had been kidnapped. It was at that moment that he noticed that there was another car ahead, and that Luther Brown and attorney Porter Ashe, one of Calhoun's lawyers, were in it. To silence his protest, one of his captors pressed a gun against his side and warned: "If you make any effort to escape, I'll have to shoot you."[8] According to Older's account, he truly believed that he was being taken to some remote location where he would be killed while trying to escape.

The kidnappers, however, had different plans and drove Older to Redwood City, about twenty miles south of San Francisco. Both cars stopped a short distance from the train station, in the shadow of the freight shed, and waited. When the overnight train for Los Angeles arrived, the captors quickly boarded and locked their charge in a Pullman stateroom that had been reserved. Apparently one of the passengers, a young San Francisco attorney, overheard attorney Ashe telling an acquaintance, with considerable bravado, about the caper in the dining car and happened to catch the mention of Older's name. Frightened for Older's safety, the passenger disembarked at the station stop in Salinas and telephoned the San Francisco *Call*.

"Is Fremont Older missing, by any chance?" asked the caller.

"My God, yes," came the answer. "The whole city is looking for him."[9] When word reached Heney shortly after midnight, he telephoned Santa Barbara, where he was able to awaken a judge and convince him to prepare a writ of habeas corpus to be issued upon the train's arrival. By the time the train pulled into the Santa Barbara station early the next morning, a large crowd had gathered. At that point local police boarded the train and took Older and his captors before the local judge, who released Older on bail. Those involved in the plot then abandoned their attempt to indict Older for libel in Los Angeles. Instead, Luther Brown was indicted for kidnapping. Over a year later, Brown was brought to trial on that charge and acquitted.

The bizarre developments outside the courtroom soon continued within. When placed on the stand, two of the former supervisors changed their stories on highly important points. Then, Alex Lathan, one of the key witnesses whose testimony would have been crucial in connecting Ford with the bribery, disappeared. Lathan was Ruef's chauffeur and had driven the boss to the United Railroads offices on May 25, 1906, the day that Ruef had allegedly entered Ford's office carrying an empty cardboard shirt-box and emerged with a box bulging with packaged currency. In addition, the treasurer of United Railroads had been unexpectedly called to the bedside of a sick relative in the East shortly before the trial began. At about the same time, officials of United Railroads announced that the corporation's account books, which might have contained a $200,000 entry, had been sent east for auditing and could not be recovered during the trial.

Despite the setbacks, the prosecution was able to produce some damaging evidence that fraud had been committed. Frank Leach, the superintendent of the mint in San Francisco, produced records which showed that on May 22, 1906, Patrick Calhoun had sent $200,000 from the East by telegraphic order, depositing that amount to his credit at the mint, and that Ford had made three cash withdrawals of $50,000, $100,000, and $50,000 after that. With this last bit of evidence, the prosecution rested its case without calling Ruef as a witness. The defense called no witnesses. In closing arguments Earl Rogers contended that the prosecution had produced no direct evidence against Tirey Ford, and only questionable circumstantial evidence. After taking thirty ballots, the jury stood deadlocked at eight votes for acquittal and four for conviction. After they had been discharged, the eight jurors who had voted for acquittal told reporters that they had done so because of the absence of Ruef's testimony. In defending his strategy, Heney responded that Ruef wanted total immunity for his testimony and that he was unwilling to grant it. Ford was tried twice again for bribing different supervisors but was acquitted both times.

On January 9, 1908, the district court of appeals invalidated the conviction of Mayor Schmitz for extortion in the French restaurant case. The state supreme court sustained this decision a few weeks later. Schmitz, who had been awaiting the outcome of the lengthy appeal process, was now released on bail on the other bribery indictments that were still pending against him. The court's reversal involved a different interpretation of "extortion" than that held by both the prosecution and the lower court. Extortion, it said, would have been the taking of money by means of a threat to do an unlawful injury to the property of the French restaurant owners. A mayor, for example, had the right to ask the police commissioners to deny a liquor license to a house of prostitution. A mayor had the right to threaten to do so. The court did acknowledge that it might be considered unethical to obtain money by such a threat, but it noted that not every moral wrong was defined by the penal code as a crime. The verdict set off a storm of protest from the prosecution and its supporters, but it came as good news to the likes of Patrick Calhoun, who changed his tactics and now demanded an immediate trial. Calhoun and others in the indictment queue now believed that Ruef would not testify against them. They based their hope on the belief that the court's decision invalidating the indictment on which Ruef had pleaded guilty had freed him from any hold the prosecution might have on him.

Daunted but unbowed, the prosecution now resolved to bring Ruef to trial on the indictment that charged him with offering a bribe to Supervisor Jennings Phillips in the Parkside affair. The selection process to field a jury for the trial began on April 7, 1908. But before jury selection could be completed, another sensational incident rocked the city. It appeared that someone had attempted to murder ex-supervisor Gallagher with dynamite. On the evening of April 22, a violent explosion severely damaged a home owned by Gallagher's brother-in-law, W. H. H. Schenck, with whom Gallagher and his wife had been living since the San Francisco fire. The explosion blew away the front porch (a pillar from the veranda was thrown 150 feet) and the entire front wall of the two-story wooden house, left the staircase hanging without a landing, and created a sixteen-foot hole in the ceiling. Fortunately, none of the eight occupants (which included three children) in the house at the time was killed or seriously injured. The Schenck family and a visitor, seated in a downstairs dining room, were thrown to the floor but miraculously protected by a chimney located between them and the explosion. Groping through the smoke and dust, they were able to stagger out into the backyard. Gallagher and his wife were upstairs and had just stepped out of the room directly above the point of the explosion. In the darkness, Gallagher felt his way down the splintered staircase to where he was able to drop to the lower floor. He then helped his wife down and they, too, took refuge in the yard.

The graft prosecution and its supporters quickly charged that the dynamiter must have been a hired assassin employed by either Ruef or the United Railroads. The explosion had occurred on the day that Gallagher had testified in the third trial of Tirey Ford. In that trial, and in the upcoming trial of Ruef in the Parkside case, Gallagher's testimony was critical since, as Ruef's agent, he had made the offers of bribes to the supervisors. Fremont Older persuaded the *Bulletin* to offer a reward of $1,000 for information concerning the dynamiters. The response shocked him. Instead of a "tip," Older received a series of alarming letters, some written in red ink, threatening to blow up the *Bulletin* building, to kill the editor and murder his family, and to assassinate each member of the prosecution if the offer of the reward was not immediately withdrawn. As a result, the homes of those threatened were placed under police protection. In reacting to the constant presence of the police in their lives, Cora Older commented that "one felt as if one were living in Russia or Turkey."[10] On May 26, while the city was still in shock from the first explosion, a second blast destroyed three residential buildings that Gallagher and a partner had recently constructed in Oakland.

A few weeks after the second dynamiting incident, a young Greek by the name of John Claudianes was arrested for the crimes. He had been apprehended when he tried to claim the $1,000 reward offered by the *Bulletin* for information leading to the arrest of the Gallagher dynamiters. Claudianes was a member of a small colony of Greek contract laborers who had been brought into the city after the fire by United Railroads to lay new trolley tracks. He confessed that he and his brother Peter had been offered $1,000 by a man named Felix Paduveris, a subcontractor of Greek labor gangs, to plant dynamite in front of Gallagher's house and "blow him to Hell." According to the story told by John Claudianes, the brothers approached Gallagher's home on a Sunday night through a vacant lot carrying eighteen pounds of dynamite in a basket. But a barking dog roused a neighbor, who challenged the intruders. Peter dropped the dynamite in the tall grass and John ran away. Realizing that they had been thwarted for the night, Peter crawled back to retrieve the dynamite. According to John, when his brother reported in with Paduveris the next morning, the dealer angrily commented: "My people are sore because nothing has been done. They are paying a lot of money for this."[11] On the following Wednesday night, Peter Claudianes, acting alone, tried again. It was a rainy evening and the barking dog was indoors. Claudianes watched the house until he saw Gallagher moving about in his upstairs bedroom. He then sneaked up to the front porch, planted the dynamite, and lit the fuse with a cigar.

The confession of John Claudianes sent the authorities in hot pursuit of Peter, who, after several months of tracking, was nabbed by one of Burns's detectives at the general delivery window of the Chicago Post

Office. In admitting to his part in the crime, Peter also confessed that Paduveris wanted him to kill Heney, Langdon, Burns, and Spreckels in addition to Gallagher. The search for Paduveris, however, proved futile as it was learned that he had fled to Europe when John Claudianes started talking to the police. He was never apprehended. As a result, questions pertaining to his motivation or to the names of his possible sponsors remained unanswered. Although no evidence was ever found to suggest conspiracy, the prosecution was able to glean enough bits of circumstantial evidence to justify their suspicion that the "graft defense" was somehow connected to the murder plot. In their confessions, both of the Claudianes brothers had expressed the belief that Paduveris was working for Ruef. The prosecution also discovered that Paduveris had periods of association with both Ruef and the United Railroads. One connection was that as a minor politician he had helped deliver the Greek vote and most of the legal business in the Greek colony to Ruef. Detectives also found a photograph of Paduveris dressed in the uniform of a United Railroads conductor while searching his room. William Burns believed that he was actually employed by United Railroads as a secret agent. But these suppositions only served to heighten the mystery and fuel the emotions of fear and animosity that were increasing with each new development in the strangely unfolding graft prosecution.

The next trial was that of Ruef for bribery in the Parkside real estate development deal. Heney had selected this case because he felt it offered the surest opportunity of convicting Ruef of bribery as he was willing to grant immunity to the businessmen involved in order to secure their testimony against the boss. When J. E. Green, president and general manager of the Parkside Realty Company, took the stand, he refused to answer questions concerning his connection to Ruef on the grounds that his answers might be self-incriminating. At that point, Heney moved that all fourteen indictments against Green be dropped and Judge Maurice Dooling, substituting for Judge Dunne, granted Heney's motion. Green then agreed to testify freely. The same offer was made to Gus Umbsen, the company's go-between in the matter, and he was granted immunity as well. Umbsen then provided the details of his $30,000 arrangement with Ruef. This testimony was followed by that of ex-supervisor Gallagher and the other former supervisors who repeated their previous stories. After deliberating for forty-three hours and taking thirteen ballots, however, the jury stood deadlocked at six to six and was discharged.

The jurors who had voted for acquittal in the Parkside case had apparently done so on the grounds that Green, Umbsen, and Gallagher were all accomplices of Ruef and that their testimony could not be credited. Heney, however, was convinced that the jury had been "fixed," either by agents working for Ruef or by members of the United Railroads detective force. This charge brought into question the entire jury selection process. At the time, lists of prospective jurors were available to both the defense and the prosecution. Even as early as the Schmitz trial, there had been complaints that Chief of Police Dinan was using city detectives as jury investigators on orders from Mayor Schmitz. Dinan had admitted this but asserted that his men were only doing what the agents of William J. Burns were doing for the prosecution. As the lists of potential jurors grew during the course of the prosecutions, hundreds and then thousands of citizens began to be harassed by legions of detectives who approached them to determine their views on the graft prosecution. This problem moved from the sublime to the ridiculous in Ruef's trial for the bribery of Supervisor John Furey in the matter of the trolley ordinance. Jury selection for that trial began on August 27, 1908, but was not completed until seventy-two days later. To obtain a twelve-member jury that was acceptable to both sides, 1,450 prospective jurors had to be called. From the beginning of the process it was apparent that agents for both sides had secretly canvassed the personal views of every individual who was summoned.

Testimony finally began in the Ruef trolley franchise case on November 6, 1908. One week into the trial, shortly after four o'clock in the afternoon of November 13, Judge William Lawlor interrupted Henry Ach's cross-examination of Supervisor Gallagher to allow the court to take a brief recess. A court official escorted the jury to an ante-room, while the defendant (Ruef) exited to the sidewalk to talk to his attorney. Although many ventured outdoors for a breath of fresh air, about two hundred courtroom spectators held their seats. Newspaper reporters lounged at their table immediately behind the line of attorney desks. After a brief conference in the judge's chamber, prosecutor Heney returned to his desk at the right end of "attorneys' row" and took his seat. Al McCabe, chief clerk in the district attorney's office, had come over to Heney's desk, and the two were casually discussing the previous day's referendum on a municipal water bond question. No one, however, noticed a small man wearing an overcoat enter the back of the courtroom and walk deliberately down the aisle toward the attorney's table. Stopping about four feet from the prosecutor, the man took a pistol from the pocket of his overcoat, raised it to within a few inches of Heney's head, and fired. The bullet entered just in front of Heney's right ear. Heney happened to be laughing at the time the gun was fired, and, miraculously, the bullet passed between his jaws and lodged in the jaw muscles below his left ear. As one reporter remembered the incident, "immediately it seemed to Heney that the walls were falling in. There followed a moment of indrawn faintness like the first effect of laughing gas—the sensation of being engulfed. As he came back from the verge of consciousness, he felt dimly that someone had smashed in the side of his face with a hammer.

'Who hit me,' he asked? 'Why you're shot!' said someone.

'Who shot me?' 'Haas! Haas!' from all sides."[12] Bystanders quickly seized the would-be assassin, while Heney was rushed to the hospital. Although many initially believed that he had been killed, he was able to recover from the near-fatal attack.

The person who shot Heney in the courtroom was Morris Haas, the owner of a small saloon and liquor store in a residential district of the city. It appeared that the assailant had been harboring a grievance against the prosecutor for nearly seven months. Haas had been accepted as a provisional juror for Ruef's Parkside trial, but Heney learned soon afterward that Haas was an ex-convict who had served a term in San Quentin for embezzlement. The crime had been committed twenty years before and the governor had eventually granted Haas a pardon. Haas then returned to San Francisco, married, raised a family, and had almost forgotten his earlier transgression. When Heney learned about the prospective juror's criminal record, he assumed that Haas had deliberately withheld the information to get on the jury and possibly sell his vote for Ruef's acquittal. He then confronted Haas with a copy of his prison photograph showing him with a shaved head and wearing prison stripes. Haas was then reprimanded and excused from duty. After an awkward attempt at an explanation, he exited the courtroom humiliated. Heney might well have handled the situation better, and there was some criticism at the time that his dramatic public disclosure was needlessly heavy-handed. But the Gallagher dynamite incident had occurred only two days before, and Heney's nerves were frayed. He saw Haas as part of a conspiracy of evil men to subvert justice. Haas's exposure had been reported in the press, but, for the most part, the incident was quickly forgotten. Haas, however, could not shake off his disgrace.

The shooting of Francis Heney led to intense public excitement. The Citizens' League of Justice, formed back in May 1908 to revive interest in the prosecution's cause, now held a mass meeting at the Dreamland Skating Rink on the evening following the shooting. A near-hysterical crowd of five thousand people packed the building, while another five thousand filled the street outside. Mayor Taylor, District Attorney Langdon, Rudolph Spreckels, and former mayor Phelan all made speeches urging the impassioned audience to refrain from mob action. Then, about nine o'clock in the evening of November 14, while the meeting was in progress, jailers reported that Morris Haas had shot himself in his jail cell. For the prosecution, and especially for William Burns, who was hoping to get a coherent confession from Haas and possibly prove that someone had hired him to kill Heney, this was shocking news. While lying under a blanket on his cot in his jail cell, and under the watch of two policemen who had been assigned to guard him, Haas shot himself in the head with a small derringer pistol. Burns and Police Captain Thomas Duke had both searched Haas at the time of his arrest and were convinced that the weapon was not on the victim's person when he was brought to jail. The death of Haas again raised the specter of conspiracy. Who smuggled the pistol in to the prisoner? Had Haas been done in by the police? Why? Angry and frustrated, Burns placed the blame for Haas's death on the negligence of the police department and, more pointedly, on its chief, William J. Biggy.

Biggy had a reputation as an honest police officer, and was a natural replacement for allegedly corrupt Chief Jeremiah Dinan, who was obviously loyal to the Schmitz-Ruef machine. Biggy believed that Haas had shot Heney simply because he had become mentally unhinged by Heney's exposure of his criminal record and dismissed the theory that someone had hired Haas. But Burns, Rudolph Spreckels, and the editors at the *Call* and the *Bulletin* publicly criticized Biggy, implying that he had shifted his loyalties to the graft defense, that he had been guilty of gross negligence, and that he may have been part of a conspiracy in which someone on the defense side, to prevent Haas from talking, had smuggled the pistol into his cell. Although the coroner's office labeled the death a suicide, Burns remained unconvinced and detailed special agents to shadow Biggy. Meanwhile, the Citizens' League of Justice kept up the call for the chief's removal.

On a foggy evening two weeks after the suicide, and in the midst of the ongoing accusations, the beleaguered chief boarded a police launch to travel across the bay to the Belvedere home of Police Commissioner Hugo D. Keil to submit his resignation. Commissioner Keil later testified that after the two had a chance to talk, he had managed to persuade Biggy to stay at his post. But sometime around midnight on the return voyage across the bay, Biggy disappeared from the launch. His body was found floating in the bay two weeks later. The only person who had been with Biggy on the return trip was the pilot, William Murphy, who was at a loss to explain how the chief might have fallen overboard. Opponents of the prosecution denounced those who had publicly hounded the chief and strongly suggested that their collective attacks might well have pushed the chief to commit suicide. His death remains a mystery.

Despite the uproar over the shooting of Heney, the suicide of Haas, and the death of Biggy, the trial of Abe Ruef resumed. Hiram Johnson, who had a reputation for boldness and cleverness in the courtroom, replaced Heney as special prosecutor. The evidence was largely a rehash of that presented during the three trials of Tirey Ford for bribery in the trolley franchise case. But where it had been difficult to prove a corrupt understanding between Ford and Ruef, it was much easier to prove a corrupt understanding between Ruef, Gallagher, and the other supervisors. On December 10, 1908, after five ballots, the jury found Ruef guilty. Two weeks later Judge William Lawlor sentenced the boss to the penitentiary at San Quentin for a term of fourteen years, the maximum sentence for the crime of bribery. Ruef was then taken back to the county jail to await the outcome of his appeal. Ironically, Tirey Ford had been acquitted on the charge of giving the bribe money to Ruef, but Ruef had been convicted of accepting it.

With the conviction of Abe Ruef, the prosecution had achieved its greatest success. In hindsight, it was also the point in time when it should have terminated its mandate. The graft investigation had been dragging on for nearly two years. Many San Franciscans had become weary of the interminable delays, the constant verbal sniping from both sides, the charges and countercharges of jury tampering, and the arcane legal technicalities that had allowed some crooks to go free. In addition, many in the city had become bitterly divided. Loyalty to one side meant hatred toward the other. As Francis Heney quickly recovered from his wound, he became even more determined to proceed against the wealthiest and most powerful of the grafters, and that meant Patrick Calhoun. To many in the opposition camp, Heney appeared as a man possessed, a man on a mission in which he must not fail. And the many admiring letters he received from loyal followers, including one from President Theodore Roosevelt, only steeled his resolve.

The case against Patrick Calhoun actually had little chance of success. The evidence presented against Calhoun was essentially the same that had been introduced during the three trials of Tirey Ford for bribery in the trolley matter. Only this time Calhoun was one more step removed from the actual briberies than Ford had been. Contentious from the beginning, jury selection required three full months and the calling of 2,370 potential jurors. Amid heated exchanges in the courtroom involving the prosecution's expenses, the motives of the prosecution, the employment of detectives on both sides, the responsibility for the streetcar strike of 1907, and responsibility for the attempted assassinations, the jury had to try and consider the actual evidence that a bribe had passed from Calhoun to Ford and then from Ford to Ruef, Gallagher, and the supervisors. Not surprisingly, the jury announced on June 20, 1908, that it had been unable to reach a verdict. The final ballot had been ten to two for acquittal. The jury seemed to find that the evidence only proved the payment of an attorney's fee to Ruef, not a bribe. The granting of several continuances delayed the start of Calhoun's second trial so long that the proceedings were finally postponed until after the fall election, which would also decide the fate of the graft prosecution.

By the time of the Calhoun trial, three distinct perspectives on the proceedings had emerged—left, right, and center. On the left there was the Citizens' League of Justice. The League published its own weekly journal called the *Liberator* and consistently held to the moral high ground in support of the prosecution. One of the articles that appeared in the *Liberator* was a letter from E. A. Ross, a noted sociologist at the University of Wisconsin. Ross had recently published a provocative little book called *Sin and Society* in which he attempted to describe a new type of social menace—the "criminaloid." The criminaloid was a powerful figure in business and politics who committed "new varieties of sin." These were offenses that had evolved with the development of a modern, complex industrial society and which law and public opinion had failed to curb. To Ross, an undiscerning public had yet to realize "that boodling [the offering of a bribe or other illicit payment to a politician] is treason, that blackmail is piracy, that embezzlement is theft, that speculation is gambling, that tax-dodging is larceny . . . that the factory labor of children is slavery, that deleterious adulteration is murder."[13] In his letter to the *Liberator* Ross wrote: "It is perfectly clear to me where honest men ought to stand in this San Francisco graft fight. . . . One might wait a lifetime before finding a simple moral issue presented in so clear-cut a form as you now have before you."[14]

The position of the right in this debate was effectively represented by the *Chronicle* and the *Examiner*. Both these dailies charged that the prosecution had been poorly conducted and that it had lasted far too long. "It would have benefited California," stated the editors of the *Examiner*, "to have had a brief and brilliant prosecution," but it could only prove harmful "to have the state advertised as a sort of criminal community where there is a perpetual prosecution." For several months during 1908, the *Examiner* ridiculed the work of the prosecutors and the graft trials in burlesque form by publishing the so-called "Mutt cartoons." Beginning in February, Bud Fisher's comic strip character Colonel Augustus

Mutt became involved in a long, sensational trial which satirized the San Francisco graft prosecutions. Heney was caricatured as a cross-eyed fool named "Beany"; Rudolph Spreckels was "Pickels"; James D. Phelan was "J. Tired Feeling"; Detective Burns was Detective "Tobasco"; and Superior Court Judges Lawlor and Dunne were Judges "Crawler" and "Finished." A triumph in low humor, the cartoon series appeared in a medium that reached a large number of people. And San Franciscans could not resist laughing. One typical exchange appeared after the court had invalidated the conviction of Mayor Schmitz for extortion on a technicality. Detective Tobasco was portrayed as commenting: "The decision merely prolongs the matter and as Pickels is paying me by the day, I should worry. I have lots of time and Pickels has lots of money."[15] The *Examiner* ridiculed Heney unmercifully and even poked fun at the rumors that an assassination of Heney and Langdon might be attempted. After the actual attempt by Morris Haas to assassinate Heney in open court, the paper abruptly stopped the series.

The center position in the graft discussion was best represented by Lincoln Steffens, the noted muckraking authority on municipal corruption. In a series of articles written for *McClure's* magazine, Steffens had argued that wealthy and powerful businessmen, in their quest for special privilege, were responsible for the corruption of American politics. Steffens, who gathered his articles together in book form in 1904 as *The Shame of the Cities*, had concluded: "The typical businessman is a bad citizen. . . . I found him buying boodlers in St. Louis, defending grafters in Minneapolis, sharing with bosses in Philadelphia, originating corruption in Pittsburgh, deploring reform and fighting good government with corruption funds in New York. He is a self-righteous fraud. He is the chief source of corruption and it would be a great boon if he would neglect politics."[16] It was Steffens who inspired Heney to pursue the higher-ups. But Steffens had come to change his mind. In an article that appeared in *American* magazine in the summer of 1908 entitled "An Apology for Graft," Steffens argued that the further punishment of individuals in the graft trials mattered little. The prosecution's real service to the country, said Steffens, had been to expose the conditions that had resulted from the system of special privilege that had gained control of municipal government—conditions that had motivated both businessmen and politicians to commit bribery. What was now needed, said Steffens, was "sympathy and understanding."

> *We Americans have been out on a manhunt. . . . We are crying to have somebody put into jail; to make some individual suffer; and we may, mob-like, catch some victim . . . [and] wreak upon him our hate. I hate this hate and this hunt. I have bayed my bay in it, and I am sick of it. . . . It is things, not men, that hurt us; it is bad conditions, not ill-will, that make men do wrong. . . . There is something unspeakably painful in the spectacle of . . . men—able, proud, successful; holding themselves and being held to be the best citizens of their city—suddenly summoned into a dirty, criminal court of justice to give bail as felons.*[17]

Whether or not the graft investigation would continue became the main issue in the San Francisco municipal election in 1909. For the previous two years, the graft prosecutions had been associated with a growing reform movement in the state aimed at ending the Southern Pacific's domination of state politics. Leading this crusade was the Lincoln-Roosevelt League, and Francis Heney had made a number of speeches for the League around the state. His participation in that political movement had convinced him that he must go into politics, and that to save the graft prosecutions he must run for the office of district attorney (Judge William Langdon had declined to run for a third term). But Heney's chances of winning were slim. The election of 1909 was the first to be conducted under the new direct primary system. Under this system a candidate could appear on the ballot of only one party, and that party had to be the one in which he had been affiliated in the general election in 1908. At that time Heney had been a registered Republican. But the Republican Party was dominated by conservative, anti-prosecution voters, and it was obvious that, should Heney file for the Republican nomination for district attorney, he would be defeated. The man eventually chosen by the Republicans was Charles M. Fickert, a former Stanford University football star who had the support of a group of anti-prosecution businessmen. Heney's only chance was in gaining the write-in nomination of the Democrats, which he was able to do by a narrow margin.

During the campaign, it was generally understood that Fickert would ask for a dismissal of the graft prosecutions if elected as district attorney. And by the fall of 1909 this was a position that had great popular appeal among voters. But Heney seemed hopelessly out of touch with popular sentiment and continued to demand, in speech after speech, a second chance to convict Patrick Calhoun. Irrationally overconfident, Heney wrote to journalist Lincoln Steffens only days before the election that he expected to win by ten thousand votes. When the ballots were finally counted, however, he lost by slightly more than that margin. The prevailing sentiment was for the trials to stop. As one historian concluded, "Heney had called for 'moral stubbornness' in the punishment of sins against the community. But in the interim, stubborn righteousness had palled on thousands of San Francisco voters, many of whom might have compared their feelings to those of the Athenian citizen who cast his ballot for the banishment of Artistides because he was tired of hearing him called 'the just.'"[18]

After the election of 1909, the graft trials finally drew to a close with something of a whimper. Early in 1910, after Charles Fickert had taken office as district attorney, James Gallagher, an indispensable witness for the prosecution, quietly disappeared from the city. The absence of Gallagher caused repeated delays in the second trial of Calhoun until finally, on August 15, 1911, the district court of appeals issued a writ ordering Judge Lawlor to dismiss all indictments pending against Calhoun and the other officials of the United Railroads. In the end, not one public utility corporation executive indicted in the graft prosecutions went to jail. Abram Detwiler, the president of the Home Telephone Company who had been in hiding for years, returned to San Francisco in 1910 and eventually secured the dismissal of all the charges against him. Theodore Halsey, political agent for the Pacific States Telephone Company, whose trial for bribery had been postponed in 1907 because of an attack of appendicitis and then later from complications relating to tuberculosis, was finally prosecuted by one of Fickert's assistants and acquitted. His superior, Louis Glass, who had been convicted of bribery in the summer of 1907, was finally able, after an appeal process that took more than three years, to see his conviction overturned on a technicality. All the remaining indictments against Halsey and Glass were finally dismissed in 1912. Mayor Eugene Schmitz, who had his conviction for extortion invalidated in 1908, was finally brought to trial for bribery on one of the gas rate indictments in 1912. During the trial, Abraham Ruef was brought from San Quentin to testify. But he refused to do so unless the court agreed to dismiss all the outstanding bribery indictments against him. This the court refused to do. Without Ruef's testimony, and with the absence of Gallagher, who was rumored to be in hiding in Canada, the evidence against Schmitz was deemed insufficient and he was acquitted.

In his *Autobiography*, journalist Lincoln Steffens offered a rather sobering assessment of the San Francisco graft investigation and trials. "San Francisco," said Steffens, "learned nothing from the graft prosecution, nothing but facts—no lessons that were applied either economically or politically." But why was that? The answer, said Steffens, rested with "our economic system, which held up riches, power and acclaim as prizes to men bold enough and able enough to buy corruptly timber, mines, oil fields, and franchises and 'get away with it,'... San Francisco's graft trials showed that."[19] He could well have extended his comments to include the Nome gold conspiracy, the war of the "Copper Kings" in Montana, and the Oregon land frauds as well.

The after stories of the major participants varied. With the dismissal of all the indictments against him in the summer of 1911, Patrick Calhoun was free from the threat of imprisonment. But the ongoing litigation had been a drain on his personal wealth and on the financial resources of United Railroads. In 1912, he came up with a scheme to rebuild his fortune by taking over $1 million out of the company and investing it in a grandiose real estate development called the Solano Irrigated Farms. Bold advertisements in the newspapers promoted the project. The idea was to duplicate the success that Henry E. Huntington had realized with the expansion of his Pacific Electric system in Southern California. United Railroads would expand into an interurban system that would extend through the farmland between San Francisco and Sacramento. With this new development, the lands that Calhoun's new company had purchased in Solano County would soar in value. The success of the project, however, hinged on the approval of a new bond issue by the state railroad commission. But the commission announced that it would not grant approval without first inspecting the company's books. Those books, however, had allegedly been "sent east" during the graft investigation and had never returned. Because those records would have likely included the details of the $200,000 that had been paid to Ruef in the trolley franchise matter, an account of the huge expenses incurred by the company for legal and detective work during the graft investigation, and a tally of the money expended on the various ventures into the newspaper business that had been undertaken as part of the company's public relations efforts during the trials, Calhoun refused to produce them. Denied access to the ledgers, the railroad commission refused to allow the new bond issue. It meant failure for the entire project and tremendous financial loss for Calhoun. In 1913, New York bankers, who held a good deal of United Railroads stock, resisted Calhoun's plans to refloat his land scheme and forced him out of the presidency of United Railroads. Calhoun declared bankruptcy in 1916, testifying that he was broke and that his wife was supporting him. He then lived for a number of years in obscurity. There is some evidence that Calhoun, at the age of eighty, was able to recoup some of his fortune after negotiating an oil lease in a newly discovered oil field in the lower San Joaquin Valley. On June 16, 1943, he was run down in front of his Pasadena home by a teenager street racing with another car. He was eighty-seven.

Rudolph Spreckels, who had financed the graft investigation, declined an offer from President Woodrow Wilson to be ambassador to Germany in 1913 and suppressed a movement to promote his candidacy for the US Senate. By 1928, he had become one of the wealthiest men in America. In that year alone, he was said to have made $18 million, mostly from an investment in the Kolster Radio Company. During the stock market crash of 1929, however, Spreckels lost heavily. In 1931, he was sued by the Radio Corporation for stock manipulation, but the case was thrown out of court. In 1932, he was forced to place the Spreckels Sugar Company in receivership. Trying to recoup his losses, he invested heavily with disappointing results. On top of his financial reversals, the Internal

Revenue Service sent him a bill for $1,402,042 due to his windfall profits in 1928. Attempts to restructure his company failed in 1934 ,and Spreckels filed for bankruptcy. After his wife died in 1949, he lived modestly in a small apartment in San Mateo, California, supported by a small legacy left to him by her. He died in 1958 at age eighty-six.

Francis Heney's career after the trials was a series of disappointments. After losing his attempt to become district attorney in 1909, Heney stepped aside in favor of Hiram Johnson in the gubernatorial contest in 1910 and then lost bids for the US Senate in 1914 and for governor of California in 1918. Pulled once again into the government sector, he served as general counsel for the Federal Trade Commission in its investigation of the meatpacking industry during World War I. Although he maintained his San Francisco law practice, he found himself boycotted by wealthier clients after the San Francisco graft trials. Feeling like a marked man in the City by the Bay, he moved to the Los Angeles area, invested in oil properties, and sold oil leases from an office in Venice, California. He finally concluded his career with his somewhat controversial appointment as a superior court judge for Los Angeles County in 1931 at the age of seventy-two. A committee from the Los Angeles County Bar Association asked for Heney's resignation in 1937, citing his "bad record of court attendance." Whether or not the action was politically motivated is unclear, but Heney rejected their request. He died in Santa Monica, California, later that same year.

William Burns, Heney's sidekick in both the Oregon land fraud and San Francisco graft investigations, was able to capitalize on his reputation as a detective to organize his own private detective agency in 1909. In December of that year, the American Bankers Association selected the Burns Detective Agency to protect the eleven thousand banks in its organization. As the detective of first resort, he added to his remarkable résumé when he arrested the McNamara brothers for the bombing of the *Los Angeles Times* building in 1910. Equally sensational was his role in the Leo Frank murder case in Atlanta, in which he produced evidence to suggest that Leo Frank did not commit the murder for which he was convicted. In 1921, President Warren Harding appointed Burns to direct the Federal Bureau of Investigation, but a scandal involving his boss,

Attorney General Harry Daugherty, forced him to submit his resignation in 1924. Back in private business, Burns became indirectly involved in the famous Teapot Dome Scandal and suffered censure from a federal judge for what was termed jury "shadowing" (regarded as a form of jury tampering) and fined $1,000. For several years after his retirement, he published detective stories based on his long and colorful career. William Burns died in 1932.

Two other prominent figures in the graft investigation, Freemont Older, the editor of the *Bulletin* who came up with the idea of crusading against graft, and Abraham Ruef, the only individual sent to the penitentiary out of the 383 indictments obtained by the prosecution from the grand jury, found themselves oddly drawn together in the end. Older's conscience began to plague him immediately after Ruef's conviction. He was the one who had started the fight to catch the boss, but now that he had done so he found the triumph hollow. He began to believe that Ruef was actually a victim of corrupt conditions for which all the citizens of San Francisco shared a responsibility, conditions which the conviction of one man would not cure. "I have ceased to believe," said Older, "that our economic difficulties are going to be solved by sending men to prison. The cure lies deeper. Men are too weak to withstand the temptations that lie in their way. So long as public necessities are controlled by private corporations there will be civic corruption."[20] To Older, Ruef was a victim of the system. He had also come to believe that the prosecution had acted unfairly—that they had debased themselves by stooping to methods that were almost as reprehensible as those of the defense; that they had forced a confession from Ruef with the promise of immunity and then broken their promise; and that Judge Lawlor had been bitterly prejudiced against Ruef at the trail. In the summer of 1911, Older visited Ruef in prison and asked for his forgiveness. He also offered to help Ruef win his early release.

In the fight to gain Ruef a parole, Older convinced him to write his memoirs, which he agreed to publish as a long series of installments in the *Bulletin*. It was to be a bid for public sympathy and presented as the confessions of a truly repentant man. Ruef's narrative, published as "The Road I Traveled," stopped short of going into the story of the graft cases so as not to open old wounds. Instead, Ruef offered eighteen additional articles entitled: "Civic Conditions and Suggested Remedies" in which he advanced his own proposals for reform. In the upper corner of many of the installments, Older inserted a petition to the prison directors which readers could cut out, sign, and mail to the "Society for the Parole of Abraham Ruef." The entire effort, however, went for naught. Ruef's sentence had been fourteen years. Good behavior reduced that number to nine. The State Board of Prison Directors had established a rule under which it did not grant paroles until a convict had served at least half of his sentence, which for Ruef would be four and a half years. Having served the minimum, he was finally granted a parole in 1915. On the day of his release, Older was there to greet him. In January 1920, Governor William D. Stephens granted Ruef a pardon. He had been disbarred by the state supreme court in 1912, an action that had disqualified him from practicing law. But Ruef had experience in the field of real estate and, upon his release, opened a new office in downtown San Francisco. The sign over the door read: "A. Ruef, Ideas, Investments, and Real Estate." One of his more successful ideas was to open a café on a property he owned at Fishermen's Wharf and to surround it with colorful stores and unique seafood shops. But Ruef's real estate enterprises, estimated to be worth about half a million dollars in 1925, soon began to fail. When he finally died in 1936, his estate was found to be bankrupt.

After unsuccessful ventures in real estate, mining, and music (his operetta, *The Maid of the San Joaquin*, failed in New York), "Handsome Gene" Schmitz decided to attempt a political comeback and run for mayor again in 1915. After being absent from political life for eight years, Schmitz made his first appearance at a campaign rally before a packed house at the Dreamland Skating Rink. A little unsure how the crowd might react, the former disgraced mayor was hesitant. But he need not have worried. As he entered the hall, the four thousand people in attendance "stood upon their seats and cheered. Men tossed their hats in political abandon and women snatched off their furs and waived them like banners." In trying to explain the surprising reaction for a man who, while mayor, had been found guilty of accepting bribes, one writer concluded that the crowd simply expressed a "forgiving spirit." They admired his "nerve" and his "courage," and as a sentimental figure they simply took a "sporting interest in him."[21] Although soundly defeated by popular incumbent James Rolph, Schmitz received thirty-five thousand votes from his supporters. In 1921, voters elected him to two terms on the San Francisco Board of Supervisors! When Schmitz died in 1928 at the age of sixty-four, the police and fire departments furnished an honor guard for his funeral and the church was overflowing with mourners. It appeared that all had been forgiven, forgotten, or both.

NOTES

INTRODUCTION

1. Louis Filler, *Crusaders for American Liberalism* (Yellow Springs, OH: Antioch Press, 1964), 14.
2. William R. Hunt, *Distant Justice: Policing the Alaskan Frontier* (Norman: University of Oklahoma Press, 1987), 73, 121.
3. Editors, *McClure's* 27 (August 1906): 346.
4. Filler, *Crusaders for American Liberalism*, 83, 84.

CHAPTER 1

1. Dr. Sheldon Jackson and Captain Michael A. Healy came up with the novel idea of introducing domestic reindeer into the Territory of Alaska. Jackson had previously served as a Presbyterian missionary in Wisconsin and Minnesota and after that in the Rocky Mountain area before sailing to Alaska in 1884 to become superintendent of missions. A year later he gained appointment as US general agent for education in Alaska and was given the responsibility of establishing a free school system. During his travels through the area bordering the Bering Sea, he noticed that the aggressive opera-tions of the unregulated whaling and fishing industries, with its wholesale slaughter by whites of whales, walrus, and caribou, was rapidly destroying the life-support base for the native Alaskans. After visiting native villages where he witnessed residents dying from hunger, he came to the realization that there could be little hope of establishing a school system until the native Alaskans possessed the essentials necessary to sustain life. From his study of the problem, Jackson concluded that introducing reindeer into the region might be the best way to provide the food, clothing, and transport needed for survival. It might also serve as a way for native Alaskans to derive badly needed income by raising their own private herds on the mossy Alaskan tundra.

Captain Michael A. Healy had come to the same conclusion. Healy, who had entered the US Revenue Marine Service in 1864, made his first trip to Alaska in 1868. Over the next twenty-five years, as he rose in the ranks of the service, he became some-thing of a legend for his many daring sea rescues. It was Healy who first appealed to Washington to stop the use of high-powered rifles and harpoon guns in Arctic hunting. Because hunting had become horribly more effective, the fur seals and bowhead whales that sustained the native Alaskans had been rendered nearly extinct by 1890. As a result, famine struck the coast of Alaska and entire villages were wiped out by star-vation. Healy, who had visited the Siberian coast, had noticed that the local Chukchi were able to sustain themselves by raising reindeer. Because large areas of western and northern Alaska were covered with moss, the primary reindeer food, and the climate favorable, Healy thought a reindeer culture could thrive there. The result was the "great reindeer experiment," and over the next several years, with government support, Jackson and Healy brought reindeer to the western shore of Alaska from Siberia and established the first permanent reindeer station at Teller on Port Clarence Bay on the Seward Peninsula.

The success of the project, however, depended upon finding experienced reindeer herders who could train the native Alaskans in the care and use of reindeer. The Chuk-chi, who were initially employed in that capacity, had proved to be unsatisfactory. The native Alaskans regarded the Chukchi as socially and culturally inferior and claimed that they were cruel to the animals. As a result, the US government sent agents to Norway on several occasions during the 1890s to recruit the services of trained herders. For this project, the government sought out nomads of northern Scandinavia known as Laplanders (Lapps), who, along with their families, replaced the Chukchi and made their new homes at the reindeer stations. Satisfied with the success of the program, the government continued to import more reindeer and Lapp herders.

2. E. S. Harrison, *Nome and Seward Peninsula: History, Description, Biographies and Stories* (Seattle: Metropolitan Press, 1905), 49.

3. Rex E. Beach, "The Looting of Alaska: The True Story of a Robbery by Law," *Apple-ton's Booklovers Magazine* 7 (January 1906): 5.

4. Ibid., 9.

5. Kenneth O. Bjork, "Reindeer, Gold, and Scandal," *Norwegian-American Studies* (online) 30 (April 1985): 13.

6. Beach, "Looting of Alaska," (January 1906): 10.

7. Dan Plazak, *A Hole in the Ground with a Liar at the Top: Fraud and Deceit in the Golden Age of American Mining* (Salt Lake City: University of Utah Press, 2006), 221.

8. James Wickersham, *Old Yukon: Tales, Trails, and Trials* (Washington, DC: Washington Law Book Co., 1938), 347.

9. Beach, "Looting of Alaska," (February 1906): 137–38.

10. William R. Hunt, *Distant Justice: Policing the Alaskan Frontier* (Norman: University of Oklahoma Press, 1987), 91.

11. Ibid.

12. Arthur J. Collier, Frank L. Hess, Philip S. Smith, and Alfred H. Brooks, *The Gold Placers of Parts of Seward Peninsula, Alaska* (Washington, DC: Government Printing Office, 1908), 25.

13. Harrison, *Nome and Seward Peninsula,* 58.

14. Plazak, *Hole in the Ground,* 226.

15. Thomas Arthur Rickard, *Through the Yukon and Alaska* (San Francisco: Mining and Scientific Press, 1909), 354.

16. Beach, "Looting of Alaska," (February 1906): 140.

17. Plazak, *Hole in the Ground,* 226.

18. Beach, "Looting of Alaska," (April 1906): 542–43.

19. Robert P. Wilkins, "Alexander McKenzie and the Politics of Bossism," in *The North Dakota Political Tradition*, Thomas W. Howard ed. (Ames: Iowa State University Press, 1981), 19.

20. David C. Frederick, *Rugged Justice: The Ninth Circuit Court of Appeals and the American West, 1891–1941* (Berkeley: University of California Press, 1994), 97.

21. Rickard, *Through the Yukon*, 354.

22. Plazak, *Hole in the Ground*, 228.

23. Wilkins, "Politics of Bossism," 18–19.

24. William W. Morrow, "The Spoilers," *California Law Review* 4 (January 1916): 110.

25. Wilkins, "Politics of Bossism," 20.

26. Ibid., 20–21.

27. Wickersham, *Old Yukon*, 359.

28. Plazak, *Hole in the Ground*, 229.

29. Hunt, *Distant Justice*, 117.

30. Frederick, *Rugged Justice*, 93.

31. The court also rendered decisions on three other members of the Nome ring. Thomas J. Geary, McKenzie's lawyer in Nome and a well-known member of the San Francisco bar, was charged with contempt for having advised his client (McKenzie) to disobey the writs once they were issued. Geary persuaded the court that evidence against him was insufficient to establish his guilt beyond a reasonable doubt, and the court dismissed the charge against him. Two other officers of the court were not as fortunate. US Attorney Joseph K. Wood, who agreed to become a silent partner in the law firm of Hubbard, Beeman, and Hume, was also charged with contempt of court for his actions in refusing to turn over the keys to the bank vault where McKenzie had deposited the gold dust when requested to do so by the federal marshals. For his misconduct, Wood received a sentence of four months' imprisonment in the Alameda County jail. The final defendant, C. A. S. Frost, who served as an attorney employed by the Justice Department as a special examiner to the Alaska district court and then as assistant US attorney under Joseph K. Wood, was charged with tampering with the names of individuals submitted for jury duty and assisting in the contempts of McKenzie and Noyes. For his involvement, the court sentenced him to twelve months' imprisonment. US Commissioner R. N. Stevens, who had traveled to Nome with McKenzie, was not charged with any crime relating to the McKenzie-Noyes conspiracy, but was later dismissed by Judge James Wickersham (Noyes's replacement) for neglecting to submit quarterly reports of his expenses and then padding those accounts when requested to do so. Stevens had also arranged outside income through his appointment as municipal judge by Nome's city council. The position provided Stevens with all the judicial powers in Nome not held by Judge Noyes. As municipal judge, Stevens earned $9,000 in fees and fines that should have gone to the US commissioner's court rather than for his own personal use. It was actually a form of fraud as Stevens was accepting a second income for services he should have provided as US commissioner.

32. Ed Hunter, "The Cape Nome Conspiracy: The Right Wing at Work?" *Mining History Journal* 11 (2004): 1; Hunt, *Distant Justice*, 121.

33. Beach, "Looting of Alaska," (January 1906): 3–4.
34. Hunt, *Distant Justice*, 121.
35. Frederick, *Rugged Justice*, 97.
36. Beach, "Looting of Alaska," (January 1906): 3–4; (May 1906): 613.

CHAPTER 2

1. Michael P. Malone, *The Battle for Butte: Mining and Politics on the Northern Frontier, 1864–1906* (Helena, MT: Montana Historical Society Press, 1995), 3.
2. C. P. Connolly, "The Story of Montana," *McClure's* 27 (September 1906): 452.
3. Malone, *Battle for Butte*, 12–13.
4. Connolly, "Story of Montana," *McClure's* 27 (September 1906): 458.
5. Malone, *Battle for Butte*, 57.
6. Edwards Roberts, "Two Montana Cities," *Harper's New Monthly Magazine* 77 (September 1888): 594.
7. Malone, *Battle for Butte*, 61.
8. Ray Stannard Baker, "Butte City: Greatest of Copper Camps," *Century* 65 (April 1903): 875.
9. Malone, *Battle for Butte*, 62, 63.
10. Ibid., 71.
11. Ibid., 80
12. Ibid., 86–87.
13. Ibid., 89.
14. Ibid., 97.
15. Ibid., 99, 100.
16. Ibid., 104.
17. Ibid., 112, 113.
18. Connolly, "The Story of Montana," *McClure's* 27 (October 1906): 632.
19. Connolly, "The Story of Montana," *McClure's* 28 (November 1906): 40.
20. Malone, *Battle for Butte*, 119, 121; C. B. Glasscock, *The War of the Copper Kings* (Helena, MT: Riverbend Publishing, 2002), 156.
21. Malone, *Battle for Butte*, 121.
22. Ibid.
23. Ibid., 126.
24. Ibid., 127–28.
25. Ibid., 129.

CHAPTER 3

1. Jere C. Murphy, *The Comical History of Montana: A Serious Story for Free People* (San Diego: E. L. Scofield, 1912), 25.
2. C. B. Glasscock, *The War of the Copper Kings* (Helena, MT: Riverbend Publishing, 1962), 135.
3. Michael P. Malone, *Battle for Butte: Mining and Politics on the Northern Frontier, 1864–1906* (Helena, MT: Montana Historical Society Press, 1995), 139.

4. Ibid., 143.
5. Ibid., 147.
6. Ibid., 155.
7. C. P. Connolly, "The Fight of the Copper Kings," *McClure's* 29 (May 1907): 12.
8. Malone, *Battle for Butte*, 156.
9. Ibid., 161.
10. Reno H. Sales, *Underground Warfare at Butte* (Caldwell, ID: Caxton Printers, 1966), 49.
11. Malone, *Battle for Butte*, 170.
12. Ibid.
13. Ibid., 171.
14. Ibid. 174.
15. C. P. Connolly, *The Devil Learns to Vote: The Story of Montana* (New York: Covici and Friede, 1938), 289–91.
16. Malone, *Battle for Butte*, 178.
17. Ibid.
18. Ibid., 188, 189, 190.
19. Ibid., 192.
20. Ibid., 195.

CHAPTER 4

1. Lincoln Steffens, "The Taming of the West: Discovery of a Land Fraud System; A Detective Story," *American* 64 (September 1907): 491.
2. Ibid., 502.
3. Ibid.
4. Richard Gid Powers, *Broken: The Troubled Past and the Uncertain Future of the FBI* (New York: Free Press, 2004), 34.
5. Jerry A. O'Callaghan, "The Disposition of the Public Domain in Oregon" (Washington, DC: Senate Committee on Interior and Insular Affairs, 1960), 89.
6. Stephen A. D. Puter and Horace Stevens, *Looters of the Public Domain* (Portland, OR: Portland Printing House, 1908), 180.
7. Ibid., 212.
8. John Messing, "Public Lands, Politics, and Progressives: The Oregon Land Fraud Trials, 1903–1910" *Pacific Historical Review* 35 (February 1966): 65.
9. Ibid., 57.
10. O'Callaghan, "Disposition of the Public Domain," 92.
11. Puter and Stevens, *Looters of the Public Domain*, 21.
12. Messing, "Public Lands, Politics, and Progressives," 62.

CHAPTER 5

1. William R. Hunt, *Front-Page Detective: William J. Burns and the Detective Profession, 1880–1930* (Bowling Green, OH: Bowling Green State University Popular Press, 1990), 35.

2. Walton Bean, *Boss Ruef's San Francisco: The Story of the Union Labor Party, Big Business, and the Graft Prosecution* (Berkeley: University of California Press, 1952; reprinted 1972), 127.

3. Thomas Walker Page, "The San Francisco Labor Movement in 1901," *Political Science Quarterly* 17 (December 1902): 684, 685.

4. Bean, *Boss Ruef's San Francisco*, 60.

5. Franklin Hichborn, *"The System:" As Uncovered by the San Francisco Graft Prosecution* (San Francisco: James H. Barry Co., 1915; Montclair, NJ: Patterson Smith, 1969), 19 fn. 13.

6. Cora Older, "The Story of a Reformer's Wife," *McClure's* 33 (July 1909): 279.

7. George Kennan, "The Fight for Reform in San Francisco," *McClure's* 29 (September 1907): 548.

8. Cora Older, "Reformer's Wife," 280.

9. Hichborn, *"The System,"* 90–91.

10. Cora Older, "Reformer's Wife," 283.

11. Bean, *Boss Ruef's San Francisco*, 214.

CHAPTER 6

1. Walton Bean, *Boss Ruef's San Francisco: The Story of the Union Labor Party, Big Business, and the Graft Prosecution* (Berkeley: University of California Press, 1952; reprinted 1972), 228.

2. Ibid., 241.

3. Philip L. Fradkin, *The Great Earthquake and Firestorms of 1906: How San Francisco Nearly Destroyed Itself* (Berkeley: University of California Press, 2005), 303.

4. Kevin Starr, *Inventing the Dream: California through the Progressive Era* (New York: Oxford University Press, 1985), 268.

5. Bean, *Boss Ruef's San Francisco*, 247.

6. Fremont Older, *My Own Story* (San Francisco: Call Publishing Co., 1919; Forgotten Books, 2012), 84.

7. Franklin Hichborn, *"The System:" As Uncovered by the San Francisco Graft Prosecution* (San Francisco: James H. Barry Co., 1915; Montclair, NJ: Patterson Smith, 1969), 280 fn. 296.

8. Cora Older, "The Story of a Reformer's Wife," *McClure's* 33 (July 1909): 289, 290.

9. Bruce Bliven, "The Boodling Boss and the Musical Mayor," *American Heritage Magazine* 11 (December 1959), www.americanheritage.com

10. Cora Older, "Reformer's Wife," 291.

11. Will Irwin, "They Who Strike in the Dark," *American* 67 (April 1909): 570.

12. Ibid., 574–75.

13. Edward A. Ross, *Sin and Society: An Analysis of Latter-Day Iniquity* (Boston: Houghton, Mifflin & Co., 1907; New York: Harper and Row, 1973), 15.

14. Bean, *Boss Ruef's San Francisco*, 292.

15. Ibid., 293.

16. Ibid., 258.

17. Lincoln Steffens, "An Apology for Graft," *American* 66 (June 1908): 120, 127.

18. Bean, *Boss Ruef's San Francisco*, 299.

19. Lincoln Steffens, *The Autobiography of Lincoln Steffens* (New York: Harcourt, Brace & World, 1958), 570–71.

20. Fremont Older, "Shall Abe Ruef Be Pardoned," *Survey* 26 (September 2, 1911): 772.

21. Arno Dosch, "Beating Back to the City Hall," *Sunset* 35 (October 1915): 675, 680.

SOURCES

Baker, Ray Stannard. "Butte City: Greatest of Copper Camps." *Century* 65 (April 1903): 875.

Beach, Rex. "The Looting of Alaska." *Appleton's Booklovers Magazine* 7 (January 1906): 3–12; (February 1906): 131–40; (March 1906): 294–301; (April 1906): 540–47; (May 1906): 606–13.

———. *The Spoilers.* New York: Harper and Bros., 1905; Forgotten Books, 2012.

Bean, Walton. "Boss Ruef, the Union Labor Party, and the Graft Prosecution in San Francisco, 1901–1911." *Pacific Historical Review* 17 (November 1948): 443–55.

———. *Boss Ruef's San Francisco: The Story of the Union Labor Party, Big Business, and the Graft Prosecution.* Berkeley: University of California Press, 1952; reprinted 1972.

Bjork, Kenneth O. "Reindeer, Gold, and Scandal." *Norwegian-American Studies* (NAHA online) 30 (April 1985): 130–96. www.naha.stolaf.edu.

Bliven, Bruce. "The Boodling Boss and the Musical Mayor." *American Heritage Magazine* 11 (December 1959), www.americanheritage.com.

Brechin, Gray. *Imperial San Francisco: Urban Power, Earthly Ruin.* Berkeley: University of California Press, 2006.

Brown, Henry S. "Punishing the Land-Looters." *Outlook* 85 (February 23, 1907): 427–39.

Bruner, Robert F., and Sean D. Carr. *The Panic of 1907: Lessons Learned from the Market's Perfect Storm.* New York: John Wiley & Sons, 2009.

Caesar, Gene. *Incredible Detective: The Biography of William J. Burns.* Englewood Cliffs, NJ: Prentice-Hall, 1968.

Collier, Arthur J. et al. *The Gold Placers of Parts of Seward Peninsula, Alaska.* Washington, DC: Government Printing Office, 1908.

Connolly, C. P. *The Devil Learns to Vote: The Story of Montana.* New York: Covici, Friede, 1938.

———. "The Fight for the Minnie Healy." *McClure's* 29 (July 1907): 317–32.

———. "The Fight of the Copper Kings." *McClure's* 29 (May 1907): 1–16; (June 1907): 214–28.

———. "The Story of Montana." *McClure's* 27 (August 1906): 346–61; (September 1906): 451–65; (October 1906): 629–39; 28 (November 1906): 27–43; (December 1906): 198–210.

Dosch, Arno. "Beating Back to the City Hall." *Sunset* 35 (October 1915): 675–80.

Fradkin, Philip L. *The Great Earthquake and Firestorms of 1906: How San Francisco Nearly Destroyed Itself.* Berkeley: University of California Press, 2005.

Frederick, David C. *Rugged Justice: The Ninth Circuit Court of Appeals and the American West, 1891–1941.* Berkeley: University of California Press, 1994.

Glasscock, C. B. *The War of the Copper Kings.* Helena, MT: Riverbend Publishing, 2002.

Hamilton, Edward H. "The Liberating of San Francisco." *Cosmopolitan* 43 (August 1907): 435–44).

——. "What Are You Going to Do About It?" *Cosmopolitan* 51 (July 1911): 149–59.

Harrison, E. S. *Nome and Seward Peninsula: History, Description, Biographies and Stories.* Seattle: Metropolitan Press, 1905.

Helms, Andrea R. C., and Mary Childers Mangusso. "The Nome Conspiracy." *Pacific Northwest Quarterly* 73 (January 1982): 10–19.

Hichborn, Franklin. *"The System," as Uncovered by the San Francisco Graft Prosecution.* San Francisco: James H. Barry Co., 1915; Montclair, NJ: Patterson Smith, 1969.

Hunt, William R. *Distant Justice: Policing the Alaskan Frontier.* Norman: University of Oklahoma Press, 1987.

——. *Front-Page Detective: William J. Burns and the Detective Profession, 1880–1930.* Bowling Green, OH: Bowling Green State University Popular Press, 1990.

Hunter, Ed. "The Cape Nome Conspiracy: The Right Wing at Work?" *Mining History Journal* 11 (2004): 1–11.

Inglis, William. "For the Kingdom of California." *Harper's Weekly* 52 (May 23, May 30, June 6, June 13, 1908): 10–12, 10–12, 10–12, 10–12.

In re Noyes, Geary, Wood, Frost, Cases Argued and Determined in the Circuit Court of Appeals and the Circuit and District Courts of the United States, *Federal Reporter* 121 (May–June 1903): 209–32.

Irwin, Will. "They Who Strike in the Dark." *American* 67 (April 1909): 564–75.

John, Finn J. D. "Senator Mitchell was the Snidely Whiplash of Frontier Oregon." *McKenzie River Reflections,* November 8, 2012.

Johnson, Paul H. "The Overland Expedition: A Coast Guard Triumph." *The Bulletin* (Coast Guard Academy Alumni Association) 34 (September-October 1972): 63–71.

Kennan, George. "Criminal Government and the Private Citizen: A Study of San Francisco." *McClure's* 30 (November 1907): 60–71.

——. "The Fight for Reform in San Francisco." *McClure's* 29 (September 1907): 547–60.

Knapp, Henry R. "William Andrews Clark." *Cosmopolitan* 34 (February 1903): 474–76.

Lokke, Carl L. "A Madison Man at Nome." *Wisconsin Magazine of History* 33 (December 1949): 164–83.

MacColl, E. Kimbark. *Merchants, Money and Power: The Portland Establishment, 1843–1913.* Portland, OR: Georgian Press, 1988.

Malone, Michael P. *The Battle for Butte: Mining and Politics on the Northern Frontier, 1864–1906.* Helena, MT: Montana Historical Society Press, 1995.

Marsh, George D. ed. *Copper Camp: Stories of the World's Greatest Mining Town, Butte, Montana.* Helena, MT: Riverbend Publishing, 2002.

McKee, Lanier. *The Land of Nome: A Narrative Sketch of the Rush to Our Bering Sea Gold-Fields, the Country, Its Mines and Its People, and the History of a Great Conspiracy, 1900–1901.* New York: Grafton Press, 1902.

McNelis, Sarah. "F. Augustus Heinze: An Early Chapter in the Life of a Copper King." *The Montana Magazine of History* 2 (October 1952): 24–32.

Messing, John Howard. "Francis J. Heney: The Making of an Economic Radical." Senior Thesis, Princeton University, 1964.

———. "Public Lands, Politics, and Progressives: The Oregon Land Fraud Trials, 1903–1910." *Pacific Historical Review* 35 (February 1966): 35–66.

Morrow, William W. "The Spoilers." *California Law Review* 4 (January 1916): 89–113.

Mowry, George E. *The California Progressives.* Chicago: Quadrangle Books, 1963.

Murphy, Jere C. *The Comical History of Montana: A Serious Story for Free People.* San Diego: E. L. Scofield, 1912.

Naval History and Heritage Command. "The Incredible Alaska Overland Rescue." Online publication sponsored by the Naval Historical Foundation, posted on January 29, 2015.

Needham, Henry Beach. "Francis J. Heney—Fighting Man." *Success* 10 (January 1907): 15–16, 55–56.

O'Callaghan, Jerry A. "Senator Mitchell and the Oregon Land Frauds, 1905." *Pacific Historical Review* 21 (August 1952): 255–61.

———. "The Disposition of the Public Domain in Oregon." Washington, DC: Senate Committee on Interior and Insular Affairs, 1960.

Older, Cora. "The Story of a Reformer's Wife." *McClure's* 33 (July 1909): 277–93.

Older, Fremont. *My Own Story.* San Francisco: Call Publishing Co., 1919; Forgotten Books, 2012.

———. "Shall Abe Ruef Be Pardoned?" *The Survey* 26 (September 2, 1911): 772–73.

Page, Thomas Walker. "The San Francisco Labor Movement in 1901." *Political Science Quarterly* 17 (December 1902): 664–88.

Peterson, Todd A. "Looters of the Public Domain Revisited: The 1903–1910 Land Fraud Trials." *Oregon Benchmarks* 6 (Winter 1990): 1–3.

Plazak, Dan. *A Hole in the Ground with a Liar at the Top: Fraud and Deceit in the Golden Age of American Mining.* Salt Lake City: University of Utah Press, 2006.

Powers, Richard Gid. *Broken: The Troubled Past and the Uncertain Future of the FBI.* New York: Free Press, 2004.

Puter, Stephen A. D., and Horace Stevens. *Looters of the Public Domain.* Portland, OR: Portland Printing House, 1908.

Rakestraw, Lawrence, and Mary. *History of the Willamette National Forest.* Eugene: US Department of Agriculture, Willamette National Forest, 1991.

Rickard, Thomas Arthur. *Through the Yukon and Alaska.* San Francisco: Mining and Scientific Press, 1909.

Roberts, Edwards. "Two Montana Cities." *Harper's New Monthly Magazine* 77 (September 1888): 585–96.

Ross, Edward A. *Sin and Society: An Analysis of Latter-Day Iniquity.* Boston: Houghton, Mifflin & Co., 1907; New York: Harper & Row, 1973.

Sales, Reno H. *Underground Warfare at Butte*. Caldwell, ID: Caxton Printers, 1966.

Saxton, Alexander. "San Francisco Labor and the Populist and Progressive Insurgencies." *Pacific Historical Review* 34 (November 1965): 421–38.

Smith, Dennis. *San Francisco Is Burning: The Untold Story of the 1906 Earthquake and Fires*. New York: Viking Penguin, 2005.

Sonnichsen, C. L. *Tucson: The Life and Times of an American City*. Norman: University of Oklahoma Press, 1982.

Starr, Kevin. *Inventing the Dream: California Through the Progressive Era*. New York: Oxford University Press, 1985.

Steffens, Lincoln. "An Apology for Graft." *American* 66 (June 1908): 120–30.

———. *The Autobiography of Lincoln Steffens*. New York: Harcourt, Brace & World, 1958.

———. "The Making of a Fighter." *American* 64 (August 1907): 339–56.

———. "The Mote and the Beam: A Fact Novel." *American* 65 (November–December 1907): 26–40, 140–51.

———. "The Taming of the West: Discovery of the Land Fraud System; A Detective Story." *American* 64 (September 1907): 489–505.

———. "The Taming of the West: Heney Grapples the Oregon Land-Graft." *American* 64 (October 1907): 585–602.

———. "William J. Burns, Intriguer." *American* 65 (April 1908): 614–25.

Stevenson, Frederick Boyd. "The Land-Grabbers: Exposure of the Conspiracy to Steal Millions of Acres of Land from the United States Government." *Harper's Weekly* 49 (June 24, 1905): 898–901, 919–20.

Stewart, William R. "F. Augustus Heinze." *Cosmopolitan* 36 (January 1904): 289–92.

"The Story of Heinze, a Tale of Copper—and Brass." *Current Literature* 44 (January 1908): 34–36.

Thomas, Lately. *A Debonair Scoundrel: An Episode in the Moral History of San Francisco*. New York: Holt, Rinehart & Winston, 1962.

Thompson, William Henry. "The People's War Against Graft in San Francisco." *World To-Day* 16 (January 1909): 82–85.

Wickersham, James. *Old Yukon: Tales, Trails, and Trials*. Washington, DC: Washington Law Book Co., 1938.

Wilkins, Robert P. "Alexander McKenzie and the Politics of Bossism." *The North Dakota Political Tradition*, Thomas W. Howard ed. Ames: Iowa State University Press, 1981, 3–39.

Zink, Harold. *City Bosses in the United States: A Study of Twenty Municipal Bosses*. Durham, NC: Duke University Press, 1930.

INDEX

Schneider, Joost H., 96–97, 98–99,
101, 102
indictment of, 103
"school lands," 96
See also Oregon, land fraud in;
California, land fraud in
Scott, Randolph, 34
Seawell, Judge James M., 150
Seward Peninsula. *See* Alaska
Shame of the Cities, The
(Steffens), viii, 178
Sin and Society (Ross), 177
Smith, C. A., 109, 116
Smith, Gov. Robert B., 56, 58, 59
Spaulding. Lt. Oliver, 8–9
Spoilers, The (Beach), vi, vii, 33, 34
Spreckels, Claus, 146
Spreckels, John, 161
Spreckels, Rudolph, 142, 145–146,
148, 150
after the trials, 182–183
on attack on Heney, 174, 175
Calhoun's accusations of, 161
newspaper caricature of, 178
response to earthquake, 148
Spriggs, Lt. Gov. A. E., 58–59
Spring Valley Water Co., 143
St. Lawrence Mine, 40
St. Paul Dispatch, on Montana
election, 54
Starr, Kevin, 162
Steece, Harry, 99, 103
Steffens, Lincoln, 93, 95, 102,
180

articles by, viii, 178–179
autobiography of, 181
Stephens, Gov. William D., 185
Stevens, Horace, 123
Stevens, R. N., 17
Stewart, Sen. William, 15, 65
Stillman, James, 68, 90
Stivers, D'Gay, 81
"Story of Montana, The"
(Connolly), vii, 36
Strong, J. F. A., 32

T

Taft, Pres. William H., 91, 124
Taggart, Grant, 102
"Taming of the West, The," viii
Tanner, Judge Albert H., 117–118
Tarpley, Dan, 105, 106, 109
Taylor, Mayor Edward, 158–159
on attack on Heney, 174
Teamsters' Waterfront Strike (SF),
130–134
Teapot Dome Scandal, 184
Teller, Sen. Henry M., 15
Territory of Alaska. *See* Alaska
Tevis, Lloyd, 40
Tevis, William S., 143, 144
Thaw, Harry K., 159
Thurston, John, 119
Timber and Stone Act, 1878,
95–96
Toole, Gov. "Honest Joe," 74, 86
Tornanses, Johan S., 3
Treacy, Dr. William, 56

About the Author

Steven L. Piott is currently an emeritus professor of history at Clarion University of Pennsylvania. He holds BA and MA degrees from the University of Utah and a PhD from the University of Missouri. He has also been a Fulbright teaching fellow at Massey University in New Zealand. He is the sole author of seven monographs—*The Anti-Monopoly Persuasion: Popular Resistance to the Rise of Big Business*; *Holy Joe: Joseph W. Folk and the Missouri Idea*; *Giving Voters a Voice: The Origins of the Initiative and Referendum in America*; *American Reformers, 1870–1920: Progressives in Word and Deed*; *Daily Life in the Progressive Era*; *Americans in Dissent: Thirteen Influential Social Critics of the Nineteenth Century*; and *Daily Life in Jazz Age America*.